THE TRUTH ABOUT
JUDAS

THE TRUTH ABOUT
JUDAS

Mysteries of the
Judas Code Revealed

YITZHAQ I. HAYUT-MAN
EDITED BY JAMES G. MEADE

Foreword by Richard Kirby

WATERSIDE PRESS

Published by Waterside Press
2376 Oxford Avenue, Cardiff, CA 92007
760–632–9190

Library of Congress Cataloging in Publication Control Number: 2007922330
ISBN 978-1-93375-402-4

Design by Jane Raese

07 08 09 / 10 9 8 7 6 5 4 3 2 1

Not just one thing, but everything that the tradition attributes to Judas Iscariot is false.

—DE QUINCY (1859)

quoted in J. L. Borges' "Three Versions of Judas" (1944)

CONTENTS

My Obsession with Judas

It is fair to ask me, the author, where I stand on the issues of Judas, and perhaps even why. To answer why, I need to explain how I became obsessed with Judas, about the decades of struggling with these matters and the surprising turns and seemingly providential clues received along the way, including highly inspiring literary works.

I was born in Israel—then Palestine—to parents who had also been born there (my father's father was one of the founders of Tel Aviv, "the First Hebrew City") in an exclusively Jewish-Israeli milieu. Christianity was something utterly foreign, briefly mentioned in classes on Jewish history, and the only Christians I knew in my early childhood were our old Arab gardener and the British soldiers who disappeared when I was five years old and "Palestine" became "Israel." When I studied architecture in England, after my military service, I had no problem, for instance, going to churches for concerts, but religion had never been a concern for me. Nor were there Christian-Jewish issues when I continued my studies at the University of California at Berkeley in the exciting years of 1967–1969, though the many cultural controversies of "the sixties" were of course present.

My dramatic, perhaps mythical, encounter with Christianity came in a very special setting—in Catholic South America, at the highly folkloric and quasi-pagan Carnival of Bahia, Brazil, in

1974. It came after three days and nights of dancing and living in the body, when I found myself in a native church almost bursting with candles, images, and statues (idols, according to my Jewish upbringing). Something happened there, and, rather than feeling alienated by the seeming paganism, I took it all in and entered into its mythical world. Memories of the movie *Orfeo Negro* came to life, and indeed I seemed to behold the Angel of Death walking the streets among the heaps of exhausted humanity. He (or it) followed behind me to the left, and for the first time in my life I realized my own mortality and the urgency and poignancy of the passing moment. I then retired to the seaside village of Itapoã, where I started furiously writing a journal of all that was passing through my mind, and there I soon experienced some divine visions, which eventually made me put away my professional career (urban planning) and dedicate my lifework to "the New Jerusalem" and the issues of the Temple of Jerusalem.

So I started a journey through the Americas, writing a personal journal, and one hitherto-unconscious theme that came out strongly in my wanderings was the historic Jewish-Christian conflict. Bogotá, Colombia, was the first Spanish-speaking place I came to, and there I spent a few drizzly days in a cheap hotel room, reading a book that a friend happened to give me in Brazil (I guess he thought it might deepen my encounter with South American culture), the English translation of Jorge Luis Borges's *Labyrinths*. I was utterly amazed that anyone could write so well.

The one excursion I made in Bogotá was to the top of the hill overlooking the city. I entered a church and felt the strongest revulsion at the sight of people walking on their knees all the way to the altar. It was right after that event that I read *Three Versions of Judas*, which must have made an indelible impression in my mind, and came to a head a year later.

During that year (in which I had been working as a visiting professor in Brazil and the United States), my copious journal notes led to a rather naive book outline: "The Architect's Guide for Building the New Jerusalem."

I embarked then in England on doctoral studies in cybernetics, under the guidance of a most remarkable and eccentric teacher, Professor Gordon Pask. I was to discover that, privately, the world's leading cyberneticians were nothing short of a modern version of the Gnostics, holding to various spiritual leanings (including Buddhist, Sufi, and Christian mysticism), and that my own adored teacher was a genuine Christian mystic who saw his work as a contemporary reiteration of the work of the Catholic mystics Saint John of the Cross and Ramón Lull. When it came to discussing the topic of my doctoral dissertation, Pask was ready to consider my writing "The Architect's Guide for Building the Heavenly Jerusalem" as my research work, but then he brought literary reservations about what I presented ("too much coffee chat, Isaac," was his verdict).

The next morning as I sat to meditate, I heard a voice inside my head, and the voice clearly said: "Write the Gospel of Judas Iscariot!" I was puzzled, but set out to write an outline and presented it to Gordon—who then agreed this would be it. For the next few years, I dedicated my creative moments to trying to comprehend the mind of Judas Iscariot. Recalling it now, I can't escape the thought of a connection between finding the Gospel of Judas, in the Egyptian desert, and my experience of hearing the voice, both of which happened during the mid-1970s.

Three events in that long process were so outstanding or emotionally charged that they merit recounting. One was soon afterward, when I decided to return to my motherland, Israel, to work on the dissertation. An English Sufi teacher whom I had met back in California in 1974, Reshad Field, had advised me then (in a semitrance state) to go to Patmos, Greece. So I decided to go there on my way from London to Israel to start writing *The Gospel of Judas Iscariot* (I was unaware at the time that Patmos was where Saint John had reputedly written the book of Revelation). Traveling to Patmos overland by train, I reached Rome on Christmas night. This opportunity to observe Christianity was too good to miss, so I drifted with the crowd to the Vatican and into Saint Peter's Cathedral, impressed by its architectural size, style, and pomp, even while classifying it in the back of my mind as idolatry. Then came the midnight hour, and the pope was led in state through the passage, with the high priests by his side, delivering the Host to the people, who were scurrying to ingest it, evidently as a high point in their life. It was then that something in me seemed to burst. (I was not aware at the time of the meaning of the Host, and only now, writing this book, have I looked at the 1987 book *Christianity in Perspective* by Robert Wolfe, which regards Christianity as heir to pagan mystery religions, whose main rite is of a mystic unification with Jesus by symbolically eating of his body and drinking of his blood, in Wolfe's even more extreme expression "ritual cannibalism.")

I looked at the pope, who appeared to be a decrepit old man, and, sensing the weight of the countless Jews who had suffered because of Jesus' Church, I let my mouth utter some invectives in Hebrew. Then the ritual was over, the crowd was leaving, and I spent the rest of the night standing by the Castello Saint Angelo, cooling my rage in the drizzle—again, still unaware of the Jewish legends of the Messiah dwelling right there, among the lepers. Years later, I found out that the pope died within a year of my visit to the Vatican and that his successor survived only thirty-three days after assuming office. I did not, however, become an enemy of Christianity—in Patmos I frequented the great monastery church, listening to the chanting, and in Israel I started writing *The Gospel of Judas Iscariot* at the Catholic monastery of Ein-Kerem, while participating in an interfaith "hope seminar."

Then I happened to go to a Shabbat morning concert of Mozart, and, at a moment when I felt a complete melding with that angelic music, I suddenly came to realize how painful it can be, and has been, to be a woman. My accumulated sympathy with the poor Judas, reviled and victimized for so many generations, suddenly shifted to all womankind, and I found myself suddenly in tears. I did not hear any voices (apart from the Mozart music), but it was suddenly clear: I should be writing not about Judas Iscariot but about Judith (the female form of the same name), about the essential, but overlooked, involvement of the feminine.

In the end, I wrote an ostensibly more conventional doctoral dissertation, which I finished within a year (Y. Khayutman: "The Cybernetic Basis for Human Reconstruction: An Application for the Middle East," Department of Cybernetics, Brunnel University, UK, 1981). Then I returned to the original task and eventually finished *The Gospel of Judith Iscariot.* I had accomplished what the voice told me to do. The voice never related to success in the marketplace, but the reader can find the play at http://www.thehope.org/jud1-1.htm.

I came upon the writer Philip José Farmer in an entirely providential and propitious manner. I was advised by two teachers to go to Scotland—to Edinburgh and somewhere farther north to the Findhorn community (the New Age capital of Europe at that time). Traveling by train for most of a weekend, I had just one night at Findhorn, where I felt unwelcome. The one thing I did there was to go to a bookstore. Stretching my hand and passing by the bookshelves with closed eyes, I picked off a top shelf one book that somehow felt right. To my surprise, it was just a Penguin science fiction novel by a writer unknown to me, something I might have easily found back at a Charing Cross Road bookstore in London. I read it later and until the last page could not see any reason I had been drawn to pick it. It was only in the very last paragraph that I found out that this book, *The Night of Light* by Philip José Farmer (1966), was a most original futuristic retelling of the story of Judas Iscariot. It seemed like an omen that I was on the right track.

I discuss Farmer in a later section of this text. My encounter with him proved to be one more milestone in what became my complete dedication to the Gospel of Judas, and to the book you see before you. The actual release of the translated Gospel of Judas provided me with the final impetus to bring my years of fascination with Judas to fruition.

A Gospel That Helps Fulfill the Other Gospels

The search for the truth about anything is not simple. The search for the truth about Judas Iscariot, the odd man out among Jesus' twelve disciples, is a demanding and delicate task. The journey taken by this book entails examining critically what hundreds of millions of people regard as the Truth, the Whole and Absolute Truth and Word of God—namely, the New Testament. Perhaps even more daunting, this investigation is made not by a Christian but by a Jew. So let me please comfort the reader and declare at the outset (paraphrasing what another Jew, whom every Christian knows and loves, has said [Matt. 5:17]): Do not think that I have come to dismiss the Gospels or the Passion of Jesus. The intention is not to dismiss them but to help fulfill them. But to do so, we shall look in many directions and examine carefully that apparent antithesis to the canonical Gospels, the so-called Gospel of Judas. Throughout, I use as our text *The Gospel of Judas*, published by the National Geographic Society, 2006.

Our investigation will gradually show how this "Gospel of Judas" could change, and deepen, the knowledge already gleaned from the Gnostic writings about the sources and original intentions of Christianity, and how it might in due course influence world events.

Judas–Most Exalted of Jesus' Disciples

In the traditional Christian reading of the events, as everyone knows, Judas is a traitor. The book of Matthew says, "While he was still speaking, Judas, one of the Twelve, arrived. With him was a large crowd armed with swords and clubs, sent from the chief priests and the elders of the people. Now the betrayer had arranged a signal with them: 'The one I kiss is the man; arrest him'" (26:47). Dante, in his *Inferno*, places Judas in the ninth (innermost) circle of hell. Suffering in hell more than the lowest, most despicable of other creatures, Judas in the *Inferno* lives condemned for eternity with his head inside the central of Lucifer's three mouths while the devil's claws skin his back.

The Gospel of Judas affords nothing less than a complete turnabout from the long-standing view of Judas as heinous traitor. Judas is holier than the holy. Judas is supremely knowledgeable. Judas is a savior, of Christ, of himself, and of mankind.

Judas Iscariot was one of the twelve apostles selected by Jesus as his confidants and missionaries (Matt. 10:1–4; Mark 3:13–19, 6:7–12; Luke 9:1–6), but he was unique among them in many ways that this book will show—but was he a villain or a saint?

The name "Judas" is a Greek form of the common Hebrew name Yehudah (יהדוה, Yehûdâh, meaning in Hebrew "thanksgiving" and "confessing"), which first appeared in the Hebrew Bible, where Yehudah was one of the twelve sons of Jacob-Israel. Yehudah-Judah came to seniority and leadership among these twelve. In Jesus' time, most of the tribes had been exiled, and of the twelve-tribe confederation of Israel, just the state of Judah, or Judea, was left, and its inhabitants were called "Judeans," or Jewish. Jesus' own pedigree and status derived from his being of the line of the Judaic House of David, the expected kings of all Israel, making him a brother tribesman of Judas.

In the Greek of the New Testament, Judas Iscariot is called Ιουδας Ισκαριωθ (Ioudas Iskariôth) and Ισκαριωγης (Iskariôtês). In English translations of the Bible the name "Jude" is also found. The name "Iscariot" (spelled more correctly "Ish-qrayot") can be interpreted in several ways. First, it could designate that he came from the town of Qiriot in Judea, making Judas Iscariot the only Judean in the group of Jesus and his twelve disciples, since the others were all from Galilee (a rustic region north of Judea, with a different culture, and even a different accent). The Hebrew word *qrayot* also means "cities," and Iscariot can mean "of the cities" or "urbane," creating a city-versus-country dichotomy with the rustic Galilean followers of Jesus.

However, "Iscariot" may instead derive from "Sikkari," the name given at the time to the more extreme zealots who opposed the Roman occupation of Judea and carried a small hidden dagger—called a Sikkah—to use against their opponents. The zealot leader Judas of Galilee founded the party of the Sikkari, so it is possible that all the Sikkari were in some way associated with Judas. Among Jesus' twelve disciples there was another, Simon, who was called "the Zealot" (Matt. 10:4). The Zealots were looking for the Jewish Messiah who, they believed, would liberate Judea from the Roman occupation.

Now why is Judas worthy of mentioning and enduring recollection for many? In the recently announced ancient manuscript of the Gospel of Judas, Judas Iscariot is portrayed as the closest and most exalted of Jesus' disciples, he who faithfully fulfilled Jesus' command and was destined to ascend to the greatest height in the Kingdom of Heaven. With the publication of that Gospel of Judas, the truth of the canonical gospels comes under scrutiny. By finding the truth about Judas, we may well find the truth about Jesus or, in even more ambitious thinking, the Truth itself.

It is a solemn responsibility but also a luminous privilege for me, as a coordinating scholar in the field of religious-future studies, to be asked to write an introduction to this remarkable book. The new Gospel of Judas is much more than a curiosity. It is a unique document whose publication at the beginning of the twenty-first century is no accident. Spirited examination and debate on the validity and meaning of this Gospel are opportunities for a new dialogue between Christians and Jews on the fundamental relationship between the two religions.

The book you hold in your hands can serve as a catalyst for this debate and as such has value far beyond its intellectual contributions alone. The relationship between Christians and Jews has been basic to the development of Western civilization as it has evolved over the past two thousand years. The possibility that Judas may in fact have been Jesus' closest friend and not a traitor at all turns on its head the myth from which anti-Semitism developed.

At this critical moment of world tensions, especially in regards to the Middle East, it is a Godsend to have an opportunity to reexamine the fundamental beliefs that have stirred negative rather than positive passions. It is in this context that the Gospel of Judas is indeed, as all Gospels have been, "Good News from God."

In reading this book may you as reader and student be open to some of the unexpected and controversial findings of author

Hayut-Man, who is not only an esteemed colleague but also one of those rare scholars who dares to explore the largest of human questions, those dealing with the future relationship between the Creator and the human family.

The Academy of Jerusalem, Dr. Hayut-Man, and his book are an inseparable trinity. The mission of the Academy of Jerusalem is to bring healing, hope, and a new spiritual vision of planetary citizenship to the beleaguered family of humankind. In the past such people as Dr. Hayut-Man were called prophets, and their job was not so much to forecast the future as to foretell the will or message of God to the people. Dr. Hayut-Man is such a foreteller, though he is assuredly a normal man, who is also clearly a dedicated religious scholar, and indeed the most morally earnest man I have ever met. He personifies the will of scholars everywhere to discover a truth so profound that it will bring infinite hope back to the human race. Dr. Hayut-Man is concerned with the global community of humanity. He has a fresh word of hope, and, although he finds this hope through his reflections on recent discoveries of so-called apocryphal documents such as the Gospel of Judas, his majestic hope is not necessarily tied to this particular text but has broken free of it and has become a new transcendental hope for all peoples.

The heroic paradigm, in Greek and other legends, permeates the thinking of Dr. Hayut-Man. In his case, the hero is not the individual; it is the human race as a whole. To think along such lines is to be consistent with the genius of Hebrew thought, as we read in such commentators as Stephen Caiger in his book written approximately seventy-five years ago, *Lives of the Prophets*, and in many other expositions of the prophetic tradition—whether from Christian or Jewish viewpoints. Some illustrious examples include J. Lindblom in his Oxford work, *The Prophets of Israel;* Klaus

Koch and his two-volume work on the prophets as thinkers published by London SCM; and many others who could be mentioned.

The new hope that Dr. Hayut-Man brings is indeed a remarkable one. It implies that there can be what Abraham Lincoln called in a different context "a new birth of freedom" for religious thought, for religious community, and for global peace. In keeping with the prophetic tradition, Dr. Hayut-Man believes that this birth of freedom can begin in Jerusalem and be a series of events that will be a kind of healing for the three Semitic religions of Judaism, Christianity, and Islam. His work is not only a vision but also a call.

It is an ineluctable fact for statespersons that the world is looking for supreme science. In reading Dr. Hayut-Man's book, one has a feeling that this hope has been fulfilled. The consummation of all political science has been thought to revolve around the idea of the end of the world. This notion sometimes has been associated with the coming of the Messiah. All too often, these Messianic futures are associated with a kind of frenzy of human suffering. No more. Dr. Hayut-Man gives us another way of reading not only the science of the time but the scriptures as well. He gives us a new way of thinking about Jesus and the Jews, about Judaism and Zionism, and about humanness and hope.

In fact, his work creates a new paradigm for comparative religion, which we might call "spiritual public health science." Dr. Hayut-Man's allusion to such notions as the "laughing Jesus" is part of his compendious thought in which he shows a new way forward for softening relations among nations. The new Messianic future that Dr. Hayut-Man envisions portends a wonderful new era for Jewish-Christian relations. It heralds and adumbrates a marvelous healing of the anti-Semitism that has besmirched

Christian history and tormented Jewish history, and instead it in-
augurates a new and marvelous era of Jewish-Christian cooperation. This cooperation means none other than the healing of
nations. We can all rejoice at the coming of a new community of
sacred social science and therefore a spiritual path for global
citizenship.

Dr. Richard Kirby
President, Academy of Jerusalem

THE TRUTH ABOUT
JUDAS

PART I

THE GOSPEL &
ITS PUBLICATION

CHAPTER 1

The Gospel's 2000–Year Path
to Publication

T HE CONTROVERSIAL GOSPEL OF JUDAS, a Coptic manuscript originally written in Greek, has been vehemently denounced by orthodox Christians as heresy, especially by Saint Irenaeus, bishop of Lyons in AD 180. Actually, the only source we have had about the existence of this manuscript until recently was the testimony of Saint Irenaeus. The Gospel of Judas was hidden in the sands of Egypt, only to be found in our era.

Through the twentieth century most ancient manuscripts were found by locals who were looking for something else and did not have a clue as to what they had in hand. Such was the case with the Gnostic library that was found in Nag Hammadi, Egypt, in 1945 and the Dead Sea Scrolls in 1947. And so was the case in the mid-1970s with the villagers in Jebel Qarara near the city of El Minya, a desert area in middle Egypt, walking distance from the Nile bank, and halfway between Nag Hammadi and Cairo. The hills there are full of caves, which the villagers keep searching, looking for treasures that were usually buried with their wealthy owners. Next to a buried skeleton, some locals discovered a box made of limestone in which the dead man's library was buried.

The books, made of papyrus and covered with leather, were written in strange characters that drew the attention of the diggers.
They knew enough to expect a nice amount of money from the
big-city antique dealers for this strange library. They consulted
the local "Man of the World," who took it upon himself to sell the
books to an antique dealer in Cairo.

The middleman, though he could not read the language of the
manuscripts, knew he had put his hands on a treasure and
wanted a suitable price. He brought the manuscripts from the
arid area of El Minya to hot, humid Cairo, and there started the
Via Dolorosa, the passage of the manuscripts into almost total
destruction, yet at the same time, very slowly, into the consciousness of the Western world.

In Cairo, in the hands of a well-known antique dealer whose
shop was placed in Han al-Halili market, the manuscripts were
appreciated for the fortune they represented. That was part of
their bad luck. Nobody yet considered them a cultural and theological treasure; only their monetary value mattered. The dealer
himself (Herbert Krosney and Bart D. Ehrman in their book *The
Lost Gospel: The Quest for the Gospel of Judas Iscariot* call him by
the pseudonym "Hanna," and so shall we), although literate,
could not identify the characters and thought them to be Hebrew.
As a matter of fact, they were Coptic, a language not much different from the language of the Pharaohs.

Discovered not far from where the Nag Hammadi Library (thirteen volumes of Gnostic writing, which included fifty-two texts—
two numbers to which we shall return) had been found some
thirty years earlier, the manuscripts would have suggested to a
scholar a link between the two. But we are talking about thieves
and buyers of antiques. Although all the persons involved were of
the Coptic Christian minority of Egypt—the villagers who found

the manuscripts, the middleman, and the antique dealer—and should have taken an interest in exposing their old and banned codex, they were only after the big money.

"Hanna" was spreading the news of the found codices among colleagues, expecting a price of no less than three million dollars. There are two main figures who contacted Hanna and take an important part in our story. One was Frieda Tchacos Nusberger, a Greek woman born in Alexandria, the second-largest city of Egypt and its main harbor, who eventually became a Swiss citizen. Nusberger, a well-to-do, highly appreciated antique dealer, had the advantage of speaking fluent Arabic. The other was Nicolas Koutoulakis, also of Greek origin, the best and most successful dealer of all the Near East. The two knew each other.

Koutoulakis, ready to help Hanna sell the manuscripts, was accompanied by two women. One of them, Mia, a redhead, was probably part of the plot to steal Hanna's goods, including the manuscripts. On her own, without consulting her partner, she arranged with Hanna to meet some potential buyers. He gathered his collection, which had usually been kept in different safes in several apartments. The buyers did visit Hanna, agreeing to buy everything without bargaining, but the next day the apartment was broken into and the safe taken and emptied. All the Cairo fortune was gone, and the manuscripts (then not known to scholars yet containing a huge Gospel to Christianity—and actually to all mankind) had vanished once again.

Eventually, it turned out that the papyrus, already damaged by the Cairo humidity and other unsuitable weather conditions, was taken to Europe and wrapped in newspapers, never to see the land of Egypt again. In Switzerland, in the Alps weather, kept in the hands of people who knew nothing of the preservation of old manuscripts, stored in bank safes, it continued to deteriorate.

Mia was on the scene once again, more than twenty years later, trying to sell to Nusberger—through a boyfriend—the few pages of the manuscripts that she still possessed. Nusberger was suddenly reminded of the pages' origin, as she had seen them many years earlier in pictures that Hanna had sent her. She did buy the pages, at about one-tenth the price the young man had requested. As for Koutoulakis, being a man of honor, he managed to find most of the precious antiques, among them the manuscripts, which he returned to Hanna.

Frieda Tchacos Nusberger met Koutoulakis in Cairo, around the time of the manuscripts' discovery, which she had heard of but never had a chance to investigate. By the time the manuscript was rediscovered after the robbery in the early 1980s, yet another Greek antique dealer, a collector named Yannis Perdios who had been advising Hanna, contacted Nusberger, showed her some photographs of the codices, and asked her to identify potential clients. She would—though not quickly.

In the meantime, Perdios showed the same set of photographs to the first scholar ever to lay eyes on the manuscripts—Ludvig Koenen, known by the Egyptian dealers as "Koenik," the king of papyrus. He was the one who informed the dealers of the importance of the papyrus manuscripts. He was probably the one to tell Hanna his manuscripts were worth millions. Koenen, who knew Hanna and appreciated his integrity, had some prior assumptions: that at least some of the material had been written in Coptic, that its content was biblical, and that it had connections to the Nag Hammadi Library. He wanted to assemble a team of experts to examine the codex.

On May 15 (incidentally, Israel's independence day), 1983, he gathered in Geneva, Switzerland, four of the most distinguished scholars in the field of Coptic codices, or "Coptology." Of the four,

I shall mention especially a young scholar, Stephan Emmel, representing the general editor of the Nag Hammadi Library, Professor James Robinson. Emmel missed the big scoop this time but would have a chance to share in the efforts to restore and decipher the texts some seventeen years later.

Facing the four scholars, three of them coming that very day from the United States, were Perdios and Hanna, who were rather impatient and strict, allowing no photographs—or writing. Emmel, who later wrote some notes, warned his colleagues that the manuscripts were in danger. He had seen that they were merely wrapped in newspaper and stored in a cardboard box.

As for the box's contents, the team managed to identify two out of at least three manuscripts that were placed before them: "The First Apocalypse of James" and "The Letter of Peter to Philip," both already known from the Nag Hammadi texts. The third part, still unidentified, was interpreted as "A dialogue between Jesus and his disciples, at least Judas is involved. . . ." But the Judas involved was thought by them to be the Gnostic character "Judas Thomas, Jesus' twin brother," known from one of the first Gnostic codices ever found, the Gospel of Thomas. Consequently, the significance of the manuscript was ignored.

The team members, each relying on his university and all expecting some fund to take an interest in the manuscripts, estimated they could raise only some one hundred thousand dollars. The demanded price of three million was far beyond their abilities. Frustrated, both parties parted, and the manuscripts were put back in the bank safe. Koenen's team left for the United States and forgot all about the fascinating, endangered codices, while the dealers also went to the States, only to find once more that the task of selling the papyrus was a tough one, and thus left it in another bank safe, this time on Long Island, for about sixteen years;

the document was becoming almost impossible to read, a mass of disintegrating fibers.

Still, there were some people who could not stop thinking about the codex. One of them was Professor James Robinson of Claremont College, who had just finished the publication of the Nag Hammadi Library in 1984—the very same year that Hanna left the manuscripts in the New York bank safe. To pull some strings that might lead to the now-lost codex, he dropped some information that found its way into a Ph.D. dissertation and mentioned the subject in a conference on Coptic studies that was held in Warsaw in August of that year. No response. It took Robinson some six years to locate Perdios, the Greek helper of Egyptian Hanna. He tried to raise the right amount of money, counting on two sources: a Norwegian collector who was known to be very rich and the sponsor of Laval University of Quebec, Canada—the Bombardier foundation—which had been involved in the translation of the Nag Hammadi codices into French. But then the First Gulf War began, the Egyptian dealer was scared to travel, and the efforts of Professor Robinson came to naught.

The other person who never gave up hope and never forgot the manuscripts was the Egyptian-Greek-Swiss antique dealer Frieda Tchacos Nusberger. And Fortuna, the goddess of luck, put the mission of revealing the Gospel to the world on her shoulders. But she still had a long way to go, as did the manuscripts.

I have mentioned before red-haired Mia, helper (and perhaps lover) of the Greek antique dealer Koutoulakis, probably one of the thieves who took all Hanna's treasures, including the manuscripts. I also recall that in 1999 her boyfriend called Nusberger, trying to sell her some pages taken from the manuscripts. Nusberger knew at once where the pages belonged, and the incident gave her the drive to go back and find the authentic owner of the papyrus.

The years softened Hanna. The millennium came. He had had the manuscripts for about twenty-five years by then and had not been able to sell them. When Frieda Tchacos Nusberger approached him this time, it seemed that he was finally ready to give up his unbelievably high selling price, realizing he would not get it but not yet realizing that soon he would have nothing to sell, as the papyrus in the vault was disintegrating into nothing.

They flew together to the States, got out the almost rotten and highly fragmented papyrus, and Nusberger, apparently with a sense of commitment, paid a certain amount of money to Hanna, certainly not three million dollars, and took the manuscripts straight to the Rare Book and Manuscript Library of Yale University, where she left them to be stored safely.

Nusberger left the manuscripts in the hands of Robert Babcock, one of the main curators of the library, who had helped her a year earlier to check the authenticity of the pages she had gotten from Mia's boyfriend. It took him a few days to understand the true contents of the manuscript: the Gospel according to Judas Iscariot, the true story of the supposed traitor who had allegedly betrayed Jesus.

For five months, the manuscripts were stored at Yale University and examined by the best Coptologists, but their sale was not realized because of matters of legal ownership (the antique goods being the property of a country, Egypt in this case) and the suspect circumstances in which the manuscripts were found.

Urged to bring the manuscripts to a safe shore, Nusberger then made a big mistake: she sold them to another dealer, Bruce Ferrini, whom she had been misled to believe had a lot of money, contacts, and knowledge. It turned out that he had financial problems, would have trouble paying her, and had questionable bookkeeping practices. On top of that, Ferrini contributed his part to the deterioration of the codices: he put them in a freezer in order to separate the pages! With the help of her lawyer and partner, Mario Roberty, Nusberger eventually managed to get the manuscripts back, bring them to Switzerland, and create her own team of experts to restore the papyrus. She hired professor emeritus Rodolphe Kasser, a leading Coptologist at the University of Geneva, to translate the texts, as well as chief restorer of the Bodmer Foundation, Florence Dabre. That was the beginning of the end.

Thousands of fibers, so delicate they turned to dust at the slightest touch, were integrated over the next three years in order to re-create a coherent manuscript. Dabre collected, connected, and glued carefully; and Kasser read, deciphered, and gave his approval. Soon another member joined the team, Gregor Wurst, of the University of Münster, Germany. He added, apart from his own knowledge of Coptology, the use of special computer programs that managed to match the most irregular parts of the jigsaw puzzle. Two funds have been supporting the work, ready to return the papyrus to the Egyptian authorities when restored and published: the Maecenas Foundation of Mario Roberty, which was founded especially for this matter, and the National Geographic Society, which carried on with the project and its publications.

On July 1, 2004, at the Institut Catholique of Paris, 150 scholars of Coptic studies were crowded together, listening to an announcement made by Professor Kasser: "Out of the sands of Egypt arose, after two millennia, documents that had been hidden by their Coptic Gnostic believers in fear that they might have been destroyed by the mainstream church. Among them was the most explosive of all—the Gospel according to Judas Iscariot. The long-banned text and its once-hidden secrets were now accessible to the world."

The next two years were dedicated to promoting the manuscript among scholars, so when the Gospel according to Judas was introduced to the public through the efforts of the National Geographic Society on Easter eve 2006, a number of books that dealt with the manuscript, its findings and its importance, were also published (including *The Gospel of Judas* by Rudolphe Kasser, Meyer Marvin, and Gregor Wurst and the previously mentioned *The Lost Gospel* by Krosney and Ehrman). Finally, the manuscript was available for reading.

CHAPTER 2

The Gospel Itself:
Judas to Exceed
All of the Disciples

T HE BASIS OF ALL OF THIS DISCUSSION is the newly discovered
Gospel itself. A reading and review of its contents illumi-
nate all the rest that I bring forth in these pages.

The Setting for the Gospel: Jesus May Have Materialized

The events reported in the Gospel of Judas occurred during a
week ending three days before the celebration of Passover. Thus,
the likely place would be the area of the Mount of Olives (which
includes Bethany on the eastern slope), today topped with the
Church of the Ascension. In the Gnostic text of the Pistis Sophia,
the appearances of Jesus to his disciples are explicitly stated to
have taken place there.

According to the Gospel of Judas (as in some other Gnostic
texts), Jesus appeared suddenly to his disciples, in a way quite

similar to the post-Crucifixion appearances reported in the canonical Gospels. Moreover, "often he did not appear to his disciples as himself, but he was found among them as a child." Likewise, it is later stated that he also disappeared suddenly, even in midsentence. It might be said that he "materialized" there, as if having "translocated" from elsewhere.

Scene I: Jesus Laughs, Tells of Judas' True Witness

The very first event reported in this Gospel is that just before or during the week of Passover, Jesus appeared to the disciples and "found them gathered together and seated in pious observance [evidently not at his request]." When he [approached] his disciples gathered together and seated and offering a prayer of [what would be called in Greek] euereukharisti over the bread, "[he] laughed." Jesus apparently laughed at the disciples' pious Christian habit of celebrating the Eucharist in a totally mistaken belief of who God the Father is. The Gnostic Gospel here claims that none of the people of that generation (of those pious disciples) could really know who Jesus was.

Most likely, this scene is knowingly anachronistic, describing the time of the establishment of the Church and the institution of the Eucharist.

Scene II: Jesus Laughs Again, Tells of a "Great and Holy Generation" (Ours?)

Jesus made another sudden appearance (materialization?) to the disciples and disclosed to them that he came from another, "great and holy," generation. The indignant disciples asked, "What is the great generation that is superior to us and holier than us, that is not now in these realms?" Jesus' response was again to laugh at them. He said that no one born of their generation would see the future generation and that "no host of angels of the stars will rule over that generation" (I'll discuss the issue of astrology next). That generation would have altogether different powers, not the powers that ruled in the apostles' generation.

This surely means that those generations—when Christianity was forming and the canonical Gospels were being prepared for the masses—could not really understand Jesus' intentions (though perhaps Judas could, as we'll see later). Could that superior generation be our generation, a generation no longer ruled by astrology and paganism? Or, if we doubt our present virtue, we can ask, are we today in a better position than the generations at that time to connect with the "great and holy generation"? If we were to meet Jesus now, what would he tell us?

The image of that "great and holy generation" is of a community of the righteous living in a separate but parallel reality (a "higher dimension," if you like), something like the Jewish image of Paradise—or the Land of the Lost Tribes beyond the Sambatyon River—and the Buddhist image of the legendary "Shambhala," the city of the righteous that disappeared somewhere in the far and unpopulated heart of Asia.

The First Temple Vision:
The Church and the Disciples Have Failed

Within this rather short document, we find several temple visions. The whole entry into Gnostic consciousness is mediated, even determined, by appropriate types of shrines. The first temple is the one seen by all the disciples, apparently in a common dream. It is a strange and troubling sight. This temple has a sacrificial altar and is officiated by twelve priests all dedicated to the name of Jesus. Jesus asks them, "What are those priests like?" It turns out some of them sacrificed their own children, some their wives (as if for praise and humility); some of them sleep with men, some are involved in slaughter, some commit a multitude of sins and deeds of lawlessness—and all the while they invoke Jesus' name, and with all their deficiencies they officiate the worship.

Jesus' interpretation of their common dream is forthright: "All the priests who stand before that altar invoke my name. . . . [They] have planted trees without fruit, in my name, in a shameful manner." (If so, those who sacrificed their children or their wives could actually be those monks and nuns who did not marry, and thus sacrificed in the name of Jesus the possibility of having spouses and children.) The altar is thus any Christian church; the tree that does not bear fruit is surely the Cross. Jesus then adds something more disturbing: Those priests are none other than his own disciples. "You are those twelve men you have seen. The cattle you have brought for sacrifice are the many people you lead astray," whereas those sacrificed are of a higher order, above the dominion of the stars and angels. These priests are "ministers of error." Jesus explains that these generations, and the twelve disciples, are ruled by the stars (or the zodiac signs). Even though these priests invoke Jesus' name, they work under the changing rulers of the world, each in his turn, automatically.

Judas discusses with Jesus the different generations. He then addresses Jesus as "Rabbi"—not as "Lord" or "God." (The word was completed by the researchers and is reasonable in a Hebrew context. However, in Arabic, "Rab" is a name of Allah.) Judas asks

Jesus a wise question: "What kind of fruit does this [superior] generation produce?" It is fruitfulness that makes the difference, and "by their fruit ye shall know them." Jesus then explains that of those who "have completed the time of the kingdom . . . their bodies may die but their souls will be alive, and they will be taken up." The others, however, may not grow their living souls, as if their soul seed fell on barren, rocky ground, somehow because of the corruption of Sophia (Wisdom).

The Two Temples—
Outer for the Other Disciples, Inner for Judas

Two temples are described in the short text of the Gospel of Judas. As mentioned, the eleven disciples tell of a first temple distinguished by its altar, upon which sacrifices are made, officiated by wicked priests. It would have been tempting to interpret it in the traditional Christian way that the temple with sacrifices is a symbol for the old Jewish religion, now superseded through Jesus' supreme self-sacrifice ("the blood of the Lamb of God"), by a new cult of bloodless sacrifice. However, in the Gospel of Judas, Jesus himself explains that this obsolete temple is in fact the Christian Church—where worship is in the name of Jesus Christ.

Then there is the temple vision of Judas. Having seen the other disciples stoning him, he seeks sanctuary in a great house with a roof of greenery. He is told by Jesus that no mortal is allowed in this holy place. The description is very scanty (two lines are missing), but it reminds one of the Jewish concepts of the tabernacle, which has a roof of greenery, and the heavenly Paradise (World to Come) where "the Just sit with crowns on their heads enjoying the brilliance of the **Shekhinah**" (the Divine Presence) (Talmud

Bavli, tract. *Berakhot*, 17a). Curiously, this is reminiscent of an earthly shrine that was built later, and which I have yet to discuss, namely, the Dome of the Rock. In that shrine are inlaid, up in the arcades, some of the finest mosaics in the world, depicting vegetational motifs, which the scholars explain as a depiction of Paradise.

In principle, these two shrines may be regarded as two aspects of the temple, the outer and the inner. The outer comprises the courts—the outer court where the crowds gather and the inner court where the sacrificial altar is situated. The inner part is the inner sanctuary, which only the elect may enter. The disciples have the outer teachings, meant for the masses, whereas Judas seeks to be admitted to the inner teachings, the Gnosis.

The Luminous Cloud and the Light Body: Judas on a Par with Moses and Jesus

There is, however, another element connected with the temple but not of it: the divine cloud, *Av ha'Anan*, or "Clouds of Glory," that marks the divine presence that may come to the temple and that the smoke of the sacrifices outside and the incense inside are meant to represent—and seek to attract. This is the cloud that appeared when Solomon's temple was dedicated: "And it came to pass, when the priests withdrew from the Holy Place, that the cloud filled the house of the Lord, so that the priests could not stand to minister because of the cloud, for the glory of the Lord filled the house of the Lord" (1 Kings 8:10–11). This is just like in the earlier dedication of the tabernacle in Sinai: "So Moshe [Moses] finished the work. Then a cloud covered the Tent of Meeting, and the glory of the Lord filled the tabernacle. And Moshe was not able to enter the Tent of Meeting, because the cloud rested on it, and the glory of the Lord filled the tabernacle" (Exod. 40:34–35). There was just one occasion when Moses entered that cloud—on Mount Sinai, after the oral giving of the command-ments uttered from fire and cloud and before receiving the tablets of the Torah: "And Moshe went up into the mountain, and the cloud covered the mountain. And the glory of the Lord rested upon Mount Sinai, and the cloud covered it for six days; on the seventh day He called to Moshe out of the midst of the cloud. And the sight of the glory of the Lord was like devouring fire on top of the mountain in the eyes of the children of Yisra'el. And Moshe went into the midst of the cloud, and went into the mountain; and Moshe was in the mountain forty days and forty nights" (Exod. 24:15–18).

One of the most remarkable ingredients in the Gospel of Judas is the vision of the "luminous cloud" that appears in it twice and resembles the cloud of the glory of the Lord described above. The first vision comes right after the descriptions of those two tem-ples, and it was granted to Judas when Jesus agreed to teach him the secret of the great invisible: "And a luminous cloud appeared there. He said, 'Let an angel come into being as my attendant.' A great angel, the enlightened divine Self-Generated, emerged from the cloud. Because of him, four other angels came into being from another cloud." Then the last vision of this Gospel took place when Jesus told Judas: "'Lift up your eyes and look at the cloud and the light within it and the stars surrounding it. The star that leads the way is your star.' Judas lifted his eyes and saw the luminous cloud, and entered it. Those standing on the ground heard a voice coming from the cloud saying [contents lost]." So Judas' "ascension" is on a par with Moses' when he received the Torah and with the transfiguration of Jesus!

This "luminous cloud" is a plastic and creative matrix from which all forms can be generated and the elect may enter to emerge with a new identity and knowledge. But this vision of the luminous cloud with which the Gospel of Judas ends is also an opening to the great Christian future—"the Second Coming"—for how would Christians who are fervently awaiting this Second Coming know who is the right one? After all, there never has been and never will be a lack of Messianic contenders and false Messiahs. So the signs that most evangelical Christians give to distinguish the true Messiah are the operation of the Temple of Jerusalem and the fulfillment of the vision in the book of Daniel about the appearance of the "Son of Man": "In my vision of night I looked, and there before me was one like *a son of man, coming with the clouds of heaven.* He approached the Ancient of Days *(Aṭiq Yomin)* and was led into His presence. He was given authority, glory and sovereign power: all peoples, nations and men of every language worshiped him. His dominion is an everlasting dominion that will not pass away, and his kingdom is one that will never be destroyed" (7:13–14). This "son of man" *(Bar Enash)* is identified with the "Son of Man" of the Gospels, with whom Jesus apparently identified (see, for example, Matt. 14:20–21)—and thus his characteristic mark is his "coming with the clouds of heaven": "In the future you will see the Son of Man sitting at the right hand of the Mighty One and coming on the clouds of heaven" (Matt. 26:64; also Mark 15:62). In the concluding section in this book we shall see how the future Temple of Jerusalem may be distinguished by this kind of a cloud.

There is another way to interpret this cloud, using the Gnostic method of gematria, which is explained and illustrated in Part VI (I use the symbol ⇔ to indicate correspondence by gematria). In Hebrew gematria *Aṿ* ⇔ 72 is a cosmological number revealed in the Gospel of Judas (and which I shall gradually explain). This is also the number of members of the Sanhedrin, before whom Jesus might be brought for a proper retrial (as former Israel Supreme Court justice Hayim Cohen showed, the judgment of Jesus as portrayed in the Gospels either could not happen or else was not a proper Sanhedrin session). So in addition to "the Son of Man coming on the clouds of heaven," this could be read as "the Son of Man coming in front of the Sanhedrin." How would "the Son of Man" emerge from this *Av?*

The Gospel of Judas presents the ruler of this world as the "autogenes," the "self-generated" entity—or, in current terms, "self-organizing system" or "autopoietic system."

Jesus' Private Cosmological Teachings: The Spirit and the Self-Generated Angel

Jesus then offers to teach Judas about secrets that no person has seen, to witness a great and boundless realm of a great and invisible spirit. Then appears a projection medium, a luminous cloud. (The commentators bring many parallel visions of luminous clouds in the New Testament and Gnostic literature. I may add the "Clouds of Glory" that Moses entered to receive the Torah, the clouds over the tabernacle and in the temple, and especially in Ezekiel's divine visions.) That invisible spirit said, "Let an angel come into being," and from the cloud emerged "an enlightened divine Self-Generated" angel, who caused four other angels from another (lower?) cloud to form and attend it. Then the Self-Generated Angel, in turn, called into being some creature (or aeon) and called into being a luminary to reign over it and countless angels to serve him. Then the Self-Generated Angel called into being an aeon of light and again created a luminary to rule over it and hosts of angels to serve him. The same creation process repeated for all the (twelve?) enlightened aeons.

That first luminous cloud, which is the first manifestation of the divine, contained "Adamas," that is, Adam of the book of Genesis, a paradigmatic Adam, the exalted image of humanity in Gnosticism. The image of a "primordial man" from whom all is created appears in various cosmologies (for example, the Vedic Purusha). But this Gnostic Adamas resembles, more than anything else, the "Primordial Adam" (***Adam Qadmon***) of the Lurianic Qabbalah (sixteenth century—see Chapter 9 and Part VI), which is still the recognized mystical teaching of Judaism. This entity then generated "the generation of Seth" (the third and perfected son of Adam in Genesis, soon later also called Christ). This generated in several stages a system of luminaries characterized by the numbers 12, 24, 72, and 360. This system of generation is somewhat like the system of Creation in Genesis, marked by the six "days" characterized by the numbers 1 to 6. Here, these numbers themselves determine the generation of multiplicity, though not in the exact order. The first term is 12, which implies prior multiplication of 3 and 4, then multiplication by 2 to 24, then by 3 to make 72, and then by 5 to make 360. The number 360 is the multiplication of $3 \times 4 \times 5 \times 6$ and so is the union of the special qualities of these four numbers.

This was evidently an astrological system (and astrology was the leading science of those times), which can be shown to relate also to "the Platonic Year" of 25,920 terrestrial years, divided into 12 ages (or aeons) of 2,160 years each. It may mean then that the next "great and holy generation" was expected to come some 2,000 years after the disciples' generation.

All this ordered (and apparently astrological) system of immortal luminaries and worlds, in the words of the Gospel, "is called the Cosmos—that is, perdition—by the Father and the 72 luminaries who are with the Self-Generated and his 72 aeons." So this (lower) cosmos that houses humanity (lower, in that it is susceptible to decay) is also "perdition." The first human, Adamas, with his incorruptible powers, then appeared in that defective cosmos. It was still a perfect aeon in which there was the cloud of knowledge, and its angel was called El. But these aeons kept rolling, and apparently (some words are missing) after that one there were called "twelve angels to come into being [to] rule over chaos and the [underworld]. Then two angels appeared from the cloud, "one whose face was flashed with fire and whose appearance was defiled by blood. His name was Nebro, which means 'rebel'; others call him Yaldabaoth. Another angel, Saklas, also came from the cloud." "Saklas" apparently means the Hebrew "Sakhal," or "Ksil," that is, "Fool" (and also means the star Orion). Rebel and Fool created between them 12 angels to run this world, each receiving a portion of the heaven. Thus, 12 astrological "houses" were created, each encompassing 30 degrees of the 360–degree zodiac. Five of these are then listed and named as "the five who ruled the underworld, and first of all over Chaos."

In the Judas Gospel (as in some other Gnostic writings), the physical creation of mankind was carried out by a lower deity (demiurge), Saklas ("the Fool"), in a manner akin to the Genesis account of the creation of Adam (1:26) and Eve/Zoe (2:23). The demiurge then blessed them with a long life—which Judas seems to question.

Judas then asks whether the human spirit dies. Jesus explains that God (apparently the higher God) ordered Michael to give souls to the people of the present generations as a loan but ordered Gabriel to grant (eternal) spirits to that "great generation" that has no rulers over it.

Jesus then explains to the disciples that the spirit in them dwells in their flesh during the generations ruled by those angels but that God caused special knowledge (Gnosis) to be given to Adam and his offspring (a knowledge that the world rulers do not have), so that the rulers of chaos and the underworld might not lord over them. Judas asks (on their behalf) what those generations will do. Jesus answers that those generations are under the (astrological) influence of the stars. When Saklas completes the span of time assigned to him, the stars of the generations will run, and they will finish what they said they would do. The disciples will then fornicate in Jesus' name and slay their children (content missing) in his name—and then Judas' star will shine over the thirteenth aeon. After that Jesus laughs again. To Judas' surprise, Jesus explains that he was laughing not at him "but at the errors of the stars" that wander about, for they will be destroyed along with their creatures.

Scene 3: Judas' Vision—
Stoned and Ascending to the Holy Generation

Judas asks Jesus in private to listen to him too, for he has seen a great vision. Jesus' reaction is to laugh (the third time in this short text) and calls him "you thirteenth spirit" (which Jesus shortly explains) "who needs not try so hard," but he lets Judas describe his vision. Judas tells of two events: being stoned by the twelve disciples (thus, he is already indeed the thirteenth) and coming to a place where there was an immense temple or house with a roof of greenery. Many people were waiting to enter, and Judas implored Jesus, "Master, take me along with these people." Jesus' response seems to refer to astrology: "Judas [Yehudah], your star has led you astray" because no mortal human being is allowed inside. He explains that the paradisiacal temple of the vision is for the holy, an eternal realm over which the stars do not rule, where they will dwell with the holy angels.

Judas then asks, "Master, could it be that my seed is under the control of the rulers?" Jesus offers something (here a piece is missing) but tells him that he will grieve much when he sees the Kingdom and all its generation. When Judas is distressed about being set apart from that generation, Jesus comforts him by saying, "You will become the thirteenth, and you will be cursed by the other generations [that is, those of the disciples and of the orthodox Church]—and you will come to rule over them. In the last days they will curse your ascent (or transfiguration) to the holy [generation]."

Judas' Star and the Covenant of Thirteen

Jesus explains Judas' unique and eventually exalted position by the image of his star and his being the thirteenth. What is that "Star of Judah" (or Judas)? Perhaps you don't have to look further than the one-dollar bill. There, to the right of the word ONE, is the great seal of the United States. There are about a half-dozen elements that count up to thirteen (the number of arrows, leaves on the olive branch, and so on), but the most prominent is the constellation of thirteen stars shining over the American eagle. I'm not initiated in Masonic symbolism but will explain the number thirteen and these symbols in biblical and Jewish terms in a later section, after I have introduced and explained Gnosis and the Qabbalah.

Judas Enters the Luminous Cloud

Judas then asks Jesus what those who have been baptized in Jesus' name will do. The answer is not clear, due to lacunae, but other Sethian texts are critical of the ordinary Christian baptism. There is discussion that the people (or the other disciples) actually sacrifice to Saklas. Then, apparently in comparison, comes the punch line: "But you will exceed all of them. For you will sacrifice the man that clothes me." Then Judas is aroused by Jesus' poetic encouragement:

Already your horn has been raised
Your wrath has been kindled,
your star has shown brightly
and your heart has [. . .].

Jesus then speaks of something (two and a half lines missing) that will be destroyed, and then the place (or image) of the great generation of Adam will be exalted—a generation that existed prior to heaven, earth, and the angels. With that, Jesus said, he has told Judas everything and instructs him, "Lift up your eyes and look at the cloud and the light within it and the stars surrounding it. The star that leads the way is your star." Then, in the very manner of Jesus' transfiguration (Matt 17:5; Mark 9:7; Luke 9:34–35) and Moses' entry into the Clouds of Glory (Exod. 19:9, 20:18), Judas sees the luminous cloud and enters it, and a voice from that cloud speaks to all below (then five lines missing).

Conclusion: Judas Betrays Jesus
as Jesus Requested

The end is as unemotional and matter-of-fact as can be. The scribes who want to arrest Jesus approach Judas; he answers them as they want, "and he received some money and handed him [Jesus] over to them." That is the end of the Gospel of Judas, with no further word of the Crucifixion or the Resurrection, and certainly no criticism of Judas.

The reason the Gospel of Judas gives for Judas' action toward Jesus is that he was responding to Jesus' own request: "For you will sacrifice the man that clothes me." But does this explanation satisfy? Could "being clothed by a man" (that is, by a physical human form and body) have been so irksome to Jesus? If so, what prevented him from giving up the body himself? In this story he can apparently come and go and seemingly materialize at will. So releasing him from this physical cover, which constrains him less than it does any person, is not such a great favor, in fact hardly necessary, all the more so since the text presents us with a surprising "Laughing Jesus" who seems to be enjoying himself.

John 16:7 gives an explicit reason for Jesus' removal: "It is for your good that I am going away. Unless I go away, the Counselor (*Paracletas*) will not come to you; but if I go, I will send him to you." It seems likely that Jesus needed Judas to take a role that was necessary for the show—it had to *look* like a betrayal in order for the show to be more dramatic.

PART II

JUDAS & GNOSIS:
THE SCHOOL OF
INNER AWAKENING

CHAPTER 3

The Judas Gospel
as Part of a Tradition:
Christian Gnosis

ORTHODOX CHRISTIANITY has one doctrine, and it is not a mystical doctrine. Ascent to heaven depends on believing in Jesus, accepting certain guidelines for behavior, and adhering to them. Orthodox Christianity, though, had a rival in the early centuries after Christ—Gnosticism. Gnosticism is mystical. In Gnosticism ascent to heaven derives from direct experience of the divine and can happen even during this life. It does not depend on accepting Church doctrines, believing in something, or behaving in a prescribed manner.

Gnosis was likely a derivative of esoteric Judaism. In orthodox Christianity, Judas is a traitor. In Gnosis, though, this mystic is a prophet, the most exalted of Jesus' followers. This controversial "Gospel of Judas," a Coptic-language manuscript originally written in Greek, had long been vehemently denounced by orthodox Christians as heresy. Actually, the only source we have had about the existence of this manuscript, until recently, was the testimony of Saint Irenaeus, bishop of Lyons. Irenaeus's attack on the Gnostic heresies in AD 180 contained descriptions of their beliefs. I shall quote some of his observations in the presentation of some of the Gnostic figures below. What we find in reading the actual Gospel for ourselves, though, is not that Judas is a heretic with respect to Jesus but rather that he is a spokesman in the Gnostic tradition that may in fact be the true teachings of Jesus.

The Gospel of Judas Is Typical of Gnostic Teachings

In many respects, the Gospel of Judas is typical of Gnostic writings. The cosmology revealed in it is much the same as that described at greater length in the Gnostic Secret Book of John and in other Gnostic books. Also, the names and figures of the aeons— such as Barbelo, Saklas, Yaldabaot—are familiar from earlier-found Gnostic texts. The unique figure is that of Judas Iscariot. Before the discovery of the Gospel of Judas, there was no primary source for a "Gnostic Judas." Judas Iscariot doesn't appear by name in any of the other Gnostic texts that have been uncovered to date, including the Nag Hammadi collection. He is, in fact, notably absent from Gnostic literature.

The Nag Hammadi Find: Hidden Gnostic Documents Discovered in the Twentieth Century

Two dramatic finds of lost religious traditions that preceded the unveiling of the Judas Gospel were the discovery in 1945 in Upper Egypt of the Nag Hammadi Gnostic library (thirteen books) and the Dead Sea Scrolls (about eight hundred manuscripts) found in the caves of Qumran in 1947. Both finds took several decades to be translated and published. Both were discoveries of sacred texts that had been hidden long ago (some sixteen hundred and nineteen hundred years) by sects now extinct, losers in a history written by their rivals. In both cases, the documents were hidden because the beliefs of their authors threatened those in power.

Looking just at the first quantitative measures of the Nag Hammadi Gnostic Library, an intriguing question presents itself: Was the Nag Hammadi collection a chance collection of whatever was there in some monastic library that had to be hidden or else destroyed, or was there an intentional design in this collection? This hidden library was made in the format of two numbers—thirteen codices that contained fifty-two distinct texts. So these two numbers may well convey special inherent meaning—and so might be the number 4 that these two numbers imply, as $4 \times 13 = 52$. As I have discussed, the number 13 is intrinsic to the Gospel of Judas and a key to its enduring message.

Why the Documents Were Hidden—
Suppressed by the Imperial Christian Theologians

In the case of the Dead Sea Scrolls, it is likely that they were gathered in this remote desert location and hidden in caves to save them from destruction by the Romans, who indeed destroyed the Temple of Jerusalem and, sixty years later under Emperor Hadrian, sought to eradicate the memory of Judea (by calling the land "Palestina" and its people "Palestinians") and to terminate the transmission of Judaism and the Torah. The Dead Sea basin offered a remote and dry place where sacred scrolls could survive for centuries and even millennia—as indeed they did.

In the case of the Gnostic Gospels, their believers must have become increasingly aware that they had lost the battle with the imperial Christian theologians over the definition of Christianity for their age. But they trusted that another age, a different aeon, would likely follow. Whether this present evil aeon would last for a thousand years, as implied by the book of Revelation (20:1–7) or be an astrological age (aeon) of some 2,160 years, they needed a dry hiding place for lengthy preservation of their delicate sacred texts.

Pre–Nag Hammadi Known Texts:
The Tradition of the Great Mysteries

Before the discovery of the Nag Hammadi Library, the British Museum purchased in 1795 an epic Gnostic manuscript, the Pistis Sophia (Power-Wisdom), and work on its translation began in the 1850s. In it, the resurrected Jesus guides his disciples (especially Mary Magdalene) into the regions of the invisible world, revealing many esoteric mysteries—in particular, he tells the story of the repentance of Pistis Sophia, a "fallen" archetypal feminine figure.

The religious scholar Morton Smith found in 1958 at the monastery of Mar Saba in the Judean desert a copy of a letter by the church father Clement of Alexandria written about 195 CE, which he then spent years validating. Clement had argued at length against the Gnostics, but some suspect him too of Gnostic tendencies. In this private letter Clement admitted the existence and authenticity of a *secret* Gospel of Mark, which had been used by some "heretics." In his own day it was also being used in the Church, "being read only to those who are being initiated into the great mysteries." He then provided its text. A section that would fit the known chapter 10 of Mark, between verses 34 and 35, for example, tells of a youth who was ritually initiated by Jesus into the "kingdom of God." In *The Gnostic Gospels,* Elaine Pagels shows several traits of Clement's own teachings, which were features of the Gnostics, such as characterizing God in feminine as well as masculine terms and advocating equality for women in religious practices. Hans Jonas's classic study *The Gnostic Religion* was based only on these texts. Yet they were enough, for example, to convince Carl Gustav Jung of the great importance of Gnosticism.

The Inner Teachings of Jesus:
Not Heaven and Hell but Spiritual Awakening

The "Gnostics" were known before the Nag Hammadi find almost only from the orthodox church fathers, who—as I have mentioned—had treated them as heretics and who had the backing of the imperial Roman authorities (the heirs to those who had crucified Jesus). But as Elaine Pagels writes: "Those who wrote and circulated these texts did not regard themselves as heretics. . . . [M]any claim to offer traditions about Jesus that are secret, hidden from 'the many' who constitute what . . . came to be called the 'Catholic Church.'" These ancient Christians are now called "Gnostics," from the Greek word *gnosis,* which means the knowledge that comes through observation or experience (rather than hearsay or reading). We could translate it as "insight," for gnosis involves an intuitive process of seeing and knowing oneself.

We know from the synoptic Gospels that Jesus spoke in parables to enable simple people to understand some of his sublime intentions. To his close disciples he revealed more, even that he was going to be killed. But he also complained that even the disciples had not understood (or could not understand) him and were unreliable (as in the case when he found them arguing who among them was the most important). The first Gnostic text found spoke of "*the Secret* words which the living Jesus spoke." Gnostic texts were intended for the few who might understand, who might attain the experiential and paradoxical knowledge they called "Gnosis." There were also non-Christian Gnostics, but the Christian Gnostic texts were said to be the *inner* teachings of Jesus, given privately on special occasions. Gnosis asked not for faith and blind conformity but for genuine self-knowledge. Rather than projecting an outer devil, Gnosis ultimately calls each person to recognize her inner demons, get rid of them, and find courage and have an open mind to face the world's problems.

For official Christianity, Paradise and hell were of the ultimate importance and the real means for its hegemony. The keys of Paradise were given to Jesus, and he gave them to the Church (so much so that eventually the Catholic Church did sell indulgences that released people from hell for a period, depending on the price). But for the Gnostics, Paradise and hell were seen not as other worlds but as states of mind in this world. Alternatively, they often taught that hell is this world, formed by some deficient creator god, and that the only way to escape it is through that special Gnostic knowledge. Although the Church insisted on the literality of the Gospel events, and especially the Resurrection, for the Gnostics these were also just parables containing an inner message. Thus, resurrection meant not bodily return from death but spiritual awakening from being a "living dead" living in a state of unconsciousness.

Three Main Religions:
Rabbinical Judaism, Christianity, and Gnostic Christianity

In the year 70 CE the Temple in Jerusalem was destroyed, leaving the Jewish people confused. The rituals in the temple were the core of Judaism and the only thing that held its numerous sects together. Soon the new rabbinical Jewish religion would be founded outside of Jerusalem, and the Christian religion would separate from the Jewish people, spreading the truth of Jesus, or actually the truth that Paul claimed about Jesus, around the entire world. But there was another little sect, a former Christian sect that did not follow the Paulian way—the Gnostics.

One of the greatest challenges that the Roman Empire ever faced was "the Jewish wars." At the core of these wars was the issue of monotheism versus paganism. Although a sort of monotheism was also advocated by some of the great Greek philosophers, it was not on a level that challenged organized religions (though Socrates was sentenced to death for heresy). But with Judaism, that was another matter. **HaShem** was considered not only "the God of the Jews" or of Judea but as always the sole Universal Lord—and all the other gods were totally denied. By the first century conversions to Judaism were so common within the Roman Empire that any statistician or augur could extrapolate the fate of the Roman Empire as becoming dominated by the One God of Israel—which in a way eventually indeed happened through Christianity.

This conflict led to the destruction of the Jerusalem Temple (70 CE) and then the eradication of Judea (135 CE) and its conversion into "Palestine." The old religion of Israel was thereby shattered into three main religions: (rabbinical) Judaism, Christianity, and

Gnostic Christianity. The first two strove to keep their coherence, whereas Gnostic Christianity was made up of many different sects and versions. Of these three split-off religions, eventually one—the "orthodox" Christian Church—prevailed and took over the Roman Empire, and in the process adopted the same imperial centrist organization and the exclusive authority to interpret the scriptures as the empire. Having done so, the Church went out to obliterate its sister religions. Christian (and all other) Gnosticism was eradicated and its literature destroyed, while Judaism was persecuted and reviled.

Yet in the process, Christianity made its own accommodation between monotheism and polytheism with the mystery of the Triune Godhead—the Three that are One. One perhaps unintended effect of this construction was that by adopting the Trinity as its foundational image, Christianity also adopted an exclusive male divinity. (As the Pythagoreans and then the Neoplatonists such as Iamblichus showed, three is "the first male number," and four is "a feminine number.") Note that Judaism and Gnosis also made their own accommodations between monism and plurality. Judaism developed its mysticism that started with the fourfold *Merkavah* mysticism (which I shall presently introduce) and the tenfold Qabbalah constructs. Gnosticism had a basic duality of, on the one hand, a plurality of daemonic-mythical agents who made our basically defective world and rule it, much like the gods of polytheism, and, on the other hand, a transcendental God that does not take part in the mundane affairs and whose exalted domain can be reached only by those who have the secret yet experiential Knowledge—the true Gnosis.

The big theological question that these three religions had to contend with after the destruction of the Temple of Jerusalem was that of the prevalence and even supremacy of evil in this world.

How could a claimed sole and omnipotent God—who is by definition good—allow evil to win? The orthodox Christianity that followed Paul of Tarsus had two answers: First, it developed the
theory of "original sin" (rooted in Paul and perfected by Saint Augustine in the fourth century) that held that back in the worldly
Paradise, the first Adam sinned and thereby made all descendant
humankind guilty and sinners by nature. So this universal sin also
brought about a vengeful world through "God the Father" and
sure perdition in hell for all. But since God still loved the world so
much, he sent his Only Begotten Son to become "the Second
Adam," and his ultimate self-sacrifice redeemed the sin of the
First Adam . . . but only for those who believe in this story and
obey the dictates of his licensed agent, the Church, and purchase
indulgences from hell through proper personal sacrifice, either
monetary or in kind. It was presumably this claimed power of the
Church to release its followers from eternal suffering in hell that
led to its greater popularity and eventual victory over its Gnostic
competitors. The second and connected answer was the building
up of the image of Satan, and his Kingdom of Hell, to such a great
power (and really glory) that borders on dualism—Satan is the
"Prince of the World" who wields immense power.

Paul presented the Hebrew Bible as a temporary measure, an
"Old Testament" that needed to be replaced by the New. But is it
possible that the Pauline interpretation of Christianity (the anti-
Judaic doctrines) was itself a temporary measure, borrowed from
the pagans (especially those of Asia Minor, his native country) to
make Christianity attractive and acceptable to them? Should perhaps the Pauline doctrines be regarded as temporary, an instrument for their time? Would they not be unnecessary for the time
of "the Great and Holy Generation" to which the Gospel of Judas
aspires? I shall return to consider Saint Paul in the next chapter.

From the Gnostic perspective, it would be Paul—rather than Judas—who was the traitor to Jesus' message. The Gnostics had different answers from Paul to the question of the source of evil in this world. According to the reports of their enemies among the church fathers, they regarded "God the Father," or "the Jewish God," not as the sole supreme God but as a secondary, and defective, "Demiurge"—the callous maker of this world. One Gnostic sect, the Ophites, thus completely reversed the story of the Garden of Eden and the "original sin."

The Ophites were a Gnostic sect that evolved during the second century CE and existed for several centuries thereafter. Their name was derived from the Greek *ophis*, meaning "serpent," and relates to the great reverence that the Ophites had toward the serpent. According to the theologians Origen, Irenaeus, and others, the essence of the Ophitic doctrine was that the God of the Old Testament was a misanthropic deity from whose power mankind had to be liberated. From this point of view the serpent in the Garden of Eden was seen as a benefactor to mankind when he urged Adam and Eve to revolt against such a God. As a mark of reverence for the serpent, it was reported, a snake took part in the sect's communion service.

Thus, Epiphanius, a fourth-century church father, reported that the snake was kept in a chest and at the beginning of the service was summoned out to roll among the loaves of bread that were on the table; the loaves were then broken and eaten. Afterward, each of those present would kiss the snake on the mouth, for it had been tamed by a spell. They would then fall down and worship the snake as a part of their Eucharistic service.

Likewise, other enemies of the Old Testament God became heroes of this and other Gnostic sects—and so, it seems, was the New Testament figure of Judas.

Gnosis as a Derivative of Esoteric Judaism,
Whose Enemy Was the Catholic Church

When the research on Gnosis began, the initial impression was that Gnosis was as anti-Jewish as could be. Superficially, the canonical Gospels and the Gnostic Gospels had something in common. Both were the result of a "clash of civilizations" of their time, the clash between the Judaic and Hellenic cultures, and both could be expected to share a basic anti-Semitic attitude. However, the Gnostics seemingly had no need to vilify Judas because they felt a need to discredit "the Jewish God" himself. Gnosis assumed a hierarchy of gods. The lower one (or ones) was the one who created this world, which the Gnostics regarded as faulty. It was created as a trap for human souls, which were from another—higher—realm of the superior god. The assumption was that it was this creator of Genesis, "the Jewish God," who indeed created this world, but out of malice or stupidity, which made his creation a disaster.

As discoveries came in, especially the great Gnostic library found at Nag Hammadi, Egypt, the picture changed. Many passages were found that regarded Judaic beliefs positively, as well as many imports from Jewish exegesis and mysticism. It started to appear that, rather than being an anti-Judaic movement, Gnosis was actually a derivative of esoteric Judaism, and its real enemy was not Judaism but the organized orthodox/Catholic Church.

The Gospel of Judas takes today's tendency to appreciate (esoteric) Judaism a step further. Ostensibly, not only is Judas, the symbolic Jew, no longer portrayed as the villain, but rather he appears as the hero. His higher position comes because of his inner knowledge, or Gnosis—he is portrayed as the only one of the disciples who knows Jesus' true identity—and this identity has to do with the Hebrew-Jewish recognition of the Godhead and the divine realm. The Gospel of Judas thus suggests that the true knowledge of God and of Jesus resides with the people of Judas.

The Challenge the Gnostic Documents Pose to Orthodox Christianity

Gnosticism was an elitist culture that did not fit in with the emerging hierarchy of the Church. The Church was developing through consolidation of the many early communities under one controlling structure, emulating the imperial Roman order, until it became synonymous with the Roman Empire. The Church developed a hierarchical structure of rule, based on the supposed authority of the first disciples, especially Peter, as the heirs to Jesus and as the only ones who could appoint other clerics, the chief criterion for appointment being obedience to the Church. The Gnostics, on the other hand, saw spiritual experience as the criterion for leadership and had no respect for the appointed clerics who did not understand the inner secrets.

As Christianity was losing its exclusive hold on the European mind, scholars started finding fascination and attraction even in the quotes of these enemies of Gnosticism and were looking with eagerness for the Gnostics' own words.

Elaine Pagels has especially noted in her books the different emphasis in the treatment of women, who in the orthodox Church have been excluded from ministry. In fact, it could be argued that the Gnostic (experiential) approach was inherently feminine, which is why there is awakened interest in it today, a time of "feminine revival."

Gnostic Teachers

To give a taste of Gnosticism, I shall present here just three of its teachers: Valentinus, Basilides, and Mani.

Valentinus, the Gnostic Who Almost Became Pope

Valentinus was considered by many the greatest of all Gnostic teachers. Rather than a marginal figure, he almost became the pope of orthodox Christianity. Valentinus was born in Africa, probably Carthage, around or before AD 100. He was educated in Alexandria and in the prime of his life transferred his residence to Rome, where he achieved a high degree of prominence in the Christian community between AD 135 and 160. Orthodox church father Tertullian wrote that Valentinus was a candidate for the office of bishop of Rome and that he lost the election by a rather narrow margin. Tertullian (who later also became a heretic) alleges that Valentinus fell into apostasy around AD 175. There is much evidence indicating, however, that Valentinus was never universally condemned as a heretic in his lifetime and that he was a respected member of the Christian community until his death. He was almost certainly a priest in the mainstream church and may even have been a bishop. Valentinus, the Gnostic who almost became pope, was perhaps the only man who could have succeeded in gaining a form of permanent positive recognition for the Gnostic approach to the message of Christ.

The cosmogony of Valentinus might be summarized thus: Something is wrong. We live in a system that is lacking in essential integrity, and thus is defective. Orthodox Christianity accounts for it chiefly in terms of the effects of human sin. This means that all evil, discomfort, and terror in our lives and in history are somehow our fault and our guilt. Valentinus, however, held that the defect is not the result of our wrongdoing but is inherent in the system of existence, attributing the creation of the world to a defective god.

Taking a psychological approach, Stephan A. Hoeller argues in *The Gnostic Jung and the Seven Sermons to the Dead* that Valentinus teaches that because our minds have lost their self-knowledge, we live in a self-created world that is lacking in integrity. The proposition that the human mind lives in a largely self-created world of illusion from whence only the enlightenment of a kind of Gnosis can rescue it has analogues in the two great religions of Hinduism and Buddhism.

In addition to baptism, anointing, the Eucharist, the initiation of priests, and the rites of the dying, the Valentinian Gnosis mentions prominently two great and mysterious sacraments called "redemption" *(apolytrosis)* and the "bridal chamber," references to which can be found in the Gnostic scriptures.

The (non-Valentinian) Gnostic Gospel according to Thomas presents us with a clear formulation of the theoretical foundation of the bridal chamber in its twenty-second logion: "When you make the two one, and when you make the inner as the outer and the outer as the inner and the above as the below, and when you make the male and the female into a single one, so that the male will not be male and the female not be female . . . then shall you enter the kingdom."

The Sophia myth serves as mythological support of this sacrament. The return of the soul into the loving embrace of her bridegroom, indicated by the return of Sophia into the arms of Jesus, represents the healing of this disruption and restoration of wholeness.

The complementary liberation from the clutches of the world of defect was accomplished by the sacrament of redemption *(apolytrosis)*, sometimes also called restoration *(apokatastasis)*. The individual in whom the dualities have been united and the splits healed is now empowered to repudiate the forces bereft of illuminating meaning. This is well expressed in one of the formulas of restoration preserved from a Valentinian source, through the writing of his opponent—Irenaeus: "I am established, I am redeemed and I redeem my soul from this aeon and from all that comes from it, in the name of IAO, who redeemed his soul unto the redemption in Christ, the living one."

Basilides, Who Thought Simon Was Crucified in Place of Christ

Basilides was a native of Alexandria and flourished under Emperors Hadrian and Antoninus Pius, about 120–140. Basilides invented prophets named Barcabbas and Barcoph and claimed to have received verbal instructions from the apostle Saint Matthias and to be a disciple of Glaucias, a disciple of Saint Peter who was vested with secret revelations from Paul. Basilides recognized Abraxas as the Supreme Being whom he worshiped. Nearly all the writings of Basilides have perished, but the names of three of his works, including twenty-four commentaries on the Christian Gospels and some fragments, have come down to us. So most of what we know of his teachings is from his Christian adversaries. However, the reporting of Hippolytus and of Irenaeus are quite contradictory.

Hippolytus sets forth the doctrine of Basilides as follows: There was a time when nothing existed, neither matter nor form, nor accident, not any of the things that are called by names or perceived by the mind or the senses. The Not-Being God was the Seed of the world. The World-seed contained in itself a threefold Filiation: one composed of refined elements, a second of grosser elements, and a third needing purification. There arose out of the World-seed the Great Archon, or Ruler. He created for himself a Son out of the heap of World-seed; this was the Christ. The same process is repeated, and we have a second Archon and his Son. Both spheres, including the 365 heavens and their chief Archon, Abraxas, know the truth. Last, the third Filiation must be raised to the Not-Being God. Jesus, the Son of Mary, through his life and death redeemed the third Filiation.

From the viewpoint of Irenaeus, Basilides taught that Nous (Mind) was the first to be born from the Unborn Father; from Nous (who was also Christ) was born Logos (Reason); from Logos, Phronesis (Prudence); from Phronesis, Sophia (Wisdom) and Dynamis (Strength); and from Phronesis and Dynamis, the Virtues, Principalities, and Archangels. By these angelic hosts the highest heaven was made, by their descendants the second heaven, and by the descendants again of these the third, and so on until they reached the number 365. Hence, the year has as many days as there are heavens. Again quoting Irenaeus in *Against Heresies:*

> Those angels who occupy the lowest heaven, that, namely, which is visible to us, formed all the things which are in the world, and made allotments among themselves of the earth and of those nations which are upon it. The chief of them is he who is thought to be the God of the Jews; and inasmuch as he desired to render the other nations subject to his own people, that is, the Jews, all the other princes resisted and opposed him. Wherefore all other nations were at enmity with his nation.

But the father without birth and without name, perceiving that they would be destroyed, sent his own first-begotten Nous (he it is who is called Christ) to bestow deliverance on them that believe in him, from the power of those who made the world. He appeared, then, on earth as a man, to the nations of these powers, and wrought miracles. Wherefore he did not himself suffer death, but Simon, a certain man of Cyrene, being compelled, bore the cross in his stead; so that this latter being transfigured by him, that he might be thought to be Jesus, was crucified, through ignorance and error, while Jesus himself received the form of Simon, and, standing by, laughed at them. For since he was an incorporeal power, and the Nous (mind) of the unborn father, he transfigured himself as he pleased, and thus ascended to him who had sent him, deriding them, inasmuch as he could not be laid hold of, and was invisible to all.

Those, then, who know these things have been freed from the principalities who formed the world; so that it is not incumbent on us to confess him who was crucified, but him who came in the form of a man, and was thought to be crucified, and was called Jesus, and was sent by the father, that by this dispensation he might destroy the works of the makers of the world. If any one, therefore, he declares, confesses the crucified, that man is still a slave, and under the power of those who formed our bodies; but he who denies him has been freed from these beings, and is acquainted with the dispensation of the unborn father.

Out of Epiphanius and pseudo-Tertullian we can complete the description of this: the highest god, that is, the Unborn Father, bears the mystical name Abraxas, as the origin of the 365 heavens. The Angels that made the world formed it out of Eternal Matter; but matter is the principle of all evil, hence the contempt of the

Gnostics for it. To undergo martyrdom in order to confess the crucified is useless, for it is to die for Simon of Cyrene, not for Christ.

Mani, Who Said He Was an Incarnation of Christ

The Persian prophet Manes or Mani founded the Manichaean sect in the third century AD. In legend his life seems to be a rein-carnation of Christ. He was born of a holy virgin named Mariham, or Mar Mariam, whose title was "Mother of the Life of the Whole World." Likewise, Mani preached, healed the sick, and eventually was crucified and flayed (by a Persian king). In legend, like Christ, Mani was tempted by the demon-god on the mountaintop. In re-turn for his worship Christ was offered "all the kingdoms of the earth." Christ refused, and so did Mani. Mani said he was the reincarnated Christ, and then he took on the powers of the Holy Spirit as he chose twelve partners, or disciples, to come out of Persia and spread his teachings.

Mani's doctrines were strictly Gnostic and puritanical. They in-cluded the strict abomination of all matter, especially the flesh. The devil created the material world and also made sex to entrap the ethereal souls in the prison of the flesh. According to Mani, the devil-god, which created the world, was the Jewish Jehovah. Mani said, "It is the Prince of Darkness who spoke with Moses, the Jews and their priests. Thus the Christians, the Jews, and the Pa-gans are involved in the same error when they worship this God. For he leads them astray in the lusts he taught them."

The church father Saint Augustine, the real author of the origi-nal-sin doctrine, was first a Manichaean for some ten years but later repudiated Mani's teachings, and thus smuggled original sin into the Christian doctrine. The Church had reasons to stamp out this heresy, as Manichaeans and other related sects stressed the holiness of their leaders and priests, which was extremely dangerous for the Church. The Church fiercely battled Manichaeism during the early centuries, thinking that it had rooted the teaching out, but it kept cropping up in the Middle Ages in sects such as the Cathars, Paulicians, Albigenses (or Albigensians), Bogomils, and many others.

Mythological Figures in Gnosis

Owing to the experiential and anarchistic nature of Gnosticism and the diversity of Gnostic teachers and prophets, there was a great multiplicity of mythological figures and of Gnostic sects. Gnosticism presents an apparent bestiary of mythical creatures; the aeons, such as Abraxas, Yaldabaoth, Saklas, and Nebro; and Seth and Sophia. On the face of it, this looks like idolatry and mythical imagination run wild. But modern advocates of Gnosis also recognize in these creatures inner archetypes that animate the inner world of individuals and all humankind.

Some such names are plain Greek terms—such as "Sophia," meaning "Wisdom." Others, which appear to be strange names, are usually Hebrew names or derivations of Hebrew words, held by the Gnostics in either respect or contempt. Thus, "Seth" (the third son of Adam in Genesis) and "Elohim" (a name that appears in the Gnostic Secret Book of John and is the same as the name of the creator-God of Genesis 1) are clearly Hebrew. A name that appears in the Gospel of Judas, "Saklas," may mean *Sakhal* (Hebrew for "Fool") or *Ksil* (also "Fool," as well as the star constellation Orion). Like many of the names of the gods of antiquity, these names are often concocted so as to have a numerical gematria value that signifies the special quality of that god. I now offer brief notes about some of these figures.

Abraxas: The Supreme Being

Abraxas is the name used by Basilides and his followers to designate the Supreme Being, from whom Jesus also emanated. The Greek name is Abraxas and has seven letters whose numerical (gematria) value is 365, the number of heavens and gods that Abraxas controls in the system of Basilides. The Demiurge ("people-worker") was ignorant of the existence of Abraxas. Jung's modern "Seven Sermons to the Dead" purport to present Abraxas.

Sophia: A Feminine Embodiment of Wisdom

"Sophia" means "Wisdom" and is feminine. Note that a feminine embodiment of wisdom already appears in the "wisdom literature" of the Jewish Bible and much of the Apocrypha. She is of great importance to the Gnostic worldview and is well known from the first discovered complete Gnostic text, the Pistis Sophia, in which she gets rather foolishly entangled in the celestial worlds ruled by the Archons but is finally redeemed by Christ. In the course of her journeying, Sophia came to emanate from her own being a flawed consciousness, a being who became the creator of the material and psychic cosmos, all of which he created in the image of his own flaw.

Yaldabaoth: Maker of This Physical World

Yaldabaoth is a common "Sethian" Gnostic name for the Demiurge, the purported maker of this (physical) world. This being, unaware of his origins, imagined himself to be the ultimate and absolute God. One Gnostic text says thus: "Ialdabaoth, becoming arrogant in spirit, boasted himself over all those who were below him, and explained, 'I am the father, and God, and above me there is no one,' his mother hearing him speak thus, cried out against him: 'Do not lie, Ialdabaoth, for the father of all, the primal Anthopos, is above you, and so is Anthropos, the son of Anthopos.'"

Many different explanations have been proposed for this outlandish name, and it is generally assumed that it derives from mystical Judaism, but this cannot be determined. It may have to do with *Yeled*, "Child" or "Son," and might be interpreted as *Yeled (ha) Ba'ot* (ילד באות), "Child of the Future" or "Child of the Sign," or *Yeled ba'at* (ילד הבצתה), "Child of the Fear" or *Yeled ba'Et* (ילד בצת), "Child of the Period."

This brings up quite an amazing possibility—that this "child," Yeled, is a reference to the concept of the "Son of God" that organized orthodox/Catholic Christianity adopted and made into the sole effective deity ("No one comes to the Father but through me") and the creator of the world (as in the Gospel of John). We shall see later the possibility that the book of Revelation is a covert Gnostic text that was "smuggled" into the Christian canon yet carries a hidden message that the Beast of 666 that it describes is the image of Jesus as used by the organized Church, indeed an idol. The openly Gnostic Gospel of Judas explicitly states that the disciples would set a false religion under the name of Jesus Christ. It is thus possible that the **Yaldabaoth** of the Gnostic texts is the purported Christian "Son of God" who sees himself as the Father, the sole creator.

The Concept of Aeons (Emanations of God) in Gnosticism

In many Gnostic systems, the various emanations of God—who is also known by such names as the One, the Monad, Aion Teleos (the Perfect Aeon), Bythos (Depth or Profundity; Greek βυθός), Proarkhe (Before the Beginning; Greek πρόαρχή), the Arkhe (the Beginning; Greek ἡ αρχή)—are called aeons. This first being is also an aeon and has an inner being within itself, known as Ennoea (Thought), Charis (Grace), or Sige (Silence; Greek Σιγη). This perfect being conceives within itself the second aeon, Caen (Power). Along with the male Caen comes the female aeon Akhana (Truth, Love).

Aeons bear a number of similarities to Judeo-Christian angels, including their roles as servants and emanations of God and their existence as beings of light. In fact, certain Gnostic angels, such as Armozel, are also aeons.

The aeons often came in male/female pairs called *syzygies* and were frequently numerous (twenty to thirty). Two of the most commonly listed aeons were Jesus and Sophia. The aeons constitute the *Pleroma*, the "region of light." The lowest regions of the *Pleroma* are closest to the darkness—that is, the physical world.

When an aeon named Sophia emanated without her partner aeon, the result was the Demiurge, or half-creator (occasionally referred to in Gnostic texts as Yaldabaot), a creature that should never have come into existence. This creature did not belong to the *Pleroma*, and the One emanated two savior aeons, Christ and the Holy Spirit, to save humanity from the Demiurge. Christ then took the form of the human Jesus, in order to be able to teach humanity how to achieve Gnosis, that is, return to the *Pleroma*. The Gospel of Judas, too, mentions the aeons and speaks of Jesus' teachings of them.

According to Tertullian's *Against the Valentinians* (Latin: *Adversus Valentinianos*), chapters 7 and 8 (we know the details of this system only from its opponents), the Gnostic Valentinus knew of thirty different aeons that emanated from each other in sequence. The first eight of these aeons (corresponding to generations one through four discussed next) are referred to as the "Ogdoad."

Barbelo

Of special interest to us is the figure of "Barbelo," who was already mentioned in the Pistis Sophia and mentioned in the Gospel of Judas and appears in other Gnostic texts—and with whom I shall deal extensively. Thus, in the Secret Book of John (which gives much the same cosmology narrated briefly in the Gospel of Judas and in the anonymous Gnostic document "On the Origin of the World"), the figure of Barbelo is portrayed as female and given a few details: "The Father of All knew his own image when he saw it in the pure water of light which surrounded him. His thought . . . stood before him out of the glory of the light: this is the power which is before all . . . the likeness of the light, the image of the invisible. She is the perfect power of Barbelo, the perfect aeon of glory." In his book *Gnosis: The Nature and History of Gnosticism*, Kurt Rudolph summarizes: "Barbelo represents the female aspect of the Father and is a kind of Gnostic mother goddess. Probably she has been since the beginning one person with Sophia. . . . However, she has at the same time also bisexual features; she is 'the first male virgin aeon.' For the Gnostics bisexuality is an expression of perfection." From third-century church father sources we know of a Gnostic sect called "Barbeliotes," after this Barbelo, which was one of the largest groups in Gnosis.

The addition of the feminine, of a "Judith," to the story of Jesus and Judas introduces a fourth element, which has been suggested all along by the name "Barbelo" (or *BeArba Elu*) as the holy domain to which Jesus belongs.

In his interpretation of the Pistis Sophia, J. J. Hurtak explains "Barbelo" in two ways: as the "Mother" in the Sethian-Gnostic divine triad and as the perfect model of seminal male-female unity in the Most High God. The name is perhaps a corrupt form of the Coptic *belbile* (seed). Our following discussion encompasses Hurtak's intentions.

Barbelo is hinted at in the Gospel of Judas, where of all the twelve disciples only Judas knows Jesus' true identity—as coming from "the Immortal Domain of Barbelo" and likewise sent from the unutterable (*haShem*).

I prefer the explanation of the scholars who translated the Gospel of Judas (as well as of Jung) that "the name of Barbelo seems to be based on a form of the Tetragrammaton, the holy four-letter Name of the Lord in Judaism, and it apparently comes from the Hebrew—perhaps 'God (El) in (b) four (arba).'" As a native Hebrew speaker and student of the Qabbalah, I would like to take this further and submit that Barbelo is the Greek or Coptic rendering for *beARBA ELU*, namely, "With/through These Four." This expression/name follows the same pattern as the first word of the Hebrew Bible (*BeREShIT*) and the first word of the source book of the Qabbalah, the Sepher Yetsirah (*BiShloshim u'Shtayim*), with the number 32. The gematria (numerical value of the Hebrew letters) of *BeARBA ELU* is 312, which equals 13 × 24 and

12 × 26, all significant numbers in the Gospel of Judas. These "four" signal the application or materialization of the four-letter holy name (YHWH) that, by Jewish understanding, should not be uttered by anyone but the high priest. So Judas, who recognized the unutterable name, is a **Ba'al Shem**—a knower or adept of the divine names.

Is the Judas Gospel a Gospel (Good News)? Good News for the Jews?

The first question that we may ask about this newly found "Gospel" is: Is it really a "Gospel" in the most literal sense? That is, does this discovery constitute "Good News" (which is what the word *Gospel* means)? In this book we shall find out for whom this discovery is indeed good news—or could become so. The first claim about this Gospel, which has already drawn the most attention, is that Judas is no longer presented as a villain and traitor but as the closest confidant of Jesus.

According to the canonical Gospels, Judas betrayed Jesus Christ to the Jewish authorities, who delivered him to the Roman authorities by whom he was crucified. The Gospel of Judas portrays this act positively, as being performed in obedience to the instructions of Jesus, rather than as a betrayal. ("But you will exceed all of them. For you will sacrifice the man that clothes me.") This positive portrayal appears to be based on the Gnostic notion that the human form is itself a confinement and that Judas' action was intended to release the Spirit of Christ from its physical constraints.

In the Gospel of Judas, Judas' act, as we have seen, is instigated not by Satan but by Christ himself and is done not as devilish betrayal but for a higher purpose. On the other hand, it warns that even Jesus' pious disciples and the Church they founded are liable to create human sacrifice through ignorance.

In the centuries during which the Christian Church has interpreted Judas as a traitor, it has also tended to equate Judas with the Jews. Hence, the Church has planted seeds of anti-Semitism. In fact, the Jews suffered terribly because of the way that Judas—and with him all Jews—was portrayed in the canonical Gospels (as will be further discussed in Chapter 16). Seeing Judas as a saint instead turns all such anti-Semitic views on their head and thereby constitutes, indeed, potential good news for the Jews. But it is also good news to many Christians who are uncomfortable with various manifestations of historic Christianity.

The Gospel According to Judas and the Church

The Gospel of Judas does not claim that the other disciples were in agreement with the teachings it brings forth. On the contrary, its message is that the disciples (by whom the Church was built) had not learned the true Gospel, which Jesus taught exclusively to Judas Iscariot. The Gospel of Judas asserts not only that the actions of Judas were necessary but also that Judas was acting on the orders of Jesus himself. The Judas in the canonical Gospels is portrayed as a villain and as cursed by Jesus in the words "Alas for that man by whom the Son of Man is betrayed. It would be better for that man if he had never been born" (Mark 14:21; Matt. 26:24). The Judas Gospel, however, portrays him as a divinely appointed instrument of a grand and predetermined purpose. The text says that Jesus tells Judas, "You will exceed all of them. For you will sacrifice the man that clothed me," and "In the last days they will curse your ascent to the holy [generation]."

Such claims cause consternation to traditional Christianity. For example, the *Catholic Encyclopedia,* which does ponder Judas' act and its contradictions in the traditional accounts and mentions the previously found Gnostic writings that exonerated Judas, concludes, "However difficult it may be to understand, we cannot question the guilt of Judas."

Does the new discovery change the picture? Early in 2006, it was reported in the news that some Vatican scholars, in anticipation of the publication of the Judas Gospel, called for the rehabilitation of Judas Iscariot. But following the publication and subsequent uproar, the pope quickly reasserted Judas' guilt. Looking into Protestant sects, the picture is complex, and even the Christadelfians who are pro-Jewish and pro-Zionist still regard Judas as a villain.

In some other Christian congregations, however, we find, even without the help of the Gospel of Judas or Gnosis, a different attitude toward Judas. For example, according to Tentmaker Ministries:

To summarize: be careful where you place Judas. He **did** the will of the Father and fulfilled the Scriptures. Peter, who we all love, tried to prevent Jesus' crucifixion and was called "Satan" by our Lord. Peter, who was not mindful of the will of God, was restored. Was it not Jesus who said, "For whoever **does the will of My Father** who is in heaven, he is My **brother** and sister and mother" (Matt. 12:50). Be careful about placing Jesus' brother, Judas, in Christendom's "hell." One day you may have to look up to Judas, instead of looking down on him. Peter denied him three times in one night while Judas declared Jesus innocent in front of the High Priesthood. Judas had a very important job in the Kingdom of God. For three and one half years, as a Priest he inspected the Lamb of God as an unbiased man. He was not "one of them," a Galilean. He was the outsider. He did his job perfectly. If

Judas really wanted to mess things up, he could have agreed with the High Priesthood and called Him a "blasphemer" who claimed to be the Son of God when He really wasn't. But Judas declared the Lamb spotless and unblemished, the Perfect Passover. Thank you, Judas, for not only being a hearer of the Word, but also a *doer* of the Word. Thank you, Judas, for giving the redemption money which purchased the Potter's field; a place for strangers in the land of Israel and the silver which speaks of the redemption of the family of Adam who sold himself as a slave to sin. You may not like how Judas got that money, but you should rejoice in what it did for you.

Whatever despised place Judas may have held in the traditional Church, then, he held no such place in the Gnosticism that flourished at the time of Christ. He was, on the contrary, a leading spokesman for a well-developed system of thinking, a system we see particularly well developed in the Jewish Qabbalah.

CHAPTER 4

The Role of the
Judaic Qabbalah in Gnosis

PLATO'S *TIMAEUS* OPENS with the words, "One, two, three, but where is the fourth?" In the Hebrew Bible there is a recurring motif of "three and four." Thus, the prophet Amos uses it eight times (1:3, 1:6, 1:9, 1:11, 1:13, 2:1, 2:4, 2:6) to announce the sins of various nations, but actually mentions only the fourth sin, which is the decisive one that would bring divine retribution. The book of Proverbs uses this pattern four times (30:15–17, 30:18–19, 30:21–23, 30:24–28, 30:29–31), where all five terms are listed. The most famous and most pertinent is the second instance: "There are three things which are too wonderful for me, yea, four which I know not: the way of the eagle in the air, the way of the serpent upon a rock, the way of a ship in the midst of the sea, and the way of a man with a maid."

By the time of the arguments with the Gnostics, orthodox Christian Church doctrine had crystallized into the pattern of the Holy Trinity. Obviously, the Gnostics were claiming that the Church was missing something (or some things). The very idea of the missing fourth principle is suggested in the Gospel of Judas by stating that all the disciples apart from Judas did not realize that

Jesus came from the exalted realm of "Barbelo"—which I have interpreted here as representing "in these four," the quaternary principle. We may find that missing fourth element by studying a living Gnostic tradition, one that has become a part of Judaism ("Judah-ism").

Whereas Gnostic Christianity has died (or has been killed by the organized Church), Judaism provided for its own Gnostic strand a niche where it could develop quite uninterruptedly for the two thousand years from Jesus until now. This Jewish-Hebrew Gnosis has gone through many phases and received various names, which are by now all subsumed under the name "Kabbalah" and—actually more exactly—Qabbalah. (By the rules of transliteration of the Israel Academy for the Hebrew Language, the letter Qof [ק] should be transliterated by the English letter *Q* [rather than *K* or *C*], which was historically derived from it.) It is correct to use Sephardic diction, with the accent on the last syllable. In this form the name Qabbalah makes a meaningful word, namely, Acceptance (or Tradition). In the following we shall look at a single strand of the Qabbalah—one that parallels the Gnostic concept of "Barbelo," the principle of the Holy Quaternary.

There is a major difference, however, between Qabbalah and Gnosis, which has to do with the Judaic special appreciation of the material and the real. Judaism does deal with spirituality and Gnosis but does not exclude appreciation of the Creation and its products. Gnostics often rejected the Creator God, often identified with the god of the Jews (and therefore of the Christians), as an evil god, and praised the Hidden God, longing to join him—just as, according to the Gospel of Judas, Jesus meant to do with Judas' help.

Yet there are many parallels between Gnosis and Jewish mysticism. Thus, the foremost modern Qabbalah scholar, Gershom Scholem, describes the Qabbalah as "Jewish Gnosticism" in his book *Jewish Gnosticism, Merkabah Mysticism, and Talmudic Tradition*. Scholem marvels how, a thousand years after the suppression of the Gnosis in Christianity, Gnostic concepts suddenly reemerged among Jewish mystics in Provence and in Spain (Catalonia and Castile). This quasi-miraculous resurrection is even more remarkable now when the Qabbalah is having a tremendous revival—among Jews and also Gentiles (with the unfortunate side effect that some of those who purport to teach or experiment with the Qabbalah do not have a clue as to what they are doing).

The main tool of the Qabbalah is the Hebrew language, and most of its insights are couched in the combinations and meanings of Hebrew letters and words. For example, the same Hebrew letters of the word **Qabbalah** (קבלה) can be permutated to **BeLaHaQ** (בלה"ק), which is a common acronym for **Be'Lshon Ha'Qodesh**—"In the Holy Language," namely, in liturgical Hebrew. Such permutation of Hebrew letters is actually a very common and basic practice of the Qabbalah. Just as one cannot study physics without knowing mathematics, one cannot really understand the Qabbalah without good command of the Hebrew language. I shall try, however, to illustrate a few pertinent concepts of the Qabbalah by using some English words in the manner of the Qabbalah. But first let us see a parallel of Gnosticism and the Qabbalah in discerning a certain multiplicity in the Godhead, in this case by the feminine divine figure of **Shekhinah**.

Mysticism in Judaism: "Divine Presence in This World"

"Two who sit and engage in Torah study, there is **Shekhinah** between them." With this image from tractate **Avot** (or "Wisdom of the Fathers") in the Mishnah, the Jewish treasury of concepts acquired one of its most loaded terms. Although it is very likely that the term *Shekhinah* had been known for generations before, in sacred writings we know of it from only two references in the Mishnah. From then on we read of it mainly after the destruction of the second temple. In the first stage, explains scholar Ephrayim Urbach, the *Shekhinah* was only a poetic literary image paralleling that of the Holy One (*haQadosh Barukh Hu*). Later, and especially in the Qabbalah (as summarized by Scholem), the *Shekhinah* became the personification of the Divine Presence in this world.

From the first century CE—or a bit before—the term *Shekhinah* served in the Talmudic literature to describe the Divine Habitation or the Divine Presence, especially when near to humans, but undoubtedly as a synonym for the Divine. Everywhere the term *Shekhinah* appears in the Talmud or the early *Midrashim* (exegesis), it is possible to use the appellation "the Holy One" (*haQadosh barukh Hu*) without changing the meaning. In spite of the attempts of later interpreters to identify the *Shekhinah* with a kind of light, in a way parallel to Gnostic conceptions, Urbach proves that "the light glow of the *Shekhina* (*Ziv haShekhinah*) is the Light of God. The expression about 'the Wings of the *Shekhinah*' parallels the verse about the Lord being 'as an eagle watches over its nest, hovers above its young'" (Deut. 32:11).

However, after the destruction of the temple, the use of the term *Shekhinah* increased and acquired another level of nearness and presence—and not just nearness to Israel but also some separation within the Godhead: "The Lord [there *haMaqom*] said to Israel . . . I have put my *Shekhina* among you."

The major dilemma debated in the *Midrashim* after the destruction was what happened to the *Shekhinah* in relation to the nation of Israel, and opinions diverge. The *Mekhilta*, on the one hand, claims: "You should know that the *Shekhina* is not revealed outside the Holy Land, as it is written 'But to escape from the Lord, Jonah set out to Tarshish' (Jonah 1:3). Could he possibly escape from the Lord? For it is already written (Psalm 139:7) 'Where can I escape from your spirit, where flee from your presence?' If I climb up to heaven, you are there' . . . But Jonah said, I shall go outside [the Holy Land], a place where the *Shekhinah* is not revealed." Rabbi Shmu'el bar Nahman supports that *Midrash*, saying, "Until the destruction of the Temple, the *Shekhinah* was situated at the holy sanctuary . . . and when the Temple was destroyed . . . he took his *Shekhinah* up to heaven."

There are two *Midrashim* that explain the direction of Jewish prayer toward the site of the temple that remain in effect today. One, according to Rabbi El'azar ben Pedat, says, "Whether destroyed or whether not destroyed, the *Shekhinah* does not move from her place," namely, the site of the temple. Similarly, the sage Rabbi Aha says, "The *Shekhinah* never moves from the Western Wall of the Temple, as it is said (Cant. 2:9), 'There he stands outside our wall.'"

On the other hand, another Midrash from the *Mekhilta* claims: "Everywhere that Israel were exiled to, it is as if the *Shekhinah* went on exile with them." At that period of confusion and searching grew the attachment to the concept of the *Shekhinah* as a close companion.

In parallel, Hellenic Judaism—especially represented by Philo of Alexandria (where the Gnostics taught)—already regarded Wisdom (*Hokhmah*) in the first century as a feminine entity and the companion of God: "And thus we can rightfully call the Demiurge who created the whole world in the name of the Father of all Creation, whereas in the name of Mother we shall call the Knowledge (or Wisdom) of the Creator. God mated with her and gave birth to the whole creation, even though not in the human manner, but she received the seed of God and gave birth . . . to the beloved only son . . . which is this world."

Wisdom and the **Shekhinah** were the models for additional feminine figures—Rachel crying over her sons, Zion, the Heavenly Jerusalem, and **Kenesset Yisra'el** ("The Assembly of Israel," or the spiritual collectivity of all the people of Israel).

Even more than the **Shekhinah**, this **Kenesset Yisra'el** was described at that time as the one who entered a holy marriage with God: "Whoever enjoys this world without thanks giving [*Berakhah*], it is as if he robs the Holy one and **Kenesset Yisra'el**, as it is written (Proverbs 28:24): 'To rob your father or mother and say you do no wrong' . . . and there is not his Father but the Holy One and not his Mother but **Kenesset Yisra'el**." There is still a clear hierarchy between the two: he acts upon her, and she is dependent on him.

Next came the personification, which is already evident in the **Midrash**. For example (**Eikha Rabbati**), we find that "whenever the **Shekhinah** was leaving the Temple, she would return and hug and kiss the walls of the Temple and its columns and cry and say: Oh good-bye my Temple, good-bye my Royal House . . ." Nevertheless, even in the Jewish mystical and Gnostic literature of that period—the **Heikhalot** and **Merkavah** literature—there is no mention of the **Shekhinah** being an independent entity, as she appears among non-Jewish Gnostics. The Mandaeans, for example, a Gnostic sect that is active even now, already attributed hypostasis (dual person, earthly and heavenly) of the **Shekhinah** in the Talmudic period and spoke of many **Shekhinahs** as places of light. Two sources, apparently written in the eighth century, indicate a new direction. The Yonatan translation of the Torah repeats three times (translating Deut. 33:3–8) the expression "The Lord your God and his **Shekhinah**." Unless this is a scribal error, this is an early division of the Godhead into two divine figures. In the **Midrash** for the Proverbs, the division is still more pronounced. Here at first the **Shekhinah** addresses not humans, as before, but the Holy One: "When the Sanhedrin sought to appoint Solomon as king . . . the **Shekhinah** stood before the Holy One and told him: 'Master of the Universe. . . .'"

It was only among the medieval Jewish philosophers (such as Sa'adia Ga'on, Judah haLevi, and Maimonides) that a separation between the Holy One and the **Shekhinah** is clear-cut. But in order to safeguard monotheism, they determined that the **Shekhinah** became the Divine Glory (**Kavod**), which was created by God. Although she is indeed the primordial creation and her nature is superior to any physical creation, she still has no part in the essence or unity of the divinity.

Just before the revelation of the Qabbalah in the late twelfth century, Rabbi Yehuda ben Barzilay of Barcelona explained the following: "And when the thought came to Him to create His world, He first created the holy spirit for all the creatures, to be a sign to His kingship, which would be recognized by the prophets and the angels. And He created the image of His Throne, to be a throne for the Holy Spirit which is called the divine **Kavod** [Glory], which is a brilliant glory and a great light . . . and the sages call this light **Shekhinah** . . ."

In the early Qabbalah, especially in the **Bahir** ("lucid") and the **Zohar** ("brilliance") books, a new concept of the divinity became formulated. The **Bahir** builds a dynamic conception of the divinity, as having the power of creation and vitality (**Ḥayut**) that flows outside (to the creation) and back again. The traditional concept of an unchanging God became open to new possibilities. A clear distinction was made between the Divinity itself and her creative and formative nature, between the hidden and transcendental

Infinite and the **Sephirot**, which are the revelation of the Divinity in the world (see more on the **Sephirot** in the extra section of Part VI). The **Shekhinah** is the last (tenth) **Sephirah**, the vessel that receives all the other **Sephirot**, that is, a feminine entity: Mother, Bride, and Daughter within the system of divinity. As a rule, the **Shekhinah** became regarded from then on as a mythical hypostasis of the Divine Immanence in the world, a feminine and passive entity. The book of the **Zohar** is attributed to the disciples of second-century Rabbi Shim'on Bar Yohay but actually appeared (and likely was written) in thirteenth-century Castilia in Spain. The name **Zohar** means "brilliance" and is based on Daniel's vision of the End Times (12:3): "Those who are wise (or who impart wisdom) will shine like the brightness (**Zohar**) of the heavens." It has the form of an exegesis of the Pentateuch and the Song of Songs by Rabbi Shim'on and his disciples. Its style is sort of a wedding between the Gospel stories and the Talmudic discourses of the sages. In the Qabbalah school of Nachmanides, the expressed connection between the **Shekhinah**—as the tenth **Sephirah**—and **Knesset Yisra'el**, the Heavenly Jerusalem and Zion, was already made. At that stage, the **Shekhinah** became split into the Higher **Shekhinah** and a Lower **Shekhinah**, where each one expresses another understanding of the role of the feminine aspect: The higher **Shekhinah**—the **Sephirah** of **Binah** (Understanding) and the person of "Mother"—is an expression of the power of creation, the birthing, the active power that gets out that which is hidden in the male God (the seed). The Lower **Shekhinah**—the **Sephirah** of **Malkhut** and the person of "Daughter"—is a passive and receptive feminine aspect, and what issues from her is not the Divinity but the Creation. The Lower **Shekhinah** is needy and is not a power but the vessel for transferring power.

The canonical book of Qabbalah is the *Zohar,* and the very first words of the *Zohar* are about the *Shekhinah* as *Knesset Yisra'el*, which is characterized by the number thirteen. According to the *Zohar*, the *Shekhinah* is the crystallization of all the feminine aspects, "the Eternal Feminine," and primarily she is the partner for the Sacred Union. Through the union of the masculine and feminine the union of the divine powers is realized.

The conjunction of the Father and Mother, the Sephirah of Wisdom (which is masculine in the Qabbalah) and the *Sephirah* of *Binah* as the higher *Shekhinah*, is not affected by human conduct. But since the expulsion from Paradise, the union of the Son and Daughter, the King and the *Shekhinah* Queen, is also of human concern and responsibility. Along with Adam the *Shekhinah* was expelled, and it is not yet clear who expelled whom from Paradise—God expelling Adam or Adam expelling God, in her role of the *Shekhinah*. Since that "Exile of the *Shekhinah*," her detachment and separation from the sustained union with the higher powers, it is up to humankind to supply what is missing.

The detachment is not only positive. Somewhat like the story of Sophia in Gnosis times, the *Shekhinah* falls at times under the rule of the *Sitra Aḥra*, "the Other (Demonic) Side," which invades and penetrates her, bringing dire consequences for Israel and for the whole world. Such a union is caused through the lack of the divine plenitude (*Ḥayut*), which should arrive in response to the good deeds of man ("Raising of the *Mayim Nuqbin*" or "The Feminine Waters" of *Knesset Yisra'el*), but also through the intensification of the powers associated with the *Sitra Aḥra*, from the contradictions of her characteristics, her being the "Hard Judgment," the Tree of Knowledge of Good and Evil, the Tree of Life and the Tree of Death.

Jewish Mysticism through the Sacred Texts
rather than a Person

The first to fourth centuries CE (paralleling the flowering of Christian Gnosticism) witnessed a growth of mysticism within (or at
the margins of) rabbinical Judaism. The second Judaic canon is
the Talmud (whose core, the **Mishnah**, is contemporaneous with
the rise and fall of Gnosticism), which alludes, cryptically and el-
liptically, to three types of mystical pursuit that can be taught
only verbally, and only to very few deserving students who are
wise and self-understanding (*Mishnah*, tract. **Hagigah**, chap. 1).
The second of these is **Ma'ase Bereshit** (The Works of Creation) in
the first chapter of Genesis. (**Bereshit** is the first word of the Torah
and the name of the whole first book of the Torah, first for Jews
and Christians alike. It means not just "In the Beginning" but also
"in the Head" [that is, conceptually] and even "With Wisdom."
The Qabbalah book of **Tiqune Zohar** gives seventy interpretations of this six-letter word. Even if one rereads of **Bereshit**
through the Gospel of John, "In the Beginning was the Logos," it
would be "**Bereshit** was logos," which is a mere tautology.) The
third type is **Ma'ase Merkavah** (The Workings of the Divine Chariot) described in the book of Ezekiel. The first type, however, is
learning **Arayot** (meaning literally "Incest"), which has to do with
the Erotic in human affairs—but also implies the erotic in the
connection of man to the divinity, as well as in the connections
and conjunctions between the personae of the Godhead, male
and female, where the earthly rules against incest do not apply.
This is connected also with the inclusion of the Canticles (Song of
Solomon) in the canon of the Hebrew Bible. On the face of it, this
book is a totally secular composition, where the name of God is
nowhere mentioned. But the greatest of the sages, Rabbi Aqiva,

said, "All the books of the Torah are holy, but the Song of Songs is the Holy of Holies." The Holy of Holies of the temple was considered the place, the Nuptial Chamber, for the ceremonial union of the Lord with the *Shekhinah*. So this means that this sage saw the Song of Songs as the love song of the Lord, with the nation of Israel regarded as a woman. The *Mequbalim* regard the Canticles as the deepest mystical text, along with the *Ma'ase Bereshit* and the *Ma'ase Merkavah*. (There were similar trends in Christianity. Thus, church father Origen taught that the Canticles are the love song between Christ and his Church, and Saint Bernard of Clairvaux, the founder of the Cistercian Order where the Christian Grail tales were composed and the patron of the Knights Templar, based all his sermons on the Canticles.)

Another mysterious mystical passage in the Talmud tells of "the Four who entered the *Pardes*" (Jerusalem Talmud, *Hagigah* 9a), of whom only one (the same Rabbi Aqiva) "entered in peace and exited in peace." The ministering angels, goes the story, wanted to push him away, but the Lord told them to leave that old sage, as he is worthy of utilizing the Divine Glory *Kavod*. So this mystical (and probably ecstatic) entry into the Paradisiacal divine realm apparently entailed a heavenly ascent and a utilization of the Divine Glory (*Kavod* is a mystical term that appears in the *Merkavah* Visions of Ezekiel).

Whereas Christian Gnosticism is connected with the personae of Jesus and of Sophia (Wisdom, regarded as feminine), the corresponding Judaic mysticism sought the living connection to God through the deeper experience of the sacred texts of the Hebrew Bible. An idea already expressed by the early *Mequbal* Nachmanides (1194–1270) in the beginning of his Torah commentary as "a *Qabbalah* [transmission] of truth," and developed throughout Jewish mysticism, is that the whole Torah (the Pentateuch) is the hidden name of God, so that mystical reading (*Qri'ah*) in the Torah amounts to a calling (the same word, *Qri'ah*) to the Lord by the true and intimate name. (See, for example, the *Or haḤayim* exegesis for Deuteronomy 33:5; *Yonat Elem* chap. 29; and *Zohar* II 7a.) Nachmanides states: "We have still a Qabbalah [transmission] of truth that the entire Torah is the Name of the Holy One," and he then mentions some of the methods of alternative readings, "deconstructions" and permutations of the letters that reveal these names, including the names of seventy-two letters. The mystical writings produced in that period are the *Heikhalot* (heavenly "Palaces" or "Mansions") texts, which are purported to be the secret teachings of the greatest Mishnah teachers (*Tanna'im*), such as Rabbi Yishma'el and Rabbi Aqiva. These writings were meant to train in performing Heavenly Ascents. The texts contain sets of angelic/heavenly domains or spiritual spaces that could be likened to our contemporary virtual or cyberspace. These spaces are described in those texts as ordered sets of heavenly mansions or shrines (*Heikhalot*)—which may be associated with the idea of the Heavenly Jerusalem Temple. The gates of these mansions are guarded by specific angels with outlandish names, and they allow passage only to those who know their proper names. To get there, the mystic seeker had to become an adept navigator, one of the so-called *Yordei haMerkavah*— literally, "Descendants of the Chariot" or the heavenly shuttle described by Ezekiel. The real navigation, however, is apparently through a semantic (or semiotic) space that contains the names of the angels who guard the gates of the heavenly mansions. Entry is then gained through the evocation or incantation of those secret names of the angels—much as Judas in this Gospel was granted knowledge and eventual entry into a divine realm only after he quoted the name "Barbelo."

The names *Merkavah* and *Ma'ase Merkavah* have two meanings that gave alternative focus for the mystics in different periods.
The *Merkavah* can be seen as a heavenly chariot for a rider on a
heavenly ascent. But *Ma'ase Merkavah* also means "Works of Assembly," putting together coherently diverse elements to form a
functioning whole system. Such a work of assembly is likely to follow the fourfold pattern of Ezekiel's visionary *Merkavah*, with its
diverse figures of bull, lion, eagle, and man and with a likeness of
man (Adam) above them. It can be likened to the Indian construction of mandalas and to the form of the pyramid that connects
four vertices on one plane through a common vertex above. This
latter emphasis of systemic assembly became the dominant one
for Jewish mystics after the publication of the *Sefer Yetsirah*, which
gave methods for such works of assembly of letters and words.

Parallels of Judaism and the Gospel of Judas

In the Gospel of Judas, Judas keeps observance of the Judaic-
Israelite principle of not uttering the Holy Name in vain, as com-
manded in the Decalogue (Exod. 20:7; Deut. 5:11)—"Thou shalt
not take the name of the Lord [*YHWH*] thy God in vain," and
since "All is Vanity" (Eccles. 1:2, 1:14, 2:11, 2:17, 3:19, 12:8), then it
is best not to utter it at all (apart from in blessing or prayer—
Zohar Exodus 88a). Jews write the Tetragrammaton with various
substitute spellings. A common substitute is to give a different order of these four letters, in the form of הויה—*HaWaYaH*—which
means "Being" or "Existence" and of course retains the same
gematria value of 26. Judas, presented by Borges as the ultimate
ascetic, becomes himself an expression of that Holy Name, and
his distinctive letter ד becomes the substitute letter for the ה, thus

making the appearance of the Tetragrammaton as ידוד—which is itself a proper verb meaning "[he] will make friendly/lovable."

A Leading Role in Gnosticism for Judas/Judaism

Contrary to widely held belief, Judaism is not the older, hence more primitive, religion among "the monotheistic faiths" (or rather "Abrahamic faiths," as neither Christianity with its Trinity nor mystical Judaism is strictly monotheistic but admits several persons in the Godhead). Normative Judaism is rabbinical Judaism, which developed after the destruction of the second temple, and is thus no older than Christianity.

Gnosis has not developed enough to replace normative Christianity. But it might enhance Christianity and make it more able to handle the collective Redemption and the "End of Days." In the following I shall borrow from the continuing Gnosis within Judaism to express Juda-ish redemption.

CHAPTER 5

Understanding the Judas Gospel
in the Light of Gnosis

FTER SEARCHING THE MYSTICAL ATMOSPHERE in which Jesus
and Judas lived and which the author of the Gospel according to Judas had probably experienced—and having
seen how Gnosis developed—we can now come back to the manuscript and watch how these Gnostic themes are expressed in the
Gospel.

In the following I shall present an original understanding of
the Gospel of Judas that is consistent with the Qabbalah and may
thereby be acceptable also to rabbinical Judaism. This understanding is built on a typical, even if original, *Midrash* and on
some Qabbalah-type assignments. But as the Qabbalah is a complex subject, I may need to introduce many readers to what genuine traditional Jewish mysticism and Qabbalah are and
differentiate them from "the occult." I shall try to select old and
new demonstrative examples that pertain to the matter of the
Gospel of Judas, and also try to present the special, perhaps odd-
looking, traditional terms in contemporary terms. At the outset, I
note that the Gospel of Judas bases the spiritual authority of Jesus on first "Barbelo," namely, the Principle of Four, and second

the Tetragrammaton, the four-letter ineffable name of **YHWH**. Third, note that the medium of revelation in this Gospel is a "Luminous Cloud," from which some Heavenly Persons or quasi-divine figures appear and into which Judas entered as Moses did. (As written in the Gospel of Judas: "Judas lifted up his eyes and saw the luminous cloud, and he entered it. Those standing on the ground heard a voice coming from the cloud, saying, [. . .] great generation.") The fourth consideration raised by the Gospel of Judas is the possible connection of this special Gnostic text with Judaism and with Israel. Let us begin with an examination of Barbelo.

Judas and Barbelo: Only Judas Knew Jesus' True Identity

Judas was the only one of the disciples to know Jesus' true identity: "I know who you are and where you have come from. You are from the immortal realm of Barbelo. And I am not worthy to utter the name of the one who has sent you." We have earlier taken "Barbelo" to mean "In These Four" (באר בע אלו—**Be'Arba Elu**) and to be associated with the principle, or pattern, of the Four. We have also assumed that the unutterable name of the one who sent Jesus was the Tetragrammaton—**YHWH.** We may now ask, what was it about Judas that made him able to sense Jesus' association with these sacred entities?

The clue, it seems, is given in the lineage of Judas-Judah and his own true name—**Yehudah יהודה**. Judah was the fourth son of Jacob (Gen. 29:35), and he is listed a few times as the fourth (for example, Num. 1:26). Yet he came to seniority to become the first of the Tribes of Israel, and he came to be listed as the first (for instance, Num. 2:3; 7:12). This is now reiterated in the Gospel of

Judas, where Jesus, who chose the twelve disciples as representatives of the Twelve Tribes of Israel, told Judas that he will exceed all the twelve apostles and that his star will lead the way. The name Judas—יהודה—is made of the combination of the Tetragrammaton with the letter **Dalet** (ד), the fourth letter of the Hebrew alphabet, and the Hebrew sign for the number four: הדוהי ⇔ 30 = 26 + 4. This name is therefore another representation of what is visualized in Ezekiel's vision of the **Merkavah**—the Divine "Chariot" in which the Lord rides over the "Four Living Beings." Judas, who had these principles embedded in his own name, was the right person to identify Jesus as their supreme representative.

Judas' vision of the luminous cloud recalls the vision of the prophet Ezekiel. In the vision of Ezekiel (1:4–28, 10:9–22), a great, luminous cloud came from the North, out of which came fire and "**Hashmal**." This mysterious word is generally interpreted as "Electrum" or bronzelike color. In Jewish mysticism it means "sensing and speaking." In modern Hebrew, **Hashmal** means "Electricity." From the **Hashmal** formed a fantastic vision of the Divine Throne carried upon a fourfold assembly of "Wheels" and four-winged "Holy Living Beings" (**Hayot**), each with four faces— of a man, an eagle, a lion, and an ox. From that fourfold vision of Ezekiel issued—in the same period as the Gnostics—the earlier version of Jewish mysticism, called **Ma'ase Merkavah,** "Works of the Chariot [**Merkavah**]." The practitioners of this early Jewish mysticism experienced ecstatic "descent of the Chariot" in order to ascend to the heavenly mansions, guarded by angels with fantastical secret names. (I trust all know the gospel song lyrics "Swing low, sweet chariot, coming for to carry me home.")

The principle of the four is also evoked in the book of Ezekiel in connection with the Resurrection: "prophesy, son of man, and say to the **Ru'ah** [wind-breath-spirit], Thus says the Lord [**YHWH**]

God: Come from the four **Ruḥot** [cardinal directions, same word as *spirit* and *wind,* but in plural], oh **Ru'aḥ** and breathe upon these slain, that they may live" (37:9). The same visionary scheme is also present in Christianity, where much the same "Four Living Creatures" appear in the book of Revelation (4:6–9). There they ceaselessly pronounce the expansion of the four-letter Holy "Name of Being" (**Shem HaWaYaH**) into "Was, Is and Will Be" (**HaYaH HOWeH WeYiHiYeH**). Significantly, these four creatures symbolize the four evangelists: Matthew as the human face, Mark as the Lion, Luke as the Ox, and John as the Eagle. So we can say that when Judas tells Jesus, "I know who you are and where you have come from. You are from the immortal realm of Barbelo," he is effectively saying, "You came from the World of the Chariot" (**Olam ha'Merkavah**). This realm is structured on the pattern of the Tetragrammaton, the four-lettered Holy Name.

Hardly a separate movement from Christian Gnosis, then, the Qabbalah in fact is strikingly parallel with the lost Christian mysticism in its message, in its symbols, and often in its very language.

Paul, rather than Judas, as the Traitor to Jesus

The Gnostic Gospel of Judas claims that the defective world was created by a demiurge whose rule was limited to a particular aeon, or age, of some two thousand years. In the hindsight of historic research it can be claimed that "the Christian world" was largely made by a giant demiurgic figure—that of Saint Paul.

We can see here a parallel between the historic development of the faith of Israel and the possible contemporary and future development of Christianity. In the Bible, first came the period of Judges, of having free inspiration—"In those days there was no king in Yisra'el, every man did that which was right in his own eyes" (Judg. 17:6, 21:25)—although there were Judgment and Judges. Later came the transition to kingdom and institutions. First of the kings was Saul—which I compare with Saint Paul, whose Hebrew name was **Sha'ul** (Saul). The name **Sha'ul** literally means "borrowed." In a slight declination, it is **She'ol**, namely, the underworld of the dead, which came later to be the same as hell. King Saul proved to have a temporary role, and he sought contact with the underworld. Saint Paul was the man who resorted to the usage of hell as the impetus for faith and for turning to Jesus' grace. From the Gnostic perspective, it is Paul—rather than Judas—who was the traitor to Jesus' message.

The first phase of preparing Christianity to become a world religion was to package it with the Pauline doctrines, based on the notion of "original sin" and the claim that every person is destined to go to hell unless he or she embraces the Pauline-Christian faith.

In the history of Israel, the temporary King Saul was succeeded by King David and King Solomon. Although David was as rough a man of war as King Saul, he was also a poet who produced spiritual works, and Jewish convention attributes all the Psalms to him. Solomon, the "king of peace," is credited with three books: the Song of Songs (Canticles), Proverbs (**Mishlei**), and Ecclesiastes (**Qohelet**).

Pauline Christianity was probably quite necessary for the first millennium of Christianity, and perhaps even for its first two millennia—yet may not be adequate and proper for the future. In the second millennium appeared love mystics such as Ramón Lull, Saint Bernard of Clairvaux, and Saint Francis of Assisi. And now Gnosis reemerged to help transform Christian spirituality from its Pauline base to a Gnostic one.

The Star of Judas and Judas Becoming
the Selected "Thirteenth" Disciple

"Judas," Jesus says in the Gospel of Judas when he listens to Judas' vision of the temple he fled to, "your star has led you astray," because no mortal human being is allowed inside. And when Judas asks if he might be one of the rulers, Jesus promises him, "You will become the thirteenth" (for which he will suffer and be cursed).

What, in the heavens or on earth, could Judas' star be? This star seems essentially associated with the Jewish Messiah. We know that the Jewish authorities of Jesus' time did not accept his claim to be the Messiah. But about two generations after the Great Revolt and the destruction of the temple, the greatest Jewish sage, Rabbi Aqiva, acknowledged (as a minority view, though) a nationalist military leader, Shim'on Bar Kosiva, as the expected Messiah and renamed him "Bar Kokhva," or "Son of a/the Star," echoing the prophecy of Bil'am (Balaam) that "in the latter days . . . there shall come a star out of Ya'aqov [Jacob] and a scepter shall rise out of Yisra'el [Israel]" (Num. 24:17). Judas' star has a Messianic color to it, but here it clearly comes in the context of an astrological discussion. Judas is constantly compared with the twelve disciples, and is blessed in being the thirteenth.

It is interesting that for Christians the number thirteen is shrouded in awe and superstition, so much so that in many hotels no thirteenth floor exists, or no thirteenth room on a floor, because people would not stay at such an unlucky address. The worst, and most feared, seems "Friday the Thirteenth," which was the day that the Knights Templar were rounded up, declared by the Catholic Church to be heretics, and burned at the stake. It is possible that for the Knights Templar, too, the number thirteen had a special and benign significance, and therefore it is likely that the king and the Church chose Friday the Thirteenth for extermination of the Knights Templar because they were considered associated with that number.

This fear of thirteen is not the case for the Jews. In Judaism, thirteen is a lucky number; boys' confirmation rites take place at the age of thirteen, and the two key holy terms, Unity (*AhaD*—אחד) and Love (*AHaBhHa*—אהבה), have a gematrical value of thirteen. The *Baraitha of Rabbi Yishma'el (Sifri* for *va'Yiqra,* opening*)* lists the thirteen methods of exegesis for the Torah, and it is read daily as part of the Jewish morning prayer. The same great sage Rabbi Yishma'el also said that there are thirteen covenants between God and Israel (Mishna, **Nedarim**, 3–11). Whereas the Christian calendar, which is solar (masculine), always has twelve months, the Jewish calendar, which is a tempered lunar (thus feminine) calendar, often has thirteen months in a year (seven times every nineteen years).

But most important are the "Thirteen Measures of Mercy"— **Midot haRahamim**. Exodus 32 says that when the Children of Israel made the Golden Calf, God told Moses that he would destroy all of Israel and start a New Covenant with him alone. Moses implored God to have mercy on Israel, and finally God agreed to spare it. Having then smitten the first set of tablets and gotten many of the people killed, Moses asked for mercy for the rest, and for maintaining his Presence (the **Shekhinah**) with Israel. Moses was then instructed to prepare two new stone tablets, went into the divine cloud, and proclaimed the Name of the Lord. The Lord then came down in a cloud. With this stupendous view of the Lord's mercy, Moses proclaimed (34:5–7): "YHWH, YHWH, El [Mighty], Merciful and Gracious, Long-Suffering, and Abundant in Love and Truth, Keeping troth to thousands, Forgiving inequity, and Transgression, and Sin . . ." (This is followed by some attributes of Judgment.) The sages counted these as thirteen "Measures of Mercy" that were revealed to forgive Israel. This became the essential expression of the Lord's mercy and of the Name of YHWH as the Name of Divine Mercy. Interestingly, in this passage (Exod. 34:5–7) there are (without hyphens and punctuation marks) exactly 169 letters; 169 = 13 × 13, or 13 squared. On the holiest day of the year—Yom Kippur, the "Day of Atonement"—Jews pray for the greater part of twenty-six hours (= 13 × 2), starting before sunset and carrying on until full, starry skies the next night, and repeat the expression of these "Thirteen Measures of Mercy" some seven times, mostly in the closing prayer.

As noted, the Jewish year has sometimes twelve and sometimes thirteen lunar months. The sect of the Dead Sea Scrolls split from Judaism because it held to a 364-day sacred solar calendar. The significance of this is that the number 364 is divisible by 7 (364 = 7 × 52), as well as by 13 (364 = 13 × 28, with 28 being a "perfect number." "Perfect numbers" are numbers whose divisors add up to the same numbers. The first two are 6 and 28, where 6 = 1 + 2 + 3, and 28 = 1 + 2 + 4 + 7 +14.) Thus, the Hebrew Bible has 6 letters in its first word and 28 letters in its first sentence. (The next two perfect numbers are 496 and 8,128. Beyond this figure they are very rare, and no more were known in ancient times. With modern computers we know about 30.)

So there is an Order of the Twelve—the fixed and immutable order of the Aeons, with their mechanical progression—an order of Judgment. But there is also a higher Order of the Thirteen, an Order of Mercy.

An interesting, and here important, feature of the number 13 is that it is a "configurate number"—a number that makes a characteristic figure. If you want to see this figure, just look at the green side of a U.S. one-dollar bill. In the center there are the words "In

God we trust" and the word ONE in giant letters (recall that in Hebrew, One ⇔ **AḤaD** ⇔ 13), followed by the great seal of the
United States with the American eagle and 13 stars over its head.
This is the configuration of the 13—the same "Star of David" form
you can also find on the Israeli flag. These 13 seem to emerge
from a cloud characterized by 28 divisions. The number 13 is repeated many times on that seal: The eagle holds 13 arrows in its
left (Judgment) talon and a branch with 13 leaves and 13 olives in
its right (Mercy) talon, and has 13 stripes on its shield. The pyramid on the other side has 13 marked courses, and two of the three
written mottoes on this great seal are made of 13 letters each—
ANNUIT COEPTIS; E PLURIBUS UNUM. Although this has to do with
the 13 original colonies, there are other associations that brought
this prominence of 13. (The symbols are largely Masonic, and
freemasons were using the "Star of David" sign before it became
characteristic of Jews and Israel. But this sign may also have been
included in gratitude to the Jews, especially banker Hayim Solomon, who helped finance the American Revolution.) We can surmise that something like the "Star of Judas" is a symbol of
spiritual guidance.

There is still another instance of 13 in Judaism, which was revealed in the most mysterious part of the Jewish mystical canon—the Holy **Zohar**. In the part called "Idra Rabba" (The Great Round Assembly) there is a description of the Godhead. The most supreme "Face of God" is called *Atiq Yomin* (Ancient of Days), and of whom can be seen only the white beard, arrayed in 13 *Tiqunim* (meaning "coverings" or "correctives"). The mystical Vision of these 13 "Corrections of the Beard" is the Vision of the Godhead. Remember Philip's request that Jesus show them the Father. In the Gospel of Judas, Jesus orients Judas to see the Father, as much as possible.

Even more significantly, the very first teaching of the **Zohar**, right in the introduction, associates 13 with **Knesset Yisra'el**—the mystical spiritual community of all Israelites (not just Jews). This collective entity, called the "Thirteen Petalled Rose," is seen as a feminine figure, which is simultaneously also the Fourth Person of the Godhead! In terms of Jewish spirituality and mysticism, **Knesset Yisra'el** is also the **Shekhinah**—the Presence of the Divinity on this earth. Both terms are feminine and personal—She is the Face of the immanent Divinity.

Of the Disciples, Only Judas Was Strong Enough to Stand before Jesus

The disciples were angered by the suggestion that Judas stood out from the others, and Jesus challenged them dramatically: "Let any one of you who is [strong enough] among human beings bring out the perfect human and stand before my face." None of them could do it, except for Judas Iscariot. Judas said to him, "I know who you are and where you have come from. You have come from the immortal realm [or aeon] of Barbelo. And I am not worthy to utter the name of the One who has sent you."

The Qabbalah's Tree of Life and the Flow of the Divine

A major concept of the Qabbalah is what came to be called the "Tree of Life" or the "Tree of the Sephirot" (the divine attributes). It is an intricate and complex multidimensional systemic concept (as will be explained more in Part VI), but its very first and immediate implications here are Trinitarian and Quaternary. We can recast this scheme in playful English: this divine Tree of Life is arranged with a stem and three branches or columns, namely, (1) **Love**, on the Right; (2) **Law** (or Awe), on the Left; and (3) **Laugh-**(ter), in the middle. Thus implied by this strange name is some of the paradoxical nature of this middle ground and of complementarity between two contradictory tendencies.

Why and whence **Laugh**ter? It is said that, as a king delights in having a speaking bird, just because it is not the nature of a bird to speak, what delights God is when humans (or the masculine and feminine sides) go beyond their egotistical nature. The natural order is that each side considers itself the more important—"**I** (M) **More**." However, the **Life** and **laugh**ter come through when each side looks at the other and claims, "**You** (R) **More**"—or simply stated, "**Humor**"—regarding oneself as less important than the other. (We may recall Bergson's theory of humor—that we laugh at the mechanical in human behavior, in others as well as in us. It is also a psychological portrait in the manner of Donald Winnicott in his 1982 work *Playing and Reality,* who regarded the middle zone between the subjective and the objective as that of "playing.")

When the self-importance melts down and the contradictory attributes of Love and Law (or Awe) are reconciled, the central column of the union of opposites becomes a channel that simultaneously lifts the "Feminine Waters" (*Mayim Nuqbin*) of human passionate striving for God, as it brings down the divine vitality (*Ḥayut*) to enliven the concrete world—"The Kingdom" (*Malkhut*)—in an ecstatic "Coming of the Kingdom." (This experiential and erotic assembly has some resemblance to the Indian Tantric concept "Kundalini," energy rising.) This stem, which is fed by the three branches of Love, Law, and Laugh, is that of really **Living**.

In this scheme, it is neither only "God is Love" nor "God is Law," but it is both and beyond these two, and God may be experienced as the union of opposites and the delightful flow of enlivening intelligence. Although there is no doubt about the importance and magical power of unconditional Love, indiscriminate love has no adequate social basis (law), and sooner or later suffers exploitation, which then often leads to tyranny. (Here lies the inadequacy of the Pauline doctrines that reject the Law and focus exclusively on faith and the love of Christ crucified.)

The Number 666, the Book of Revelation, and Restoring Christian Gnosis

The main knowledge we had about Gnosticism before last century's findings derived from the writing of Saint Irenaeus. From Irenaeus's description we learn, for example, that the Gnostics attached much importance to numbers and employed the technique of gematria.

It is possible that Gnosis did penetrate the orthodox canon through the veil of Gnostic practices of gematria. In his 1988 book

The Dimensions of Paradise, author and freethinker John Michell discusses the infamous number 666 of the book of Revelation (13:18). Showing the prevalence of this number in ancient cosmology as the respected "Solar Number" and as a number signifying the principles of reason, will, and authority, Michell shows it as an ingredient of the plan of the New Jerusalem, where it is held in balance with the "Lunar Number" 1,080, which symbolizes imagination and mystery. The number 666 is, however, the most notorious of all symbolic numbers, being that which Saint John ascribed to the Beast in the last verse of Revelation 13: "Here is wisdom, let him that hath understanding count the number of the beast: for it is the number of a man; and his number is six hundred and threescore and six." Michell sees these words of Revelation as shedding light on Saint John's true Gnostic attitude toward the Roman Church.

Michell first shows the abuse of the principles denoted by 666 both by the Roman Church and by its Puritan detractors, and then gleefully surveys the history of the use made of this number to disparage whoever the interpreter willed. (It was most commonly attributed to the pope by Protestant and English authors up to the nineteenth century, but it can also fit Hitler and Stalin. In fact, in an old *Scientific American* article, "666 and All That," Martin Gardner gave some mathematical rules for how to attribute the number 666 to whatever name one may want.)

Calling all this "diverting nonsense," Michell then proceeds to an interpretation of Saint John's words through the use of the same Gnostic-Cabalistic methods that, according to Irenaeus and other ecclesiastical writers, were practiced by the Gnostic masters and were presumably known to John himself. This should, in fact, be evident, as this infamous number 666 is given in the Greek text of Revelation 13:18 spelled in letters, χξϛ' with a gematria value of

600, 60, 6. Michell writes: "We are told to 'count the number of the beast.' The number 666 does not need to be counted or computed, for it is openly given, so evidently there is another number behind it, which does need calculating. That number is the final, key phrase of Revelation 13 'and his number is 666'—και ὁ ἀριθμος αυτου χξς'." The value of the words in this phrase is as follows: καυ = 31, ὁ = 70, ἀριθμος = 430, αυτου = 1171, χξς' = 666. The sum of these numbers, and therefore the value of the whole verse, is 2,368, which is the number of Ἰησους Χριστος —the name "Jesus Christ." The esoteric meaning of the whole verse is therefore: "Here is wisdom. Let him that has understanding [that is, Gnosis] count the number of the beast: for it is the number of a man: 2,368, Jesus Christ."

At first sight this interpretation may seem shocking and paradoxical, but John Michell proceeds to put it in the context of the disputes between the Gnostics and the established Church, and discusses the stance of the Gnostics as opposed to "the personality cult" of Jesus (on which much of Christianity is still based), and its utilization by the Church. He thus notes that the claim attributed to the pope, "I am God on Earth" ('θεος εἰμι ἐπι γαιης), also has the value 666.

Jesus and the Jews: The War of Christianity and Judaism Need Not Have Arisen

It is interesting to note that the only place in the Talmud that was considered to have mentioned Jesus and his rejection by the Jews is bracketed before and after by the admonition that "Always should the Left Hand be rejecting and the Right Hand accepting."

This is the very characterization of the Right and Left hands/lines of the Qabbalah (which, as noted, means "Acceptance"):

> "Always should the Left Hand be rejecting and the Right Hand accepting"' said the sages, "and not like the way *Yehoshu'a ben Praḥyah* behaved." What wrong did he do? Ask the Talmud, and answer: *King Yanai* fought the sages of Israel and killed them. *Ben Praḥyah* and his student, *Jesus,* escaped and fled to Egypt. On the way back to Israel, when peace was reached, in an inn where they had been greeted gracefully, *Jesus* criticized the hostess' looks. *Ben Praḥyah* got so angry, that he had four hundred ram's horns blown, and ostracized *Jesus*. *Jesus* came time and again to ask his forgiveness, but *Ben Praḥyah* pretended not to see him. Last time he came, *Yehoshu'a ben Praḥyah* was deep in prayer, and signalled for him to wait. But Jesus, misreading the motion, went away and adopted idolatry.

This could suggest that if Jesus' assumed rabbi, *Yehoshu'a ben Praḥyah*, had been a **Mequbal**, the tragic war of Christianity and Judaism might have never arisen. But the irony of this passage is that this sage, *Yehoshu'a ben Praḥyah*, taught a century before Jesus was born, so Jesus could not have been his student, and Jesus' name must have been interpolated centuries later. Yet the whole passage regrets the separation of Jesus from the Jewish Israel.

The Laughing Jesus: Ecstatic Rapture on the Cross

In Umberto Eco's novel *The Name of the Rose* there is a stern monk who insists that "Jesus never laughed"—and proceeds to murder his "brothers" who might look at heretical or humorous texts. The usual Christian claim is that Jesus was the Messiah prophesied in Isaiah 53, that he was the "man of sorrows" who suffered on the cross for the sins of the many. But the heretical texts of Gnosis portray a different Jesus. In both "The Apocalypse of Peter" and "The Second Treatise of the Great Seth" from the Nag Hammadi Codex appears a "Laughing Jesus"—and the very short Gospel of Judas gives four distinct occasions when Jesus laughed (recall the importance of the number 4 in this text).

There is power in laughter. It is often the only power that can cut through paranoia, superstition, and prejudice. But is it correct, or is it a blasphemy, to portray a "Laughing Jesus"? There are those such as Timothy Freke and Peter Gandy in their 2006 book *The Laughing Jesus* who argue in great seriousness for the Laughing Jesus. Let us try here to examine what is "perhaps the greatest blasphemy"—that Jesus was in fact having the time of his life on the cross.

Theologically speaking, Jesus' (self-)sacrifice on the cross was a replication or surpassing of what Abraham did in offering his beloved son Isaac for sacrifice (Gen. 22). In Christianity, it is God the Father who sacrificed his only son for the salvation of humankind. In John's reputed words: "For God so loved the world that he gave His one and only Son" (3:16). The offering of Isaac was thus a model for the sacrifice of Jesus.

There is another similarity between Jesus and Isaac, which has hitherto escaped all commentators but adds insight to the core mystery. This has to do with the meaning of their names, because in the Bible (as in much fine literature and drama) often the name of the protagonist explains his essence. The remarkable thing about Isaac's name is that God himself gave it a year before Isaac was born (Gen. 17:19, 21), and it is this God-given name that provides the key to the meaning of the offering, or rather the binding

(*Aqedah*) of Isaac. The original Hebrew biblical word is "***Yitzḥaq***," which means "[he who] will laugh" (in future tense), perhaps even "he who will have the last laugh." Isaac's distinction was to be destined to go through the most terrifying spectacle imaginable—his own father getting ready to slaughter him—yet laugh at it. But how could Isaac laugh at such an hour? As I see it, he was not a baby but a strong young man (most Jewish interpreters assume he was thirty-seven years old at the *Aqedah*) who *chose* to go through this deadly ordeal, playing a kind of "Russian roulette" with the Almighty and prevailing—God could not afford to have him killed. As I see it, Jesus had a similar name and a similar view of his destiny.

The original Hebrew name of Jesus was most likely *Yeshu'a* (ישוע), which is a derivation of the double root word *Sha'asha* (שעשע). In modern Hebrew, ***sha'ashu'a*** means "amusement," and ***Sha'ashe'a*** means "to amuse." But as Arie Kaplan shows in his study of "word archeology" in *Meditation and the Bible*, the word ***Sha'ashu'a*** as used by the prophets meant "ecstatic rapture." So the name ***Yeshu'a*** means not only "salvation" (which is the feminine form of his name) but also "he who will have ecstatic rapture." I suggest that Jesus, who was so serious about his destiny and mission, could not have ignored pondering over the meaning of his own name and what it implies. Going with his cross toward Golgotha, Jesus might have entertained several possibilities—one that he would be saved through divine intervention, the other that he was about to have the most ecstatic experience imaginable.

The Jewish mystical understanding is that the first light of creation, the light of the first day, much before the sun and moon where created, enables one to see "from one end of the world to the other end," where "world" (*Olam*) means both space and time. It is the light of prophecy that allows one to see the past and the future—and God then hid it, so that the wicked would not be able to exploit it. The legends say that Isaac received this enlightenment at the *Aqedah*. One who loves Jesus would surely concede that Jesus also received it. And if so, then he could see how he would become glorified and actually deified, become the God for countless people. Was not this worth the agony of a few hours on the cross? Would this not be reason enough to have an ecstatic experience?

Of the two men who sacrificed themselves that day—Jesus and Judas—only the latter would become "the man of sorrows." One objection made to the claim of the laughter of Jesus on the cross is his famous last words of "My God, my God, why have you forsaken me?" (Matt. 27:46). Saudi Islamic scholars Dr. Muhammad Taqi-ud-Din al-Hilali and Dr. Muhammad Muhsin Khan in their translation, *The Noble Qur'an*, argue on that basis that the Gospels must be false, because a true prophet cannot lose faith. Both missed the point (of which the Bible New International Version is aware) that this expression comes from Psalm 22:2, the hymn to the morning star, which starts with the suffering of David (the accepted Messiah) at the hands of his enemies, including events that were repeated at the Crucifixion (for example, their casting lots for his clothes), but ends in salvation and glory. In the King James Bible the verse reads, "O my God, I cry in the daytime, but thou hearest not; and in the night season, and am not silent." So Jesus was quoting this Psalm—and was acting his Messianic part until the very end. The Gospel of Judas as a Gnostic text, then, shows the inner mechanics by which Judas was not truly a traitor at all but the thirteenth, and most devoted, of Christ's disciples.

PART III

THE MODERN
REVIVAL OF
CHRISTIAN GNOSIS

CHAPTER 6

Traditional Christianity's Missed Principle: The Trinity Becoming "the Four"

H AVING SEEN GNOSIS FLOWING so clearly through the Gospel of Judas, we can turn to traditional Christianity itself and see that Gnosis was there, potentially, as well. Though the Church may have given ascendance to its own interpretations, the themes of inner awakening were there in the words of the Christian sacred scriptures, both the Old and the New Testaments, particularly in the form of "the Four."

"In These Four": Barbelo in the Design of the Gospels

The Christian Bible is made in a quaternary fashion: The entire New Testament adds a fourth to the tripartite division of the Hebrew Bible (*Tanakh*—acronym of the three parts: *Torah* [Pentateuch], *Nevi'im* [Prophets], and *Ketuvim*). The New Testament itself is made up of four divisions: the Gospels—themselves selected as Four; the Acts of the Apostles; the Letters of the Apostles; and the book of Revelation.

The Christian mystics have always been fond of the biblical Song of Songs (the Canticles of Solomon). For example, Saint Bernard of Clairvaux, the founder and head of the Cistercian Order and the patron saint of the Knights Templar, made eighty-six sermons and homilies on the Song of Songs (and eighty-six happens to be the gematria of *Elohim*, the biblical God). The canon of the Qabbalah is the *Zohar*, which includes an exegesis of the Song of Songs. Let us look at a passage in the introduction of the *Zohar* to the Song of Songs, which treats the theme of the future Messiah, "the Son," "Four Spirits," and "the Whole Spirit":

Rabbi Reḥumai quoted (Isa. 11:2), "And the spirit (*Ru'aḥ*) of the Lord shall rest upon him, the spirit of wisdom and understanding, the spirit of counsel and might, the spirit of knowledge and the fear of the Lord"—here are four spirits, which no man has merited, apart from the King Messiah alone. ("Spirit" is in Hebrew *Ru'aḥ*, which also means "breath," "wind," and "cardinal direction." In the next two quotes, "spirit" and "wind" are rendered by the same word, and are equivalent for the Hebrew reader.)

And so it is written (Ezek. 37:9), "[Thus says the Lord God] Come from the four winds [*Ruḥot*], O breath [*Ru'aḥ*]." It is not written "four winds" but "from four winds"—this is the whole Spirit. He was asked—how? Answered: this is the one that comes from the Kiss of Love (*Ahavat Neshiqah*). How? A kiss of love is through the mouth, and then a breath (*Ru'aḥ*) connects with a breath, and each one of them is composed of two spirits, his own spirit/breath (*Ru'aḥ*) and his mate's spirit, so the two of them are found with four spirits. And all the more so when a man and a woman unite, there are four spirits together. And the son who issues from them, this is the spirit that comes from four spirits. As it is written, "Come from the four spirits (*Ruḥot*), O spirit (*Ru'aḥ*)," and this is a Whole Spirit.

The Holy Quaternary in the Psalms:
Truth Grows from the Earth

Psalm 85:11–12 says: "Love/Mercy (*Ḥesed*) and Truth (*Emmet*) are met together, Righteousness (*Tsedeq*) and Peace (*Shalom*) have kissed each other. Truth shall spring out of the earth, and Righteousness shall look down from heaven." Here is a quaternary system that is patterned like the *Merkavah* and the fourfold Tree of Life—Love on the right-hand side, Righteousness (and hence Judgment-Din) on the complementary left-hand side, Peace above (from heaven), and Truth holding it up from the bottom, the earth.

How do we know the truth? The above verse says, "Truth grows from the earth" (*Emmet me'Eretz titsmaḥ*). Truth rises from the ground, from the concrete, the empirical. There are endless concepts and theories, and each may seem convincing, but, as Jesus said, "by their fruit ye shall know them."

For Judaism (and for Judah-ism), the Tree of Life is the Torah. The Torah (generally equated with Wisdom) is described as follows: "She is a tree of life for those who lay hold on her, and happy are those who hold her fast" (Prov. 3:18). The concrete (the earth, the feminine) is needed in addition to the three supernal/spiritual entities of the Trinity to make the Torah's benefit real.

As an illustration of Qabbalah methodology for expounding "The Truth about Judas," we can look at one instance of how Truth is encoded in the Hebrew Bible. Let us arrange the verse above about Truth (*Emmet:* "Truth shall spring out of the earth") in Hebrew (***Emmet me'Eretz titsmah*** [Ps. 85:12]) and in Hebrew letters (אמת מארץ תצמח) along three columns (recall that Hebrew is written right to left).

One Instance of Truth Encoded in the Hebrew Bible

ת (T)	מ (M)	א (A)
צ (Ts)	א (A) ר (R)	מ (M)
מ (M) ח (Ḥ)	צ (Ts)	ת (T)

We get a square table where the same expression, "Truth shall spring out of the earth" (***Emmet me'Ereṭs titsmah***) can be read from two perspectives—both horizontally, from right to left, and vertically, from the top down. The gematria (numerical value of the constituent letters) of ***Emmet***—אמת—is 441, which is a square number, 21×21. (In English, as an adjective *square* means fair and honest.)

This may be enough to demonstrate an essential point about the concrete Truth, worldly as well as heavenly. In three places in the Talmud it is asserted that "Truth [***Emmet***—אתמ] is the Seal of God" (***Shabbat*** 35a; ***Yoma*** 69b; ***Sanhedrin*** 64a).

The Christian Trinity Becoming a Gnostic Holy Quaternary

There are some similarities between the Christian Trinity and the visions of the Godhead in the Qabbalah. They could be understood as subsidiary divine manifestations, much like the vision of the Heavenly Chariot and Throne of God.

The Gnostic concept introduced in the Gospel of Judas, "the domain of Barbelo," from which Jesus comes and to which he returns, suggests a Quaternary that includes at least one female image—such as Sophia and/or the **Shekhinah**. There can be posited, for example, a quaternary of the Father, the Mother, the Son, and the Holy Spirit—or of Father, Mother, Son, and Daughter—as is common in the Qabbalah.

Reentering Paradise by the Fourfold Path

The concept of "four" has further implications in Gnosis and beyond, including the suggestion of a path to Paradise. The word *Paradise* comes from the Persian language, and it denotes a watered garden that grows fruit, hence its similarity to the Garden of Eden. The Muslim Paradise, for example, is this watered garden. In Hebrew, the word is פרדס (*PaRDeS*)—a four-letter word. The Jewish image of Paradise is a rather intellectual one—a delightful endless study of the **Torah**.

Where the Talmud discusses the mystical issues, such as the "Working of the Chariot" of Ezekiel (**Ma'ase Merkavah**), it alludes to the mystical practices of the sages as "entering the **Pardes**" (Babylonian Talmud, tract. **Ḥagigah** 14b). According to Tuvia Wechsler in his 1968 book **Tsfunot beMasoret Yisra'el** (Hidden Codes in the Tradition of Israel), this **Pardes** is the very Torah itself, and the entry of the sages into the secrets of the Torah. (Thus, Wechsler interprets "The Pure Marble Stones" mentioned in the Talmudic story as denoting the squared number of letters in the key passages of the Torah, which allowed the sages to assess whether there was a superfluous letter in the Torah.) It has become customary in Judaism to interpret this four-letter word **PaRDeS** as an acronym for the four modes or levels of interpretation of the Torah: **Pshat**, the literal meaning; **Remez**, meaning "hint" or allegory; **Drash,** or exegesis; and **Sod**, secret teachings. It can be seen that these methods give enough latitude to enable virtually any interpretation. Therefore, the Jews added another principle—that the interpretation should never contravene the literal meaning.

This Jewish method of interpretation (hermeneutics) is in fact quite parallel to the medieval Christian method of exegesis on four levels, as used (among others) by Dante, Bonaventura, and Thomas Aquinas: literal, moral, allegorical, and "anagogic" (which relates to eternal glory). (This method was first formulated by Gregory the Great, who reached it, significantly, by interpreting Ezekiel and who compared the words of the scriptures to square stone blocks, which can stand on any of their four sides.) An added value in the Hebrew scheme is the association of **PaRDeS** with Paradise; recalling that the original Paradise, the Garden of Eden, had four rivers issuing from it, we may regain Paradise by going back along all four paths.

In his study *Christ of the Twenty-first Century*, Ewert Cousins compares the four modes of interpretation to four levels of the psyche, as affirmed by contemporary research of altered states of consciousness. The world may be threatened by literalist-Fundamentalist interpretations of the Bible and the Qur'an. But by studying the Torah (or the scriptures) through **Be'ARBA ELU,** namely, by these four levels of study (and not only literalism), we may reenter Paradise.

Turning the Cross from the Tree of Death into the Tree of Life

The primary Christian symbol—the Cross—has often been called the "Tree of Life," which is quite paradoxical. In fact, it is a rela-

tively late, fifth-century, Christian symbol, and according to
Robin Margaret Jensen in her 2000 book *Understanding Early
Christian Art* it was originally an anti-Christian sign. The cross of
Golgotha was no doubt a Roman instrument of torture and death,
and the sight of cross-carrying soldiers and mobs and of knights
with the sign of the cross on their shields or chest was the face of
death for countless Jews, Muslims, Cathars, and Native Americans (and perhaps also for many women). No wonder that the
canon of the Qabbalah, the ***Zohar***, explicitly called the Cross the
"Tree of Death." But in truth, the Cross is both.

As a primary symbol (which had been in use long before Christianity), the cross represents two clefts or divisions: the first is a
vertical cleft that separates two sides—Right and Left, Right and
Wrong, Good and Evil. It is also the basic separation of You and I
(I'm on the Right Side, and you on the Other Side), Male and Female. It denotes a basic dualistic view of the world. Then the cross
has also another, horizontal, cleft, which separates Up and Down,
Heaven and Earth, the dualism of Spirit and Matter.

Thus, in fact, the cross cleaves the Unity into a Quaternary of
four quadrants: Up-right, Down-right, Up-left (uplifted), and
Left-down (or let-down). This is a tragic view of the world. The figure of Christ impaled on the Cross symbolizes the desperate
heroic endeavor to connect that which has been cleft asunder.
The bleeding heart of Christ symbolizes the means for binding together the two sides that were severed from each other. The sink-
ing head of Christ on the Cross generally touched the middle
point, where the upper and lower intersect. The middle point is
the heart; you cannot have both heart and head at the same spot.
It symbolizes the knowledge (Gnosis) of overcoming these distinctions, of joining Heaven and Earth, or Spirit and Body—as
well as uniting Right and Left, Male and Female, You and I, and so

on. When this head rises, when Jesus is laughing even in this dire state, the figure of Christ on the Cross turns the Tree of Death into the Tree of Life of the Qabbalah.

Saint Francis of Assisi received the most celebrated mystical experience of the Middle Ages; in 1224, on Mount La Verna, two years before his death, he had an ecstatic vision: He saw a seraph descending toward him from heaven with six fiery wings, and between the wings the figure of Christ crucified. Immediately after the vision disappeared, Francis received the stigmata on his hands, feet, and side. This form of Christ crucified ushered in a major trend in the history of Western Christianity: devotion to the humanity of Christ, especially his suffering and death, as discussed, for instance, in Ewert Cousins's above-mentioned book.

But the form that he saw can be interpreted as the Cross, transformed (through Christ's Passion) into the form of the Tree of Life of the Qabbalah, with three elements/wings to the Right and three to the Left. At about the same period, the *Mequbalim* were describing, and apparently experiencing, the Tree of the *Sephirot*. I can personally vouch for this, as I have been fortunate to have once seen such a seraph myself, and, not associating the figure with any dire images, I was transported to the most intense joy I've ever felt.

The figure of the Tree of Life of the Qabbalah—with its Three elements on the Right, Three on the Left, and Four in the Middle—opens and explicates this redemptive pattern and allows its application in every instance. In fact, this is the pattern and the meaning I have already described for the symbol of the collective soul of the United States: the American eagle on the great seal of the United States, reproduced on the right of the one-dollar bill. It has ten elements, which I shall set here in a table. But whereas in the dollar bill the eagle is facing us, I shall set the elements of the Tree of Life pattern from the eagle's point of view:

The Elements of the Tree of Life of the Qabbalah

	The 13–Star Constellation	
UNUM Unity		E PLURIBUS Out of Many
	(Right Pointing) HEAD	
Left Wing STRENGTH		Right Wing LOVE
	The 13–striped Shield (the 13 initial states)	
13 Arrows/ Missiles WAR		Olive Branch with 13 leaves PEACE
	The Tail/Yesod GUIDANCE	

So the great seal of the United States has a secret, esoteric meaning connected with the number thirteen and the Qabbalah, which was meant to inspire the collective spirit of the American people.

Gnosis, then, has a strong presence in the Holy Scriptures of both Judaism and Christianity. It should not come as a complete surprise that it might one day, our day, enjoy a revival.

CHAPTER 7

Jesus' Travels:
Was He Looking for Keys to
Gnostic Spiritual Awakening?

UCH LIKE GEMATRIA, geometry is connected with Gnostic thinking. There are those who claim that both words used to be one. We shall now try to trace Jesus' written and acceptable, as well as unorthodox and speculated, whereabouts, trying to figure out sacred intentions and patterns.

The Gospel of Matthew tells us that the infant Jesus was brought to Egypt for a few years (2:13–23). None of the Gospels tell us anything about Jesus' whereabouts between the ages of twelve and thirty. There are thus various speculations as to where he received his education. The Muslim tradition (probably based on Nazarene and/or Gnostic sources) is that Jesus did not die on the Cross. Traditions placed Jesus' grave in Kashmir, southern France, or Glastonbury, England.

To this speculation we may add other legends and traditions, which claim that Jesus was already familiar with the lands that lie in the eastern-northeastern direction, and to which he had already been before he made his appearance in Galilee and Judea at the age of thirty. In her book *The Lost Years of Jesus,* Elizabeth-Claire Prophet gathers four independent testimonies from ancient documents telling that the young Jesus had been in Ladakh until the time he decided to return to the Land of Israel. These claims are reiterated in Holger Kersten's book *Jesus Lived in India.*

All these theories, speculations, or forming myths are contemporary ways of trying to connect Jesus to an emerging global civilization, where different cultures are examining their interrelations and trying to find some sympathetic connections. Some might argue that they are not more fanciful or fantastic than the more familiar orthodox views about Jesus (for example, "the Only Son of God")!

However fanciful, it might be constructive to ask the obvious question: What was Jesus seeking there, of all places? Why would he go there, and, if he did, why return to Galilee and Jerusalem? And where does his purported desertion of Judea leave Judas, the one who might have been crucified in his stead?

There are two possible answers that could tie Jesus' wanderings to two important traditions, or even both. One is the Jewish Messianic quest for the Ten "Lost Tribes of Israel," and the other is the Asian (including Buddhist and Indian) tradition related to the quest for Shambhala.

Finding the Ten Lost Tribes as a Messianic Quest

The most likely answer, at least for a Jew, is that Jesus was keen to find the "Ten Lost Tribes" of Israel. To quote him: "I was only sent for the Lost Sheep of Israel" (Matt. 15:24).

The "God the Father" that Jesus and his disciples referred to was "the God of Israel" (Exod. 4:22)—neither a pagan God nor only "the God of Judah" or "the Jewish God." There has never been among the Jews such a term as "the Jewish God." Such a term would be blasphemous for Jews, and only their enemies would use it. Yet in Jesus' time there was no Israel, only the province of Judea, already subject to the yoke of Rome, unable to fulfill its prophetic world role. There was also a large Jewish diaspora both within the Roman Empire and outside it to the East, on the Parthian-Persian side. All these were assumed to have issued from the Tribes of Judah and Benjamin with an admixture of Levites. But farther to the northeast resided, so it was supposed, the other Ten Tribes, exiled by the Assyrians.

Expectations of the reunification of the Tribes of Israel were part and parcel of the prophetic and Messianic agenda, already prophesied, among others, by Jeremiah (31:1–20) and Ezekiel (37:16–19), whose prophecies Jesus strove so hard to fulfill. That is why he appointed exactly twelve disciples (Matt. 10:1–4; Mark 3:13–19) in whom he confided (Matt. 20:17–19), a number that after Judas' exit had to be refulfilled (Acts 1:23–26). In the Talmud we find discussions and debates, two generations after Jesus and after the destruction of the temple, about whether the Lost Tribes are likely to return (tract. Sanhedrin 110/b). Even in the most normative Judaism of the Maimonides codex, the test for the true Messiah of Israel is that he would gather all the Lost Tribes of Israel:

And if there will rise a king from the house of David, who considers the Torah and Commandments as his father David, according to the written Torah and the oral Torah and will make all of Israel walk by it and strengthen its upkeep, then he is a candidate to be considered Messiah, and if he succeeded and built the Temple in its proper place and gathered those expelled from Israel, then he is certainly the Messiah, and he will restore the whole world to worship the Lord together, as it was written (Zephaniah, 3:9): "For then I will convert the peoples to a purer language, that they may all call upon the Name of the Lord (YHWH), to serve him with one consent." (Maimonides: *Mishne Torah, Hilkhot Melakhim*, 11:4)

Here is what Maimonides wrote about Jesus himself:

Even that man [Jesus] who thought he will become Messiah and was killed by court, was already prophesied by Daniel etc. But no man has the capacity to comprehend the thoughts of the Creator of the World, because our ways are not His ways and our thoughts are not His thoughts. And all those things [of Jesus] and of that one who rose after him [Mohammad], are but means to make a straight way for the King Messiah and to rectify the whole world to worship the Lord together, as was said, "For then I will convert the peoples to a purer language, that they may all call upon the Name of the Lord (***YHWH***), to serve Him with one consent" (Zephaniah 3:9). How would that be? The world has already been filled with knowledge about the Messiah and about the Torah and the commandments, and these things have already spread to far away isles and among many nations uncircumcised of heart and uncircumcised of flesh.

In the explicit prophecy of "the Good Shepherd" and the future king, son of David (Isa. 23:3–8), it is made plain that, through him, God will gather the lost sheep and the seed of the house of Israel "out of the north country, and from all countries into which I [the Lord] have driven them."

There was widespread expectation for a holy and righteous Messiah, Son of David, about whom sectarian prophecies of that period have also told:

And he shall gather together a holy people, whom he shall lead in righteousness: and shall judge the tribes of the people that has been sanctified by the Lord his God. And he shall not suffer iniquity to lodge in their midst; and none that knoweth wickedness shall dwell with him. For he shall take knowledge of them that they be all sons of their God, and shall divide them upon the earth according to their tribes. . . . [H]e shall judge the nations and the peoples with the wisdom of his righteousness. Sela." (Ps. of Sol. 17:28–31)

So, for ceremonial as well as practical reasons, a serious Messianic bid on Jesus' part would have necessitated contacting the "lost" tribes.

Seeking an Enlightened Society, Shambhala

The Shambhala legend is known throughout Asia by various names but is best known by its Sanskrit name, Shambhala, meaning "the place of peace/tranquility/happiness." Among the various names for the leaders of this place is also the "Children of Seth," which is a Gnostic name. There are various ideas about where this society might be located, but it is often placed in central Asia, north of Tibet, and especially today in the Altai region at the meeting of Russia, China, and Mongolia (see Victoria LePage's book *Shambalah: The Fascinating Truth Behind the Myth of Shangri-la*). The inner and secret meanings refer to more subtle understandings of what Shambhala represents and are generally passed on orally.

The great late-nineteenth- and early-twentieth-century explorer Sven Hedin, who made many important discoveries in China, Mongolia, and Tibet, found a lost Buddhist city in the Gobi

Desert, which might well have given rise to the legend of Sham-bhala. The great-twentieth-century Russian artist, mystic, and vi-sionary Nikolay Roerich traveled extensively in 1926 and 1928 in central Asia, including in the Altai region, to discover Shambhala. (After the communist revolution Roerich went to the United States, where he engaged in global cultural matters, including re-institution of the usage of the great seal of the United States with all its symbolism.) Also, the twentieth-century Georgian mystic G. I. Gurdjieff tells in his autobiography, *Meetings with Remarkable Men*, that he started his career by establishing a group of "seekers for Truth" who tried to cross the Gobi Desert of central Asia to find the remains of an ancient mystical city. This is very likely Sham-bhala—the fabulous city of so many esoteric Asian traditions.

The late exiled Tibetan teacher Chogyam Trungpa, in his book *Shambhala, the Sacred Path of the Warrior*, posits that the Sham-bhala kingdom is an enlightened society that people of all faiths can aspire to and actually realize. The path to it is described as the practice of compassionate warriorship—meeting fear and tran-scending aggression—joining the wisdom of the past with that of one's own culture in a practice of openheartedness.

Jesus' Travels and the Earth's Currents

In their book *Twelve-Tribe Nations and the Science of Enchanting the Landscape*, John Michell and Christine Rhone present "the Astrological Geography of Pentecost," where they recall that at Pentecost, the twelve disciples (after replacement of Judas) spoke in the tongues of the many nations whose pilgrims were present in Jerusalem for the (Jewish) feast. The authors then relate a tra-dition current at that time and referred to in Eusobius's fourth-century *Church History:* that the twelve apostles divided the world into twelve regions and then drew lots to decide which region each of them would target for his ministry. The Nicean Council, convened by the emperor Constantine, identified the twelve apostles with the twelve zodiacal signs around Christ the Sun. The Gnostic codex of "The Acts of Thomas"—which originated from the same milieu as the Judas Gospel that we are discussing—also tells of the apostles dividing the world among them, with Jesus' twin brother going to India, which could be a metaphorical way of saying that "the Second Jesus" should have gone in that direction.

Whatever else, Jesus was the great teacher of the apostles, so they could hardly know something that he did not. And allowing for the knowledge that his divinity should confer, we can assume that Jesus had knowledge of geomancy and was a "Master Builder," according to Gordon Strachan in his 1998 book *Jesus: The Master Builder.* So, to be thorough, we should consider the possibility that Jesus' claimed long treks were guided by the arcane knowledge of geomancy.

The most far-reaching works on sacred geography have been written by the French scholar Jean Richer, who detected an ancient astrological scheme in the placement of temples and sacred monuments. He identified four sacred centers of cult in Greece, with clear geometric relation between them, each arranged like hubs of zodiacal wheels, marking twelve sectors of thirty degrees each. Among these hubs he identified Sardis, the capital of Lydia in Asia Minor, as a symbolic world center, the hub of a zodiacal wheel that contained all the nations of the ancient world.

Sardis is mentioned in the book of Revelation among the seven churches of Asia Minor, and Asia Minor was the chief area for the mission of Saint Paul, who came from Tarsus in Asia Minor. Asia

Minor was also the hotbed of the mystery religions, which some such as Robert Wolfe in his 1987 book *Christianity in Perspective* claim became the pagan core of the forming Christian religion. Noting that the first Christian emperor, Constantine, founded his capital at Constantinople and convened the Nicea Council, which identified the twelve apostles with the twelve zodiacal signs, such an astrological world center would have been quite acceptable to him. But would it have been acceptable to Jesus, the Judaic messiah?

In the Gospel of Judas, Jesus is calling for another world order, which is beyond the astrological order—an order characterized not by the twelve but by the thirteen. Such world order is ruled not by the twelve aeons but by the Lord whose unpronounced Great Name has the value of twenty-six—the God of Abraham.

The Abraham Triangle and the Jerusalem Cross

At the inception of "The Academy of Jerusalem," twelve scholars gathered to ponder the past and future of Jerusalem. John Michell, the world's leading authority on "Ley Lines," was one of them, and so was Mohammad Sabet, an Egyptian who lives in the Netherlands and who used to work in the Architecture Department at Delft University.

Researching an earth pyramid that Napoléon's army built out in the fields near Utrecht, the "Austerlitz Pyramid," Sabet found that while a long, straight line drawn from Paris to Giza would continue straight to Mecca, the Islamic center of the world, a parallel line drawn from the Austerlitz Pyramid would go through Jerusalem. This led him to look closely at the geographic relations of Giza, Jerusalem, and Mecca and to make a startling discovery: a triangle of Giza (the Great Pyramid), Jerusalem, and Mecca would have a right angle at Jerusalem, and the direction from the Great Pyramid to Jerusalem is about twenty-six degrees (the angle of the slopes of the passageways in the pyramid itself) north (or left) of the cardinal direction east.

Recalling that the book of Genesis described Abraham as a great traveler who measured the whole Land of Israel and had also visited Egypt (12:10–20), and recalling the Qur'an passage that Abraham visited Mecca to build there the Qa'ba with his son Ishmael, Sabet called this configuration the "Abraham Triangle," and urged us to search within this pattern for some key to inter-faith reconciliation in Jerusalem. At first I was cautious, as there is no end to speculations about the Great Pyramid and most of them are crackpot. Thus, there are "pyramidologists" who have divined in the dimensions of the Grand Gallery of the Great Pyramid a time line announcing the birth of Christ thousands of years later and so on. Yet that twenty-six-degree angle certainly caught my attention, as the number twenty-six is the numerical value (gematria) of the Hebrew letters of the Name of the Lord, YHWH.

John Michell, who wrote a lot about the pyramid, stuck to a solid find: that the ratio between the circumference of the base and of the height of the Great Pyramid is 2π—the same ratio of the circumference of a circle and its radius. He showed in *The Dimensions of Paradise* that the pyramid's proportions were an application of the same geometrical construction, which he called "The New Jerusalem Diagram," that was also used in the prehistoric astrological temple-observatory at Stonehenge and can be gleaned from the measurements of the New Jerusalem in the book of Revelation and from traditions about the encampment of Saint Joseph of Arimathea in Glastonbury, England. This is a pattern of "squaring the circle" that divides the circle into 28, and thus also 14, equal sectors, and 360 degrees divided by 14 is very nearly 26 degrees. (The Dead Sea sectarians used a 364–day calendar as an indication of the heavenly order. The Last Supper was apparently served according to that calendar; 364/14 is exactly 26.)

It was then found that if the triangle of Giza-Jerusalem-Mecca is extended to a cross, which is centered at Jerusalem, the other arm of the cross, opposite the direction of Mecca, the Muslim capital, goes through Istanbul, originally Constantinople—the first Christian capital. And while the head of that cross points to the ancient Great Pyramid, its foot is pointing to the very center of Asia, the Altai region, pointing to the legendary Shambhala.

This can be seen as an engaging legend for our times—a pattern that balances Christianity and Islam, as well as the mysterious centers of Africa and Asia, centered on Jerusalem. Jesus' Crucifixion in Jerusalem and his possible trek to the east-northeast, toward the center of Asia, suggest a global cross that places Jerusalem as the spot and fulcrum for some ceremonial global events.

We shall return to the "Jerusalem Cross" at the end of our investigation, to ponder the location of the temples envisioned in the Judas Gospel.

PART IV

OTHER STREAMS
OF GNOSIS:
ISLAMIC, LITERARY,
& PSYCHOLOGICAL

CHAPTER 8

Some Gnostic Views Shared by Islam

THERE ARE QUITE A FEW REFERENCES to Jesus in the Holy Qur'an, but the most remarkable of them is a clear denial of Jesus' death on the Cross:

And on account of their [the Jews'] disbelief, and uttering grave false charges against Maryam [Mary]. And because of their saying: "We killed the messiah, Issa [Jesus] son of Maryam, the Messenger of Allah." But they killed him not, nor crucified him, but the resemblance of Jesus was put over another man [Harun Yahya's translation: but it was made to seem so to them], and those who differ therein are full of doubts [about it]. They have no [certain] knowledge of it, they follow nothing but conjecture. For surely, they killed him not. But Allah raised him up to Himself. (Sura 4:156–58)

(The Qur'an quotations are mostly from the translation by Hilali and Muhsin Khan, with some insertions from Harun Yahya's index to the Qur'an.)

If Jesus did not die on the Cross, then the whole edifice of Christian dogma is left without a foundation. How does Islam explain such a bold statement?

There is a text called "The Gospel of Barnabas," which surfaced in Holland in 1709 and gives a detailed alternative, quasi-Muslim account of the life of Jesus. Most Westerners regard it as a Muslim forgery, which copies various passages from Dante. But for many Islamic propagandists, this is the true account of what happened to Jesus. This "gospel of Barnabas" explains the survival of Jesus by transfiguration: When Judas came to kiss Jesus, he was changed to look like Jesus' identical twin, and it was he who was then tried and crucified. As for Jesus, he slipped away, later going off east by northeast, and his grave is displayed to this day in Kashmir. In this the Qur'an, revered by hundreds of millions of people, sides with the Gnostic view against the orthodox view of the canonical Gospels and the Acts of the Apostles.

The claims of Jesus' stay in Ladakh and Kashmir, discussed as well by Holger Kersten in *Jesus Lived in India* and Elizabeth-Claire Prophet in *The Lost Years of Jesus,* were picked up and promoted by Mirza Ghulam Ahmad (1835–1908), founder of the Muslim-Christian Ahmadiya movement, who found it a good way of explaining the verse in the Qur'an that claims that Jesus did not die on the Cross. According to the Ahmadiyans, Jesus (or Yus-Asaf) survived on the Cross four hours and—taken as dead—was put in the tomb, in which he gained consciousness and fled to Kashmir, to find the Lost Tribes of Israel.

The treatment of Jesus in the Qur'an gives some clues to critical study of the origins of Islam, a line of questioning that is totally taboo in Muslim-ruled countries. The Dead Sea Scrolls scholar Robert Eisenmann suggests that Muhammad's informants, or those that the Prophet chose to listen to, were neither rabbinical Jews nor orthodox Christians, but remnants of the original Jerusalem Church of Jesus' own family, originally headed by Jesus' own brother James. The Christian Church eventually declared the original Jerusalem Church to be heretical. This original Jerusalem Church did not believe in the unique divinity of Jesus or his "Son of God" status, but saw him as a great teacher and even Messiah, though no greater than his brother James, and not in essence different from the rest of Israel.

The Qur'an does not necessarily strive for the replacement of Christianity and Judaism by Islam, but sees itself as the addition of a scripture for Arabic speakers:

> To each among you, We have prescribed a law and a clear way [practice]. If Allah willed, He would have made you one nation [a single community], but that [He] may test you in what He has given you. So strive as in a race [compete] in good deeds. The return of you [all] is to Allah; then He will inform you about that in which you used to differ. [Sura 5:48]
>
> And had Allah willed, He could have made you [all] one nation, but He sends astray whom He wills and guides whom He wills. But you shall certainly be called to account for what you used to do. [Sura 16:93]

What else does the Qur'an itself (as distinct from traditions and legends) mention about Jesus, Judas, or the Jews?

Judas himself, who would have been called **Yahuda**, is not mentioned in the Qur'an. But the Jews are, and they are called **Yahud** (plural) or **Yahudi** (singular). A part of the Qur'an mentions "the Children of Israel" and treats them in a respectful way. There is a Sura of the Qur'an (17) called **Bani Isra'il** or **Al-Isra'** (the direction toward Jerusalem). In it, after the story of Moses and Pharaoh, there is an address to the Children of Israel: "And We said to the Children of Israel after him: Dwell in the land [of Israel], then, when the final and the last promise comes near [that is, the Day of Resurrection or the descent of Jesus, son of Mary, to the earth, according to *Tafsir Al-Qurtubi*], we shall bring you all together as a mixed crowd [gathered out of various nations]" (17:104).

Islam, then, has within it (currently unheeded) teachings that seem to parallel those of the Gnostics rather than those of the traditional Christian Church and expect the Second Coming of Jesus and the in-gathering of the Tribes of Israel.

CHAPTER 9

Qabbalah and Christian Mysticism in the Middle Ages and Beyond

T HOUGH WE KNOW OF GNOSIS especially from the time of Christ, and though the organized Church effectively suppressed it for the centuries that followed, it continued to appear at various times around the world. Those appearances tend to suggest that the thinking in mysticism remained attractive to some segment of the population throughout the centuries of suppression.

Two peaks of Christian Qabbalah were in the Renaissance time and in the nineteenth century. But we shall start with a most remarkable Christian mystic of the Middle Ages, Ramón Lull, and his amazing Jewish parallel (*Maqbil*), the *Mequbal* rabbi Abraham Abulafia.

Abraham Abulafia: The Ostracized Gnostic Messiah

Rabbi Abraham Abulafia (1240–1291) could be described as a Gnostic. His teaching was of methods for personal revelation. Often he even wrote an individual practice and personal instruction manual for each student! Yet he was moved to appear in public more than most of the **Mequbalim** and to take upon himself messianic missions—including an attempt to convert the pope to "Universal Judaism" (**Yahadut Klal**)!

Abulafia is an Arabic name meaning "Father of the Powers," a name that fits his style of "prophetic Qabbalah" (where Qabbalah literally means "receiving")—his was an ecstatic yet cognitive path of what today would be called "raising the frequency," turning the human brain into a vehicle of instantaneous hermeneutic deconstruction and reconstruction.

Abraham Abulafia was born in Saragossa, Spain. When he was twenty he left Spain for the Holy Land, apparently excited about the Mongol invasion of the land. He intended to find the legendary Sambatyon River beyond which the Ten Lost Tribes of Israel were supposed to dwell. Perhaps he thought those Mongols, who opposed both Christianity and Islam, were themselves Israelites. But he did not get beyond the disembarkation port of Acre. He went back to Europe, got married in Greece, and returned to Spain about 1270. In Barcelona he joined the **Mequbalim** and discovered the root text of the Qabbalah—the **Sefer Yetsirah** and the ecstatic study of the Hebrew letters and Holy Names. There he received his first revelation that he should meet the pope. The major Spanish-Jewish Torah authority and Mequbal Nachmanides (**Rabbi Moshe ben Naḥman**), who was forced to hold public disputations with Christian leaders, taught that the test of the Messiah according to the Jews is that he would appear to the Gentile ruler (like Moses appeared to Pharaoh) and demand of him, "Let my people go!" Yet Abulafia understood the Messianic training as entailing two stages: a private one of contemplating the divine names to achieve liberation from materiality and the lure of the imagination and attaining the power of prophecy to discover the time of the redemption, and then the second and public one of becoming accepted by the people.

Messiah (*Mashi'ah*—מָשִׁיחַ) comes from being anointed (*Mashu'ah*—מָשׁוּחַ) with special oil (*Shemen*—שֶׁמֶן—which for Abulafia meant the experience of the Divine Name (*haShem*—הַשֵׁם) and becoming thus anointed to prophecy—that is, his words would themselves become divine names and messages. This training took him another nine years. Abulafia understood the word *Messiah* to have three simultaneous meanings: one spiritual-collective, one public, and one spiritual-individual. It is common potential "Active Intellect" (*haSekhel ha'Po'el*) becoming manifest and liberating the human mind; this is the man who will return Israel from the exile; and it is the individual material brain/intellect that liberates the soul from the physical powers, passions, and imaginings. So without forgetting the worldly context of redemption, his was a spiritual-psychological Messianism.

Discussing Abulafia's Messianic concepts, Moshe Idel shows in *Messianism and Mysticism* that Abulafia believed in a "natural Messianism," which does not require supernatural interventions. It may have to do with a quasi-astrological theory of recurrence when the people of Israel may return to sovereignty or with an Aristotelian explanation that whatever exists in potential will sooner or later be realized or from historic observation of the life of nations that fall and rise. Abulafia started his career when great powers—crusading Christianity, retaliating Islam, and invading Mongols—were contending over the Holy Land. Abulafia explicitly wrote that those contentions could also lead to the restoration of Israel. Abulafia's own messianic career is characterized by ten-year cycles. Born in 1240—which is exactly year 5000 in the

Hebrew calendar—he went to find the Lost Tribes in 1260, received his first revelation in 1270, tried to meet the pope in 1280,
and prophesied 1290 as the year for final redemption.

Abulafia's attempted meeting with the pope in 1280 was to be
the realization of the mission he had received in a vision ten years
earlier. He left Greece in 1279 and did all he could to meet the
pope before the end of the Jewish year of 5040. He spent more
than a month in Rome, apparently making his intentions public
and seeking an interview. The pope, Nicholas III, a Franciscan,
completely rejected this idea. As he was going to his palace in Sori-
ano outside Rome, the pope sent the message to Abulafia that he
would be burned at the stake if he set foot there. In fact, the stake
had already been prepared at the town gate, yet Abulafia went
there undaunted as a likely martyr. When he arrived at the town,
he heard that the pope had died just the night before from a sudden stroke. Historical sources testify that the pope had died suddenly, not even making a confession before his death. Returning to
Rome, Abulafia was arrested by the Franciscans, but released after
twenty-eight days and ordered never to return to Italy.

What did Abulafia try to achieve? Professor Moshe Idel, the
foremost Qabbalah scholar whose specialty is Abulafia, presents
two common theories and proposes another, in *Messianism and
Mysticism* and *Studies in Ecstatic Kabbalah*. These theories try to
explain what Abulafia meant when he wrote that he wanted to
present the pope the subject of **Yahadut Klal** (in the modern usage of the word, **Yahadut** would mean "Universal Judaism"). One
interpretation is that as a Jewish Messiah he tried, like Moses before Pharaoh, to present him with a political request for the Jews.
The other, more daring, theory is that he tried to convert the pope
to Judaism. Idel, however, analyzed Abulafia's own usage of the
word **Yahadut,** which is derived from **Yehudah**—a name derived

from **Hodayah**—which has to do with confessing (or thanksgiving). A **Yehudi**—namely, a Jew—is one who confesses a certain principle. For Abulafia, the special principle that ought to be confessed is the special potency of the Holy Names, especially the Tetragrammaton—**YHWH**, which is the pivot of the methods of Qabbalah that Abulafia developed. Thus, **Yahadut Klal** would mean "Universal Witnessing of **YHWH**."

If that was his own interpretation, it is possible to see the goal of the failed meeting as an attempt to discuss with the pope the true essence of **Yahadut**-Judaism—and, I would surmise, the true essence of Christianity. He wanted to discuss the religion built around the Holy Name, rather than the Judaic Halakha (Idel also shows that Abulafia could hope that this Franciscan pope knew the great reverence that Saint Francis had for Jesus' name and the Franciscan development of devotion to the Holy Name as explained in P. R. Biasiotto's book *History of the Development of Devotion to the Holy Name*).

In the context of discussing the Truth about Judas, all this is strangely significant. What Abraham Abulafia was trying to present to the pope was **Yahadut**, that is, **Yehudah**—which is Judas! Moreover, and just as amazing, going over Idel's *Studies in Ecstatic Kabbalah,* specifically chapter 3, "Abraham Abulafia and the Pope," he brings a citation from Abulafia's book **Sefer haḤayim** (The Book of Life) that shows Abulafia engaged in public Messianic work. In it he describes himself as knowing Jesus and Muhammad, and ways to relate the extent of the moon and the sun and how to "build over them" and "Square in[stead of] the Triangle." This is to understand marvels through tasting "the honey of the Wisdom of the Names." (In the expression "Square in the Triangle"—**uterabe'a bameshulash,** ותרבע במשולש—both words have the same gematria number of 678.) This is apparently an elliptical reference to turning the Christian Trinity into a Quaternary, based on the Tetra-grammaton—the Hebraic four-letter Holy Name.

Expelled from Rome, Abulafia moved to Sicily, where he spent his last eleven years and acquired some notoriety as a prophet and a Messiah. The Jews of Sicily then wrote to a major Jewish-Spanish authority, the **RaShBA** (Rabbi Shlomoh ben Aderet), who denied Abulafia's Messiahship and led his excommunication. For many centuries Abulafia's writings were banned and known in manuscripts to only a few people, but today they are enjoying a renaissance, and many are being published.

Ramón Lull, User of Qabbalah "Lullian Wheels"

The Spanish theologian and geometer Ramón Lull (1232–1315) is considered by some as the forefather of the computer, as he created a mechanical device to generate what he considered logical proofs for religious and scientific questions.

In 1274, repenting his carnal drives, Lull climbed Mount Randa in Majorca in search of spiritual guidance. After fasting and con-templating for several days, he experienced a divine revelation, which he later tried to explicate in more than 265 works.

Lull's strongest desire was to settle the Christian-Muslim con-flict of his time through rational debate rather than continuation of the century-long military conflict of the Spanish Reconquista. In the year 1285 he traveled for the first time (out of three) to North Africa, trying to convince Muslim leaders of the Christian Truth. Coming back, he began to preach for a unification of the three monotheistic faiths—Judaism, Christianity, and Islam—which together, he hoped, would be able to defeat the Asian in-vaders then threatening Europe and the Middle East.

As a geometer, he wrote a book of geometrical constructions, starting with a method for squaring the circle, followed by a method to square the triangle.

His magnum opus was *Ars Magna* (The Great Art), which described a number of logical techniques. The one of which Lull was most proud (and which received the most attention) was based on concentric disks containing a number of different words or symbols, which could be combined in different ways by rotating the disks. For example, he used his disks to show that "*God's mercy is infinite*," "*God's mercy is mysterious*," "*God's mercy is just*," and so forth. Some of Lull's devices contained as many as sixteen different words or symbols on each disk. His masterpiece was the *figura universalis*, which consisted of fourteen concentric circles. In later days, his works were known as "Lullian Wheels."

And here we come to Lull's connection to the Qabbalah: The eminent Qabbalah researcher Moshe Idel found prayer books of **Mequbalim** that already contained "Lullian Wheels" decades before Lull used them and in his article "Ramón Lull and Ecstatic Kabbalah" he shows contacts between Lull and **Mequbalim**.

The **Mequbal** who was the undisputed master of combinatory arts was Rabbi Abraham Abulafia, and Ramón Lull seems to have unwittingly walked in Abulafia's steps. Thus, Abulafia's revelation in 1270 predated Lull's revelation of 1274, and Abulafia's Messianic mission to the pope in 1280 to speak with him about **Yahadut Klal** predated Lull's mission to the Muslim king of Tunis in 1285. Abulafia's desire was to show the pope how "to Square the Triangle"—apparently to replace the Trinity with the Tetragrammaton. Lull's geometry book, on the other hand, dealt with a method for squaring the circle and the triangle—and he was attempting to convince the Moors about the Trinity!

Lull was more successful than Abulafia. But from a Qabbalah

perspective, there is trouble with Lull's usage of the Latin letters, which are quite arbitrary and ambiguous, rather than the Hebrew letters of the original biblical revelation. Those words, the **Mequbalim** believe, have intrinsic meanings that make their combinatorics akin to the very creation of the world. In particular, the True Name of the Lord and the (four) letters that constitute it substantiate the biblical message and its inherent understanding of the Divine—and all those are lost in translation.

Lull's followers flourished in the late Middle Ages and the Renaissance, and Lullism spread far and wide across Europe. Lull's work eventually fired the imagination of Gottfried von Leibniz, who invented the mechanical calculator called "the step reckoner." Although Leibniz had little regard for Lull's work in general, he believed there was a chance it could be extended to apply to formal logic. Leibniz even conjectured that it might be possible to create a universal algebra that could represent just about everything under the sun, including moral and metaphysical truths.

Qabbalah at the Renaissance

Historians generally associate the beginning of the Renaissance in Italy with the fall of Constantinople to the Turks in 1453, ending the Byzantine Empire, so that waves of Greek refugees spread knowledge of classical Greek philosophy throughout Europe. The newly available Greek manuscripts included the *Corpus Hermetica,* and the Neoplatonists' works.

But as eminent cultural historian Frances Yates shows in his 1979 work *The Occult Philosophy in the Elizabethan Age,* an even greater impetus for the Renaissance was the expulsion of the Jews from Spain in 1492. This sent waves of Jewish refugees through-out Europe, spreading knowledge of Hebrew and the Qabbalah.

Renaissance Christian Qabbalah was derived from a number of sources. First were the Christological speculations of a number of Jewish converts from the late thirteenth to the late fifteenth centuries. Second was the philosophical Christian and Renais-sance speculation concerning the Qabbalah that developed around the Platonic Academy founded by the Medici family in Florence, directed by Marsilio Ficino.

The initial motivation of the Christian Qabbalah was similar to Lull's: to prove to the Jews the divinity of Jesus from the Jews' own science of the Qabbalah. Thus, the Christian Cabalists tried adding the letter **Shin** to the middle of the Tetragrammaton to read "YaHShUH."

In the process, however, like with the tar baby, by undertaking the translation of Qabbalah classics they integrated many Qab-balah constructs into their own systems and compiled several books of Christian Qabbalah, which became the forerunners for the Rosicrucian, Freemasonry, Illuminati, and Hermetic Qab-balah movements.

The main Renaissance Christian Cabalists were Marsilio Ficino (1433–1499), Giovanni Pico della Mirandola (1463–1494), Johan-nes Reuchlin (1455–1522), Heinrich Cornelius Agripa (1486–1535), and later Athanasius Kircher (1601–1680).

Giovanni Pico della Mirandola

Pico della Mirandola was an Italian nobleman who left the life of nobility to study and single-handedly brought the Qabbalah into the heart of the Renaissance. He came to Rome from Florence in 1486 and brought with him nine hundred theses to expound on all possible subjects, which he proposed to publicly debate within a year. (In a way, it was similar to what Martin Luther did later, nailing his ninety-five theses to the doors of the church in Württemberg.) These theses included two series of theses according to the Qabbalah: forty-seven were based on Hebrew Qabbalah's explanation of the world, and seventy-two (a most significant number, as I repeatedly show) were Pico della Mirandola's own understanding of the Qabbalah. He intended to validate the Christian Truth on the basis of the Qabbalah. For instance, he used a free rendition of the word **Bereshith**, the first word of the Hebrew Bible, as proof of the Trinity. By taking apart and then putting together the letters of **Bereshith** in various orders, he made a discourse such as: "The Father, in the Son and through the Son, the beginning and end, or rest, created the head, the fire, and the foundation of the great man with a good agreement." He then explained the Sephirot and placed Christ at various positions on the Tree of the Sephirot. Pico della Mirandola appreciated the Qabbalah for the promoting of the subject of Love. He was fascinated by Solomon's Song of Songs—"Let him kiss me with the kisses of his mouth"—and connected it with the ecstatic "Death by Kiss" (**Mitat Neshiqah**). Chaim Wirszubski, who studied the life of Pico della Mirandola, shows that with him started a Christian Qabbalah that is no longer a Christian interpretation of Jewish Qabbalah but a mystical interpretation of Christianity proper that uses the same method that a Jewish **Mequbal** uses to find the truth hidden in the Torah.

Though Pico della Mirandola studied Hebrew expressly to learn the Qabbalah firsthand, he was mainly influenced by translations made for him by a Jewish convert to Christianity. The translator, known by many names but chiefly Flavius Mithridates, rose to notoriety by rehashing the arguments of an older Christian disputation as if these were genuine Jewish secret writings that validate Jesus' divinity, according to Chaim Wirszubski in his 1989 book *Pico della Mirandola's Encounter with Jewish Mysticism.* In his translations Mithridates also planted Christological ideas that Pico della Mirandola picked at times, unaware of the forgery.

The theses Pico della Mirandola was trying to promote were preceded by his now famous *Oration on the Dignity of Man* that expressed the spirit of the Renaissance. It is possible to recognize many kinds of gods hidden in the *Oration.* Man's freedom is due to the fact that man contains all the gods within his incarnate form, yet he has the power "to have that which he chooses and be that which he wills." Despite the papal search for heresy, this Gnostic-like fundamental teaching went unnoticed by the censors. But the theses were censured. Seven of them were condemned by Rome as heretical, and six others as "dubious," including the contention that "the science of magic and the Qabbalah prove the divinity of the Christos." Pico della Mirandola then wrote the lengthy *Apologia* in which he defended his views, but he was forced to flee Rome under threat of persecution from Pope Innocent VIII, and the public debate did not take place. Yet shortly before his death he was fully exonerated by Pope Alexander VI, who was deeply interested in magic himself.

In the words of Frances Yates: "The profound significance of Pico della Mirandola in the history of humanity can hardly be overestimated. He it was who first boldly formulated a new position for European man, man as Magus using both Magia and Qabbalah to act upon the world, to control his destiny by science."

Johannes Reuchlin

Reuchlin, Pico della Mirandola's disciple, wrote a book called *De Arte Cabalistica* published in 1517. It is a conversational treatise in which he portrays the role of the Cabalist Jews as a channel to transfer Christian Cabalistic symbols that are illegible to the Jews but make perfect sense to the knowledgeable Christian reader! For example, Simon the Jew, the main character of the book, makes a veiled reference to Christ: "Just as God wears a Crown in the kingdom of the world, so is the mind of man chief among the ten sephiroth." Jesus, who is God, wears the Crown of Thorns (Keter) in this world, and the mind of Christ is chief among the **Sephirot**. The book gives a procession of biblical almost-savior figures (Enoch-Enosh, Noah, Shem, Abraham, Isaac, and Jacob) who strove to become the Messiah and who desired "to be killed by Wood," till finally Jesus came with his wooden cross. Reuchlin puts the task of proving the Trinity onto another conversant, the Pythagorean Philolaus.

Reuchlin followed Pico della Mirandola's lead that created from the Tetragrammaton (YHWH) the Pentagrammaton (YHSWH). He was familiar with a Jewish belief that the letter **shin** was missing from a proper understanding of the Torah (however, this Jewish belief has to do with the four-headed **Shin**, rather than the known three-headed form); the coming of **shin**, Reuchlin argued, made the unpronounceable name Yahweh pronounceable, and salvation came to Israel. "When the Tetragrammaton shall become audible, that is effable," Reuchlin wrote. "It will be called by the consonant which is called **shin**, so that it might become YHSWH, which will be above you, your head and your master." He also noticed that the letter **shin** is shaped like a lamp with three lights— ש—symbolizing the Trinity giving off divine light and fire.

Athanasius Kircher

Kircher (1601–1680), who lived in Baroque times, was called "the last Renaissance man." He was taught Hebrew in his childhood by a rabbi, in addition to his studies in a Jesuit school. Kircher taught and researched almost any imaginable subject, notably the Egyptian hieroglyphs, and was a professor of ethics and mathematics at the University of Würzburg and the Roman College in Italy. He wrote well over forty works and was probably the first scientist who made a living from the sale of his books. One of these books was *Oedipus Aegyptiacus* (Rome, 1652–1654), Kircher's major (and rather erratic) work on Egypt. It included a chapter called "Qabbalah Hebraeorum," which is an extensive dissertation on the Qabbalah, dealing with, among other things, the 72 Names of God and the Name of 72 (**Shem Av**). One of Kircher's main glyphs, **Sigillum Dei Aemeth** (Sign of Truth), had a five- (or six-) pointed star inside a seven-pointed star and surrounded by a circle that contained 72 letters derived from the Qabbalah and thus, in a way, giving an image of the "Luminous Cloud" of theophany (**Av ha'Anan**).

The Renaissance was eventually crushed, but its hermetic and Cabalistic teachings then found their way into the various types of European esotericism, such as of the Rosicrucians and the alchemists. Thus, the Hebrew Tetragrammaton became included in many Renaissance and later esoteric and alchemical illustrations, most often as coming from the clouds, as can be seen in Klossowski de Rola Stanislas's *The Golden Game: Alchemical Engravings of the Seventeenth Century*. For example, in Heinrich Khunrath's *Amphitheatrum sapientiae aeternae* of 1602, we find a cosmic diagram in Hebrew with the Tetragrammaton on top in the form of a triangle (sign for the Trinity) yet containing what the **Mequbalim** called "The Squaring of the Name" (with the pointlike letter Yod in the apex, then Y'od and H'e below, then Y'od H'e W'aw and the full Y'od H'e W'aw H'e below). In this way, the triangulated yet "squared" Holy Name has the gematria of 72, in Hebrew the Name for *Av*—עֲ"ב—meaning the Cloud of Glory.

The Holy Name with a Gematria of 72

		Y			10
	Y	H			15
Y	H	W			21
Y	H	W	H		<u>26</u>
					72

Frances Yates, who sees Shakespeare's king in *King Lear* as modeled on the British esotericist Doctor Dee, also finds influences of the Qabbalah in Shakespeare. We shall soon examine the role of the translated Qabbalah in the great esoteric revival of the end of the nineteenth century. But it needs to be pointed out that these developments of European occultism used mainly the (often erroneous) Renaissance translations and books, which were not yet aware of the contemporary original development of the Qabbalah of the ARI in the sixteenth century ("The Lurianic Qabbalah," developed by Isaac Luria [1534–1572], who was also known as Ari), which soon became the theology of Judaism. Thus, we have the ongoing "Hermetic Qabbalah" using the old "Cabalistic" constructs and still unaware of the current Jewish Qabbalah (as discussed below).

Renditions of Lurianic Qabbalah were eventually made by Harera and by Christian Knorr von Rosenroth and Francis Mercury van Helmont, who edited the *Kabbala Denudata* (1677–1684), the largest collection of Lurianic Cabalistic texts available to Christians up to that time. Helmont himself became a prisoner of the

Inquisition, accused of "Judaising," but his efforts contributed to the development of religious toleration.

As Allison Coudert exposes, the codiscoverer of calculus, Gottfried Wilhelm Leibniz, became deeply interested in the Lurianic Qabbalah through Helmont, and the Lurianic Qabbalah shaped his concept of the monads and defense of free will.

The currently flourishing (and greedy) "Kabbalah [sic] Center" claims that Leibniz's great (and even more known) rival developer of infinitesimal calculus, Sir Isaac Newton, "wrote 80 books of Qabbalah," but according to Coudert, the truth seems quite the opposite. Not that he did not encounter it—Newton's *Zohar* exists in the library of Cambridge University in England to this very day and his mentor More was a Christian Cabalist—but in fact Newton strongly disapproved of the Qabbalah he encountered, according to G. W. Trompf in his 2005 book *Isaac Newton and the Kabbalistic Noah*. Newton sensed similarities between Qabbalah and early Christian Gnosticism, which he disapproved of. Ironically, it was precisely because he strongly objected to the Trinity, which he regarded as idolatry, that Newton was as much out of temper with the older run of Christian Cabalists, like Reuchlin, Paracelsus, and their like who sought to deduce both the Trinity and the Divinity of Christ from Jewish theosophy.

Fringe Qabbalah Influences

In the wake of the Lurianic Qabbalah there arose in Judaism the movements of the false Messiahs Shabbetai Tzevi (1626–1676)—who was forced to convert to Islam—and later of Jacob Frank (originally Leibowicz; 1726–1791) and his fringe messianic movement. The Frankists taught and practiced a doctrine of salvation through sexual ecstasy, and Frank himself eventually converted to Christianity and became a baron. The Frankists anticipated the sexual magic that emerged a century later under the influence of Max Theon and, ultimately, Aleister Crowley. It is in fact possible that Frankism influenced Max Theon.

In the nineteenth century there appeared an enigmatic Polish Jew, the son of Rabbi Judes Lion Bimstein of Warsaw, Louis Maximilian Bimstein, better known as Max Theon. Theon came to teach quite similar sacred-couple work, along with visualization, and acted as the grand master of "the Hermetic Brotherhood of Luxor" according to the book *The Hermetic Brotherhood of Luxor: Initiatic and Historical Documents of an Order of Practical Occultism* by Joscelyn Godwin, Christian Chanel, and John Patrick Deveney. Theon, it is claimed, traveled widely in his youth, and in Cairo he became a student of a Coptic magician named Paulos Metamon. He was authorized, it is claimed, to teach Qabbalah to the Gentiles. According to Sri Aurobindo, Theon taught a "fully Tantric" approach to spirituality. He exercised a profound influence on Sri Aurobindo's teacher and companion, Mirra Alfassa "the Mother," and on Helena Blavatsky, the founder of the Theosophical Society, and on Peter Davidson, who, in turn, was a profound influence on Papus and other luminaries of the "occult revival." Yet Theon relinquished his association with that occult brotherhood, and his legacy eventually moved to Israel and reintegrated with orthodox neo-Hassidic Judaism.

The Nineteenth-Century Occult Revivals and Their Qabbalah

The Western esoteric (or hermetic) tradition, a precursor to both the neopagan and New Age movements, is intertwined with aspects of Qabbalah. Within the hermetic tradition, much of Qabbalah has been changed from its Jewish roots through syncretism. Core Cabalistic beliefs are still recognizably present—but are really like a parody of the Qabbalah.

"Hermetic Qabbalah," as it is sometimes called, probably reached its peak in the "Hermetic Order of the Golden Dawn," a late-nineteenth-century organization that was arguably the pinnacle of ceremonial magic (or, depending on one's position, its ultimate descent into decadence). Within the Golden Dawn, "Kabbalistic" principles such as the ten Sephiroth were fused with Greek and Egyptian deities, the Enochian system of angelic magic of John Dee, and certain Eastern (particularly Hindu and Buddhist) concepts within the structure of a Masonic- or Rosicrucian-style esoteric order. Many of the Golden Dawn's rituals were publicized by the occultist Aleister Crowley and were eventually compiled into book form by Israel Regardie (they are nowadays much published by Llewellyn Publications). As we shall see, many if not most of the occultists and hermetic Cabalists tended toward anti-Semitism.

Aleister Crowley

Aleister Crowley, who called himself "the great beast" (an allusion to the book of Revelation) and was notorious for his advocacy of sexual magic, made his mark on the occult use of Qabbalah with several of his writings; of these, perhaps the most illustrative is *Liber 777*. This book has a set of tables relating various parts of ceremonial magic and Eastern and Western religion to thirty-two numbers representing the ten spheres and twenty-two paths of the Cabalistic Tree of Life. From genuine Judaic Qabbalah, these look nonsensical.

Aleister Crowley was an anti-Semite who committed the offense known as blood libel, the accusation that Jewish rites are celebrated using sacrificed Christian children. He would until his death continue to wrestle with the difficulty that the Qabbalah is Jewish. One persistent rationalization was that the Jews stole the Qabbalah from the Egyptians, which seems clearly mistaken in light of current knowledge. At times he implied that the blood libel myth had a redeeming esoteric meaning, but usually he presented the accusation as a plain assault on the moral character of Jews.

Gerard Encausse (Papus)

"Papus" was the stage name of Gerard Encausse (1865–1916). As a young man, Encausse spent a great deal of time at the Bibliothèque Nationale in Paris, studying the Qabbalah, the Tarot, the sciences of magic and alchemy, and the writings of Eliphas Lévi. In 1893, Encausse was consecrated a bishop of l'Église Gnostique de France by Jules Doinel, who had founded this church as an attempt to revive the Cathar religion. In 1895, Doinel abdicated, leaving control of the Church to a synod of three of his former bishops, one of whom was Encausse.

Encausse joined the French Theosophical Society shortly after it was founded by Madame Blavatsky in 1884–1885, but resigned soon after joining because he disliked the society's emphasis on Eastern occultism. In 1888, he cofounded his own group, the Cabalistic Order of the Rose-Croix. That same year, he and his friend Lucien Chamuel founded the Librarie du Merveilleux and its monthly revue *L'Initiation,* which remained in publication until 1914. Encausse was also a member of the Hermetic Brotherhood of Light and the Hermetic Order of the Golden Dawn temple in

Paris, as well as Memphis-Misraim and probably other esoteric or paramasonic organizations, as well as being an author of several occult books.

In October 1901 Encausse collaborated with Jean Carrère in producing a series of articles in the *Echo de Paris* under the pseudonym Niet ("no" in Russian). In the articles it was suggested that there was a sinister financial syndicate trying to disrupt the Franco-Russian alliance and alleged that this syndicate was a Jewish conspiracy.

In his occult writings Encausse drew heavily on the scriptures and Cabalistic mystical writings of the Jews, yet he can be labeled an anti-Semite. This contradiction between occultistic Judophilia and political Jew-hatred was neither explained nor acknowledged in his writings. One theory is that, as a Christian, he wished to appropriate the Qabbalah for his own spiritual ends, and to facilitate this, he fomented a climate of fear and paranoia that he hoped would result in the removal of Jews from Europe.

Madame Blavatsky

Helena Petrovna Blavatsky (1831–1891), of Russian origin, was the prophet and founder of the Theosophical Society that still has many adherents today.

With the aid of Henry S. Olcott, she established the Theosophical Society in September 1875. "Theosophy" referred to subjects such as the Egyptian mysteries and the Qabbalah, which had been discussed in a lecture previously given to an informal group by J. H. Felt, an architect and engineer. Its name was furnished by Charles Sotheran, who was of independent means, a high Mason, a Rosicrucian, and a student of the Qabbalah. The direction of the society was claimed to be directed by the secret Mahatmas, or Masters of Wisdom, although there is not any certain evidence of these Mahatmas or Masters of Wisdom and many claims that they were fabrications, such as those in the book by Chanel, Godwin, and Deveney mentioned earlier. Blavatsky's first book, *Isis Unveiled* (1877), outlined the basic precepts and the secret knowledge, which they protected. In the book's preface she inserted "a plea for the recognition of the Hermetic philosophy, the ancient universal wisdom."

Much of Helena Blavatsky's writing contained strong racial themes. She regularly contrasts "Aryan" with "Semitic" culture, to the detriment of the latter, asserting that Semitic peoples are an offshoot of Aryans who have become "degenerate in spirituality and perfected in materiality," as she does in *The Secret Doctrine*. Blavatsky also sorted the races of the world by their relation to the "Fifth Race" (the Atlanteans), putting the Aryans on the top and describing Native Australians and Tazmanians as "semi-animal creatures."

Blavatsky was probably not more anti-Jewish than she was anti-Christian. But her student and eventual successor Alice Baily (whom some consider as the mother of the "New Age" trend) was a blatant anti-Semite, and in her theories on the karma of the Jews she presents many negative stereotypes that sound as if they were written by Adolf Hitler, as affirmed in the work of Rabbi Yonassan Gershom.

THESE EPISODES OF OCCULT ANTI-SEMITISM are a variant of the problem that accompanied the establishment of Christianity in the first centuries, to which I shall turn in Chapter 14. Trying to exploit the spiritual treasury of Judaism without paying respect to its keepers parallels the original sin of Christianity that adored Jesus but denigrated Judas—the figure of the Jew. The current rise of interest in the Qabbalah that shows more respect for the Judaic legacy parallels the modern exoneration of Judas that we have been surveying.

These occultists and their appropriation of the Qabbalah have caused the Qabbalah to be regarded by many Christians as a negative "occult" teaching and "New Age" fashion. It is hoped that the distinctions I made here may help these Christians to accept the value of the Qabbalah as genuine Judaic spirituality (recall that "Qabbalah" literally means "Acceptance") and to further develop their Christian Qabbalah also as a means of sharing with the Jews.

CHAPTER 10

Judas and Gnosticism
in Psychology:
Carl Jung

O NE OF THE FIRST to deal with Gnosticism through the
twentieth century, even to readopt it, was the famous
Swiss psychologist Carl Gustav Jung (1875–1961).

The Nag Hammadi hidden Gnostic library contained, as I have
mentioned, thirteen codices. Twelve of them were recovered for
the Coptic Museum in Cairo, but the thirteenth was purchased
separately, presented to Jung and kept by him, so it is even called
"Codex Jung."

Jung was known for his attachment to esoteric beliefs, and his
"first love" was Gnosticism. From the earliest days of his scientific
career until the time of his death, his dedication to the subject of
Gnosticism was relentless. As early as August 1912, Jung inti-
mated in a letter to Sigmund Freud that he had an intuition that
the essentially feminine-toned archaic wisdom of the Gnostics,
symbolically called Sophia, was destined to reenter modern Western culture by way of depth psychology. Subsequently, he stated
to Barbara Hannah that when he discovered the writings of the

ancient Gnostics, "I felt as if I had at last found a circle of friends who understood me."

Jung was the only non-Jew among Freud's coterie. Freud, who took pains that his teachings should not be regarded as "Jewish" and used Greek mythology and kept his reading of the *Zohar* hidden, was very happy to have this Gentile disciple, and Jung was heralded as the "crown prince" of the fledgling movement. But he broke with his teacher because of a difficult personal and intellectual dispute. In their last meeting and dispute, Freud fainted from his agony that Jung had betrayed him. Yet Freud did not use the association of Judas, but complained that Jung engaged in an Oedipal father-murder, like the children of Israel who killed and ate Moses in Freud's later fantasy about Moses.

The separation proved to be much more complicated than either of the men first envisaged, and Jung fell into a long period of depression and introspection—and into a period of self-analysis that he wrote about in his autobiography, *Memories, Dreams, and Reflection.*

That was about the time that Jung wrote a very strange text called *Seven Sermons to the Dead,* in which he "channeled," or impersonated, the second-century Gnostic teacher Basilides of Alexandria. Jung wrote those sermons between December 1916 and February 1917, during World War I. He reported that before the writing, strange phenomena began in his house: loud retorts from invisible sources and a series of disturbing dreams experienced by Jung and his children. At one point he said the house seemed to fill with an invisible presence, a crowd. It was at this stage that he was compelled to write, ordered, in a sense, to scribe what is now known as *Seven Sermons to the Dead.* The esoteric, magical, and ultimately Gnostic overtone of the work is without question. Jung did not claim to be the "author" of the text, but said the author was the ancient Alexandrian Gnostic heretic Basilides. Many decades later Jung commented thus upon these sermons: "All my work, all my creative activity, has come from those initial fantasies. . . . [E]verything that I accomplished in later life was already contained in them."

The text opens with the words: "The Dead came back from Jerusalem, where they found not what they sought. They prayed me let them in and besought my word, and thus I began my teaching." It seems that the disappointing "Jerusalem" was both the Judeo-Christian tradition and Freud the Jew. The fertile place to search for truth seemed "Alexandria, the city where East and West meet"—and the home of the Gnostic heretics.

In these sermons Jung/Basilides taught of the Pleroma and of the God Abraxas:

> There is a God about whom you know nothing, because men have forgotten him. We call him by his name: ABRAXAS. He is less definite than God or Devil. In order to distinguish God from him, we call God HELIOS, or the Sun. Abraxas is activity; nothing can resist him but the unreal, and thus his active being unfolds. The unreal is not, and therefore cannot truly resist. Abraxas stands above the sun and above the devil. He is the unlikely likely one, who is powerful in the realm of unreality. If the Pleroma were capable of having a being, Abraxas would be its manifestation.

Aware that the Gnostic tradition was dead, Jung sought a living, connecting tradition and believed he found it in alchemy, according to Steven A. Hoeller. One of Jung's academic associates, Professor Gilles Quispel, who studied Gnosis, came to coin a phrase reflecting Jung's point of view: "Alchemy is the Yoga of the Gnostics."

Yet Jung also supported an alternative path for seeking continuation between the terminated Gnosis and our times and developed an academic association with the greatest Qabbalah scholar
of his time, Gershom Scholem, who often referred to the Qabbalah as "Jewish Gnosticism." Jung used to invite Scholem from
Jerusalem to his yearly Eranos conferences and paid him hand-
somely to produce a series of excellent studies of Qabbalah that
were published in the *Eranos Yearbook* and were later also published separately (as *On the Kabbalah and Its Symbolism* and *On
the Mystical Shape of the Godhead*). Jung had great respect for Scholem's work (though apparently Scholem did not think much of
Jung's theories).

It seems that, in a way, Jung's life and teaching recapitulate
what we find in the Gospel of Judas, both in terms of an ambiguous "betrayal" and a revision of doctrine. As mentioned above,
Jung was the only non-Jew among Freud's coterie. The irony is
that Jung might have been more loyal to the Jewish/Mosaic tradition than Freud was.

As Israeli scholar of "Jewish psychology" Hebrew University
professor Mordechai Rotenberg claims, Freud's psychology was a
"Christian psychology" based on an "original sin" (in this case, the
Oedipal one) and the authoritarian position of the psychoanalyst
as heir to the confessor priest. We may claim that Freud was a
Trinitarian, and that the Freudian trinity of id, ego, and superego
was a secular materialistic heir of the Holy Trinity. Jung, on the
other hand, held much to the Quaternary, as evidenced in his
fourfold typology and recognition of the fourfold Mandala as the
symbol of the Self. Jung writes about the Three and the Four in his
books *Psychology and Religion* and *An Answer to Job*. But perhaps
the most revealing are his diagrams of the structure and dynamics
of the Self in his book on Gnosticism, *Aion*, in which he constructs

around the figure of Moses a fractal of a quaternary of quaternaries. Rather than Freud's Oedipal nonsense concerning Moses, Jung takes Moses as the universal man, enmeshed with all the connections with family figures and with the higher and lower worlds. The full analysis requires four quaternaries, each with added top and bottom points, which makes the figure a three-dimensional octahedron rather than just a two-dimensional square. But at the base, what turns the Trinity into a Mandala is the addition of a fourth element for each analysis—be it the added feminine element, or the element of Evil (for example, the Serpent), or the higher Anthropos-Adam. It is especially the addition of "the Black Woman" that Moses took (Num. 12:1) to the Trinitarian scheme that allows greater psychological depth and connection to the lower and higher worlds.

This transition from the Trinity (which is considered all masculine) to the Quaternary (which is all-feminine or half-feminine) is, I have claimed, the message of the Gospel of Judas and was the very message that the prophetic *Mequbal* Abraham Abulafia tried through the thirteenth century to convert Pope Nicholas III to (and risked being burned at the stake had the pope not died the very same day)!

CHAPTER 11

Gnosticism in Literature:
Borges and Others

NOSTICISM HAS ENJOYED a strong presence in literature, particularly in modern times. Three instances in which the imprint of Gnosticism is unmistakable are Hugh Schonfield, P. J. Farmer, and Jorge Luis Borges.

Schonfield's Salutary Jewish Perspective on Jesus

Until modern times, Jews preferred to stay silent on Jesus. If we look for a Jewish perspective on Jesus, which poses alternatives to Christian views yet treats Jesus with reverence and empathy, we can turn to Hugh Schonfield.

Hugh Schonfield (1901–1988) was a Jewish British scholar who published forty-five books, including *A Popular Dictionary of Judaism, The Secrets of the Dead Sea Scrolls*, a modern translation of the New Testament that he called *The Authentic New Testament*, and some dozen books about the origins of Christianity. His book *The Passover Plot: New Light on the History of Jesus* was quite a sensation when it came out in 1965, went through many editions, and has influenced many of the subsequent discussions about Jesus. We can see it now as a precursor to the discovery of the Judas Gospel, and as having substantial bearing on the issue of Judas.

Schonfield embarked on trying to find the truth about Jesus. As he subsequently wrote: "It finally dawned on me, and I have in honesty to say this, that Christianity was still much too close to the paganism over which it had scored a technical victory to be happy with a faith in God as pure Spirit. There had never been in the Church a complete conversion from heathenism." He believed that the image of Jesus that emerges from serious historical inquiry about him does not, when honestly examined, detract from the greatness and uniqueness of Jesus. Rather, it does confirm the earliest Christian conviction, that awareness of being the Messiah meant everything to Jesus. Jesus directed his life to affirmation of that office, anticipated his execution, and envisioned his resurrection.

The "Passover Plot": Did Jesus Seek to Be Crucified?

Schonfield shows that Christianity began not as a new religion but as a movement of Jews, who held Jesus to be their Messiah in the Jewish terms of that office. From this perspective, much mooted material becomes clear. It was Jewish Messianism (without a trace of the subsequent Pauline doctrines) that shaped the life of Jesus and so brought Christianity into being. It was the same Messianism that provided the impulse behind the Jewish war against Rome that broke out in 66 CE., a generation after Jesus—a war that brought about the critical separation of Gentile from Jewish Christianity. "Jesus, as much as any Jew, would have regarded as blasphemous the manner in which he is depicted, for instance, in the Fourth Gospel," Schonfield states.

The Jewish expectations about the coming of their deliverer, the Messiah, have been closely linked with the anticipated historic period of the Last Times or the End of Days, which would precede the inauguration of the Kingdom of God through Israel. The conception of the Last Times drew on biblical prophecies, combined with Babylonian and Persian ideas of the succession of ages. Although it was not known how long the Last Times would last, Jews believed that it could be known approximately when they would begin. This was found in the prophecy of the Seventy Weeks (of years) in the book of Daniel (9:24), interpreted as 490 years after the decree of Cyrus to restore Jerusalem (2 Chron. 36:23)—that is, after about 46 BCE. Those who lived in Herod's time could accept that the Last Times had begun, and the Messiah could be expected soon. Schonfield, who has also studied the Dead Sea Scrolls, shows how from the time that the books of the Prophets and the Psalms became recognized as sacred, the way opened to see these books as oracles of God, subject to all kinds of interpretations to draw out of them hidden meanings and prognostications. At the same time came the clash between Hellenism and Judaism, leading to the Hashmonean revolt, in whose victory was seen the hand of God helping those obedient to his commandments. This opened a new age of extraordinary fervor and religiosity, in which any event was scrutinized to discover in what way it might be a Sign of the Times. There was a widespread expectation of the coming of a holy and righteous Messiah Son of David, about whom also sectarian prophecies told.

At the time when Jesus lived, not only was there a widespread anticipation of the coming of the Messiah, but also for many there was nothing inconsistent with the way that Jesus understood the functions of the Messiah. From this perspective, there was no presumption of the Deity of Jesus, and no authority then identified the Messiah with the Logos, or conceived of the Messiah as an incarnation of God. All of this came later, with the spread of Christianity to the Gentiles.

Jesus acted as he did because he was consciously fulfilling what Jews saw in the Hebrew Bible. He died in Jerusalem not because the Jews hounded him, but because he was persuaded that, as Messiah, he must journey to Jerusalem in order to be rejected and to die. With the help of the Oracles, Jesus deduced that he was required to suffer ignominiously at the hands of the rulers at Jerusalem. This was also demanded by the actual political realities, that a ruler of Judea had to be confirmed by the Roman Senate, and the Roman and Jewish authorities were required to apprehend anyone claiming to be king. A claimant who was not a Roman citizen would be condemned to death by crucifixion (a Roman, not Jewish, mode of execution).

Jesus inherited a faith that Israel was chosen by God to lead all nations to him, that his land, and especially Jerusalem, was the Holy Land, and that his time was the End of Days. Becoming convinced that he was the Chosen One, he had to act dramatically—and it is even likely that he was familiar with the theater, affirms Richard Patey in his book *Jesus and the Theatre*. As Schonfield writes: "His visualization of the role of the Messiah was highly theatrical, and he played out the act like an actor with careful timing and appreciation of what every act called for. . . . But the portrayal of the Messiah's tragedy, and the anticipation of the happy ending, was utterly sincere. This was not make-believe." Schonfield's analysis of the actual situation in the Land of Israel at those times also stresses the differences between the social conditions and beliefs in Galilee and in Judea—the region of Jerusalem and its environs.

When Jesus started becoming prominent in Galilee, and with that attracted the danger that the authorities there might stop him, he appointed twelve of his more intimate followers as envoys. Their number was symbolic of the twelve tribes of Israel, and he gave them precise instructions as to how they should travel and speak. Only to them did he reveal himself as the Messiah. Of these twelve, all but one were from Galilee. The odd man out was Judas Iscariot, a Judean.

In Schonfield's analysis, Jesus then went alone, without the twelve apostles, to Jerusalem to set the stage. There he also met his Judean accomplices, including Lazarus and his sisters, the unnamed "beloved disciple," and Joseph of Arimathea, all unknown to the twelve. He then returned to Jerusalem a few months later with his disciples among the throngs of pilgrims for Passover. There he was going to suffer torture on a Roman cross, to be followed by resurrection. In Jerusalem he was preaching in the temple by day, to attract the attention of the people and the apprehensive authorities, but careful to return in the evening to Bethany, outside the city. With his accomplices he arranged his royal entry to Jerusalem according to prophecy (Zech. 9:9) and prepared the upper room for the Last Supper—and the new grave next to Golgotha.

Schonfield on Judas' Betrayal

Among the prophecies Jesus sought to fulfill was also that of being betrayed by a friend. This had been foretold in Psalm 41:9: "Even my close friend, whom I trusted, he who shared my bread, has lifted up his heel against me." Ever since the revelation of his Messiahship at Caesarea-Philippi, Jesus told—but only the twelve—that his end would come from rejection by the chief priests, elders, and scribes. He kept repeating this, adding that he would be betrayed to these rulers.

In his last days in Jerusalem, Jesus repeated to the apostles that he was going to be betrayed. He did not say that it would be by one of the twelve, and only the Fourth Gospel says he had foreknowledge it would be Judas. Schonfield sees this as improbable, but agrees he might have suspected it. In Schonfield's view, Jesus' stratagem was to pile on the pressure at the crucial moment and provoke the traitor to act, and that he had prearranged with Mary the incident of the precious ointment in order to say the words about his body being anointed for burial. With the value of the ointment and Judas' role as treasurer, he became the weakest link and registered the conjunction of the idea of wealth and the anointing for burial. Mark's testimony is that this decision by Judas followed immediately after the incident of the precious ointment. Here are Schonfield's further reflections about Judas:

> Judas knew that Jesus expected to be betrayed. He had been saying so again and again, and once more now he had spoken about his death. We may believe, however, that not until this moment had Judas thought of himself as the betrayer. It was the worth of the ointment and Jesus talking about his burial that put it into his head. Suddenly like an inspiration it came to him that money was to be made by doing what Jesus plainly wanted. It seemed as if in a subtle way Jesus was telling him this, inviting him to profit by doing his will. The tempter came in the guise of his Master.
>
> What else may have been in the mind of Judas it is impossible to judge. It has been suggested that he was bitterly disillusioned about Jesus, having imagined that he would speedily establish his kingdom and that there would be great material rewards for his followers. But

Jesus had said he would be killed, and the rewards would come to an uncertain future in the circumstances of the performance of strange prodigies incomprehensible in practical terms. Judas therefore betrayed Jesus, on this estimation, because he felt that Jesus betrayed him.

Schonfield then continues to analyze the unfolding of the "Passover Plot," stage by stage: the Last Supper, when Jesus announced that one of those eating with him would betray him, but refusing then to say who, either because he did not wish to put Judas to shame or to prevent any chance that he might be stopped. He told only the beloved disciple that he would indicate, as he did, by passing the sop, and then telling Judas: "What you have to do, do quickly." Judas then did whatever he knew Jesus wanted, and the company in general thought nothing of this. Schonfield then continues to relate the events of Judas with the council and comments: "The council might imagine that they were exercising their own free will in determining to destroy Jesus, and Judas Iscariot might believe the same in betraying him; but in fact the comprehensive engineer of the Passover Plot was Jesus himself. Their responses were governed by his ability to assess their reactions when he applied appropriate stimuli. Thus it was assured that the scriptures would be fulfilled."

It eventually comes to Jesus' Crucifixion, which lasted only about three hours—in other words, not enough time to kill a person, and eased by stimulants and simulated death, but then exacerbated by the soldier's unexpected stab at his side with a lance. Joseph of Arimathea, who claimed the body from Pilate, took the body to the prepared grave and the medications.

Schonfield tells of a similar incident related by Josephus of three people removed from the crosses, one of whom survived.

He does not dwell on why and how the revival of Jesus failed. The second part of this book, and all of the book that came next, *Those Incredible Christians,* was dedicated to proving that the religion that followed, that is, Christianity, had nothing to do with Jesus' own intentions.

Schonfield on "Jesus and India"

In chapter 6 of Hugh Schonfield's book *The Essene Odyssey,* the writer asks the crucial question: "Did Jesus survive?" This is a question that Schonfield had attempted to answer in previous works and had arrived at his own hypothesis—as in *The Passover Plot.* Taking this up again, he opens the contemporary discussion on the person of the enigmatic Yus-Asaph whose tomb is in Kashmir.

It has been speculated that Jesus and Yus-Asaph are the same person, and there are a number of elements of circumstantial evidence to support this. Schonfield points out that without the survival of Jesus, this of course would not have been possible. In investigating the issue of whether Jesus went there to proclaim his message to the Ten Lost Tribes of Israel, he argues that this is a misinterpretation of Matthew's Gospel, where Jesus' mission is "to the lost *sheep* of the house of Israel," not to tribes that had gotten lost. He thus contends that Jesus' mission was clearly defined as the Land of Israel and that he did not enter Gentile cities. With a number of other plausible arguments, Schonfield doubts the theory of Jesus having gone to India, romantic and appealing though it is. He argues that even if Jesus had survived the Crucifixion, he would not have been in the best of health. Schonfield reiterates his earlier theory that Jesus expired shortly after being removed from the cross because he had not reckoned with the soldier's spear. He does, however, give some credence to the idea that the wounds of Jesus might have healed in a few days due to special ointments and that the Turin Shroud, if genuine, points to a temporary covering and not burial clothes. However one sees it, according to Schonfield, there would seem to be little evidence to support the idea that Jesus could immediately travel long distances. Schonfield is left with the conviction that Jesus had left this life.

At this point, I shall make a pause in discussing Schonfield's writing and go back to a cardinal question that was raised in the Gnostic Manuscript.

Was Judas Jesus' Twin?

Until the recent discovery of the Gospel of Judas (and its early mention by Irenaeus), no mention of Judas Iscariot by the Gnostics was known. But once we are open to the possibility that the presentation of Judas in the orthodox Gospels is confused, drawing three Judases (or Jude, as in the Greek texts; the three being Judas Iscariot, Judas Thomas, and Jude) out of what might have been only two persons or one, we can try to detect Judas also in other Gnostic texts.

The first Gnostic Gospel to be discovered was called "The Gospel of Thomas" and purported to bring "the secret words which the Living Jesus spoke and Didymous Judas Thomas wrote." Thus, it already gave the expectation of offering a deeper level of teachings, more esoteric (secret words). This it does indeed, much in the manner of Zen Koans. The scholars, who wanted to differentiate clearly between the beloved disciple and the accursed Judas, coined the name "The Gospel of Thomas." So they took "Thomas"

to be a proper name—"the doubting Thomas." Yet various researchers have already argued that "Thomas" was no other than a
Greek corruption of the Hebrew word "*Te'om*," namely, "Twin," the
same as the Greek word "Didymous," which was put in as an explanation of the Hebrew-Aramaic "*Te'om*." Thus, the opening of
that Gospel would be "The secret words spoken by the living Jesus
to his twin brother Judas."

So far, this has caused no great problems, since another major
Gnostic work has been found, named "The Acts of Thomas," implying that Jesus' twin brother was the apostle Thomas. After Jesus' death, this story tells, the twelve apostles divided by lot
among themselves the world to be converted, and Thomas received India. He was reluctant to go there, but Jesus tricked him,
reappearing on earth to sell him into slavery for twenty pieces of
silver (thus introducing a haunting similarity to Judas' act).
Thomas's new master took him to India. In India he was able,
with the help of Jesus who appeared as his identical twin, to convert princes, build a heavenly palace for the king, revive the dead,
return people from hell, and so on. This entire Gnostic tale has a
dreamlike quality.

But what may happen to our conceptions if this beloved disciple and twin brother of the Lord Jesus turns out to be none other
than Judas Iscariot? Such a claim has already been made by Hyam
Maccoby in his book *Judas Iscariot and the Myth of Jewish Evil,* a
claim similar to Borges's tapestry of stories with "Three Versions
of Judas," which is related below. Could this lead to a new twining
of Jesus and Judas, of Jesus and the Jews, and perhaps even of Jesus deriving his divinity from his transactions with his twin Judas?
The Judas Gospel opens the gates to hitherto inconceivable possibilities. In the contemporary world the implications could be
explosive.

RETURNING TO SCHONFIELD'S BOOK, in the following chapter, "Thomas's Twins," Schonfield continues the discussion as to who this person Yus-Asaph could have been. This will not be discussed here, except to say that he sees a clear link to Judas Thomas (the twin). This myth has been put about by the Nestorians, who were Persian Christians and spread the Gospel eastward. His conclusion is that we are dealing not with an individual but with a movement of ideas, which in turn created legends about certain persons.

In discussing the myth that Jesus and Judas Thomas were twins, he points to the Islamic literature *Rauza-tus-Safa* by Mir Muhammad (AD 1417). In it, Jesus and Judas Thomas are made to travel to Iraq. On this journey, Jesus supposedly visited the tomb of Shem, son of Noah. This has Essene relevance, especially relating to the Essenes' alleged practices of medicine. He goes on to say that "Shem" in Iraq could easily be substituted for the Babylonian Sun-God Shamash, whose story mirrors the underlying Messianic idea.

After considering a number of other theories and speculations, Schonfield comes to the conclusion that there is confusion between Jesus and the True Teacher of the Dead Sea sect, and that it is the body of the True Teacher that was buried in the tomb in Kashmir.

Schonfield's Interpretation of the Secret of the Knights Templar

Hugh Schonfield carried on studying the Passover Plot, to the point of what he considers to be later Gnostic legacy. During the reign of the Crusaders' "Kingdom of Jerusalem," the mightiest power in the Holy Land was the "Holy Order of the Poor Knights of the Temple of Solomon," or the Knights Templar. The order came to build and hold many castles in the Holy Land, but their

original and central domain was at the Temple Mount of Jerusalem. They retained the formerly (and future) Islamic shrines
and renamed them. The al-Aqsa Mosque was renamed "Templo
Solomonis" (the Temple of Solomon) and used as their residence.
The underground halls became the knights' stables. The Dome of
the Rock was renamed "Templo Domini" (the Temple of the Lord)
and was used for whatever religious rites they held. After the fall
of Jerusalem to the Muslims, the Knights Templar still thrived in
many places throughout Europe. They had a great enclave in
southern France by the Pyrenees Mountains, where they apparently performed secret rites. In the year 1314—on Friday the Thirteenth—the king of France, Philip le Bel, in league with the pope
crushed the Knights Templar, and many were tortured by the
"Holy Inquisition" and burned at the stake as heretics. One of the
claims extorted by torture was that the Templars worshiped an
idol they called "Baphomet." Many researchers have tried to comprehend whether such a being/idol existed, and if so what this
outlandish name could signify.

It is here that Schonfield had another inspiration. Applying the
esoteric Jewish practices of letter codes, Schonfield used the
ATBaSh code on the name "Baphomet" (which written in Hebrew
is בפומת) to substitute its letters, and extracted the name "Sophia"
(written as שופיא in Hebrew, where the letter ש is pronounced as *s*,
which is entirely admissible). In this code, the first Hebrew letter
(א) is substituted with the last letter (ת) and vice versa, the second
letter (ב) with the second-to-last letter (ש), and so on. So the hidden God (or Goddess) of the Templars, he suggested, was Sophia,
implying that the Templars were secret Gnostics.

Schonfield's twentieth-century version and analysis of the
Gospel stories approaches that of the Judas Gospel but actually
falls short of it. Although Schonfield's declared intention was to

honor the historical Jesus, and his implicit aim (as a Jew himself) was to exonerate the Jews, the old-new Judas Gospel is more thorough in respecting both Jesus and Judas. Noting that Judas was the exception among the disciples by being a Judean (and thus more of "a Jew"), he might have included Judas among Jesus' Judean accomplices. In the Schonfield interpretation, Jesus tricks Judas and thus betrays him, and Judas reciprocates, thus taking on himself the blame (and the eternal damnation).

Were he alive today, Schonfield might have been happy with the old Gnostic Gospel. But even that is not certain. Looking up his name on the Internet, I found that his legacy was intended to establish a nation of world service. It seems that he kept faith neither with the Christians nor with the Jews, but set out to accomplish what he thought had been Jesus' true aim.

The Vision of the Servant Nation

While writing *The Passover Plot*, reports his trustee Stephen A. Engelking, Schonfield had no intention of writing a best-seller, but the book's enormous success in selling millions of copies helped put him into the position of being able to make publicly known what was nearest to his heart—the development of a Messianic Servant Nation for the sake of mankind.

He had been active before the Second World War, together with a number of others, in trying to establish such a holy nation. By 1952 such a nation had already been officially and legally formed in the name of "the Mondcivitan Republic" and was gaining growing international recognition as an instrument toward bringing peace among men. Schonfield's work in this area was recognized in his nomination for the Nobel Peace Prize.

After the success of *The Passover Plot*, he was able to publish a book titled *The Politics of God* promoting this idea. It became a catalyst for many new projects and proved that it was possible to unite thinking people from all religions with those of none.

He would have wanted to see the realization of the messianic vision of a united servant people of God to bring peace and salvation to mankind. Maybe his experimental republic has so far not proved sustainable, but the search must go on to find a way of achieving this goal as the fulfillment of human destiny.

P. J. Farmer's *Night of Light*:
Judas of the Galactic (Anti?) Christ

In science fiction (SF) and fantasy literature circles, Philip José Farmer is a classic author. Farmer has won the Nebula and Hugo SF Awards, and there is even a museum about him (he is still alive). Farmer's use and reuse of classical literary themes and characters has won him the title of "the North American Borges." He has reached such a status that he writes a book outline, creates a framework universe, and invites readers/writers to compose books of adventures that take place within that universe, obeying the guidelines he as "master creator" has set.

The variety of Farmer's output makes it nearly impossible to label him. But for our purposes, we may regard Farmer as a modern Gnostic, much like the Gnostics of the first centuries, who claimed that this world had been created by some secondary and quite deficient god. The theme of flawed creator gods is prevalent in several of his book series. He has written, for instance, a series called *Makers of Universes*, each universe created by a different scion of William Blake's very Gnostic myth of Urizen and his offspring, and even this earth, it eventually turns out, was created and is run by one of them (whose most recent residence is in Hollywood).

One theme that Farmer has treated quite obsessively is that of resurrection and of the preservation of identity beyond death and hibernation, and of being trapped for successive lives. All humankind is resurrected over and over again (the River World Series and many others), mixing companies of explorers of various times, including Samuel Clemens (Mark Twain), Alice from Lewis Carroll's Wonderland, and Richard Burton, the adventurer who also translated the *Arabian Nights*. Farmer treated resurrection in various ways, some of them seemingly on the verge of being realized in the modern world. In one book, *Traitor to the Living*, resurrection (or its denial) is combined with the theme of the Traitor.

His 1966 *The Night of Light* was, as mentioned, a wholly original retelling of the story of Judas Iscariot. The hero of the story is Father John Carmody, a serial hero in five of Farmer's short stories (collected as *Father of the Stars*). He is traveling in a spaceship, incognito, to the planet "Dante's Joy." The reader discovers that Carmody is a secret agent, a former professional assassin who at some past time had had a conversion experience, embraced Christianity, and eventually became a bishop of the Catholic Church, which is in the process of expanding throughout the galaxy. The planet Dante's Joy, it turns out, holds some threat to the further expansion of Catholicism in the entire Milky Way.

At that planet, every seven years there are tremendous magnetic storms, which have the curious effect of materializing people's thoughts, creating both heaven and hell. For most people, their inner demons come out and materialize. All who stay awake and take the Chance become what their innermost longings dictate: a beast howling with lust and depravity or a godlike being flowering with truth and light. Thousands are transformed into monsters, while others find perfect happiness. The majority, who are afraid to take the Chance, escape by going down into underground shelters and lying drugged in the Sleep. But there are always twelve courageous souls who venture out to reach the Temple, forming two opposing bands.

On that "Night of Light," twin babies are born to the creator goddess Mother Boonta: the good Prince of Light, Yess, and the wicked Prince of Darkness, Algul. The task of each of these tribes is for each to find its baby god and beat the other band in bringing their god to his appropriate temple. The god who makes it first quickly grows and destroys the other, and the next seven years are under his reign—for good or for evil.

John Carmody has no ethics, no morals, and no conscience. Until he takes the Chance on Dante's Joy, living through seven nights of his wildest fantasies come true, he can't even imagine why anyone would want a conscience. Father John Carmody is a man who knows evil intimately, and comes to know good with an equal intimacy.

Eventually, Carmody makes his choice for Yess, thereby tipping the scales—but in this act he betrays the repressive Church that had sent him there to make sure that what comes of that planet poses no threat to it. He then finds out that his conversion to Catholicism, many years earlier, had actually been effected by the still unborn god Yess, with the intention that at the right moment, he would become the Judas who betrays the organized Church in order to install the good Yess.

The Night of Light focuses on the dark and light sides of human nature as represented by the demonic and benevolent aspects of power and religion. Typically, Farmer does not allow one side to defeat the other, insisting on the recognition and acceptance of both. *The Night of Light*'s plot dramatizes how transcendental forces can unlock the true heroic self that is trapped inside even the most alienated antihero.

With our attention to the Judas theme, which Farmer brings in the last page as the key, we can be alive to the way Farmer's *Night of Light* further opens the inquiry—even into "galactic" vistas.

Obviously, Farmer, who comes from the U.S. Bible Belt, is searching for an equal, but less repressive, alternative to the Bible as it is taught there. In so doing, he re-creates a version of the ancient Persian religion that rivaled Christianity at its inception.

The remarkable aspect in Farmer's story is that Evil is created ever anew, just as Good is. It is not there from the start, a priori, fixed, and determined. And hence it is susceptible to change.

The figure of Judas in the Farmer story is certainly highly paradoxical—he is sent as an agent provocateur to help the evil side to win so that the Church of God shall not be challenged. But then by choosing the good, he in effect betrays the Church.

But all this comes about because this time, Yess has his own imperialistic aspirations, to extend his rule beyond that one star, and thus challenge the galactic expansion of Christianity. So in effect here Yess—a name certainly intentionally redolent of Yeshu'a-Jesus—is the "Antichrist" (that is, unless the Antichrist is the Church).

Borges's Three Versions of Judas

The Argentinean author Jorge Luis Borges (1899–1986) was the ultimate writers' writer. The cover of the Penguin edition of his *Labyrinths* calls him "probably the greatest 20th-century author never to win the Nobel Prize." When the Colombian writer Gabriel García Márquez received the Nobel Prize for Literature, the story goes, he told the judges: "Gentlemen, you should have given this prize not to me, but to Borges." Borges never wrote a piece of more than a dozen pages, but in those short stories, essays, and fantasies he managed to pack greater intricacy than most writers do in entire novels.

Borges was drawn to the Gnostics, and I, for one, first saw the word *Gnostic* when I read his "Three Versions of Judas"—and my life has never been the same since. Borges had a talent to always see the other side, the surprising, the uncommon, and the magical beneath the everyday, the full hidden pattern.

The Hidden Redeemer: Borges's Many Versions of Judas

In 1944, when Germany was exterminating the Jews and his native Argentina was sympathizing with the Nazis, Borges began—in addition to his fiction—to write political articles. These articles didn't so much support any one political system as criticize many of the general trends of the time: anti-Semitism, Nazism, and the increasing decline into fascism. But he did not give up literature, and published his second collection of short stories, *Artificios,* six new stories that ingeniously mixed philosophy, fact, fantasy, and mystery. Of these six stories, three deal in some way with Judas Iscariot: "The Shape of the Sword," "Theme of the Traitor and the Hero," and "Three Versions of Judas."

In "The Shape of the Sword," Borges tells of having been forced to spend a night on the border of Argentina and Brazil in the estate of a taciturn and reclusive Englishman, whose face was marked by a crescent scar. He turned out to be an Irishman who had taken part in the Irish rebellion against the English in 1922. Late that night, when both were drunk, he told Borges the story of that mark. It was a story of a rebellion by romantic Catholics, during which he hid in a deserted labyrinthine villa along with a shallow Marxist materialist by the name of John Vincent Moon, who also proved to be a miserable coward. His cowardice made the teller ashamed: "Whatever one man does, it is as if all men did it. For that reason it is not unfair that one disobedience in a garden should contaminate all humanity; for that reason it is not unjust that the crucifixion of a single Jew should be sufficient to save it. Perhaps Schopenhauer was right. I am all other men, any man is all men, Shakespeare is in some manner the miserable John Vincent Moon." On the tenth day of hiding, the story goes, when the English took the city, the storyteller returned to hear Moon on the phone, betraying him in exchange for safe passage for himself. The storyteller chased the traitor around that labyrinth and caught him just before the soldiers caught him and took him to execution. He just managed to cut a bloody crescent on the traitor's face. Here the storyteller stopped his confession, his hands trembling. "And Moon?" asked Borges. "He collected his Judas money and fled to Brazil . . ." He stopped, and eventually Borges asked him to continue. He sobbed, pointing to his scar: "You don't believe me?" he stammered. "Don't you see that I carry written on my face the mark of my infamy? I have told you the story thus so that you would hear me to the end. I denounced the man who protected me. I am Vincent Moon. Now despise me."

Looking back at the Judas Gospel, which Bishop Irenaeus defined eighteen hundred years ago as a "Cainite Gnostic," we have here a story about a man carrying his "Mark of Cain." He has to tell it through the tale of his accuser in order to be heard, to confess.

Borges followed this story with another short story—"The Theme of the Traitor and the Hero." That was a deliberate story-in-the-making, where the author consults the readers as to the setting, time, and place for enactment of the story—which might take place elsewhere as well—but then landed it again in Ireland, still earlier, in the early nineteenth century, during another (fictitious) revolt against the English.

Ryan, a great-grandson of the national hero Kirkpatrick—who like Moses (or, if you prefer, Jesus) did not live to see the Promised Land or the victory of the revolt he had prepared, as he was assassinated just before the revolt—investigates the circumstances of his great-grandfather's death. But the historic or detective investigation turns into a literary one—the hero was shot in a theater (as if anticipating Lincoln's death)—but the murder starts looking more and more like the assassination of Julius Caesar, in the very style and with the literary allusions of Shakespeare's play.

The investigation is taken from what the author calls "the naïve circular labyrinths of incarnation cosmologies" by a stranger literary discovery—a quotation from *Macbeth* by a beggar who last spoke with the hero before the murder. That history imitates history is pretty amazing, but that history would imitate literature seems inconceivable.

The investigator then discovered that the hero's closest friend, Alexander Nolan, was the one who had translated Shakespeare into Gaelic. He also found in the archives a manuscript of an article that Nolan had written about the Swiss "Festspiele," traveling theaters where thousands of participants reproduce historic events. Another unpublished document revealed that a few days before his end, the hero had presided over the tribunal that passed a death sentence on a traitor whose name had been erased, a verdict out of keeping with his character. Ryan found that the hero—his great-grandfather—had signed his own death sentence. Afterward, it was irrefutably proven that he had betrayed the revolt. But he asked to die in a way that would not harm the revolution and that might redeem his betrayal. Nolan thought up a plan whereby the execution of the traitor would assist the liberation, by his being assassinated in a dramatic setting, and the hero/traitor agreed. With the time being so short, Nolan had to borrow much from Shakespeare, repeating scenes from *Macbeth* and *Julius Caesar.* Hundreds of participants acted out their roles, and for the hero it was his finest hour.

In the last paragraph of the story, Borges adds that the Shakespearean parts were the weakest, perhaps deliberately, and the investigator assumed that they were added for his own sake—that he was also a part of the plan. Finally, after much painful deliberation, the investigator decides to hide his discovery (and still wonders if this part was planned by Nolan).

The "Three Versions of Judas"

Here we come to Borges' best and most explicit treatment of betrayal and of Judas. The name of the story already contains a paradox. As we saw, this is the third story of Borges that deals with these themes, the third version. In this story, there is an ambiguity about which are the three versions of Judas—the protagonist successively considers three interpretations of Judas' act, but he writes only two books. Thus it may be that the third version is his own destiny—or it may be the fourth version. There is here the same ambiguity between the principles of the Three and the Four, which is the very secret of Borges's famous story "Death and the Compass," commented on in the following. Thus, "Three Versions of Judas" also hints at the alternatives of the Christian Trinity and the Quaternary of the Qabbalah.

The hero of this story, wrote Borges, should have been a second-century Gnostic leader—likely the author of the recently found Judas Gospel! But instead, God appointed him the twentieth century, the university town of Lund in Sweden, and the name Nils Runeberg. The discoveries he made might have also been made in a literary circle in Paris or in Borges's Buenos Aires, but there they would have been nothing more than an exercise in heresy. But for the deeply religious Nils Runeberg, member of the National Evangelical Union, they were the key to deciphering the central mystery of theology, which justified his life and destroyed it.

Borges relates that the first edition of Runeberg's *Christ and Judas* carried the epigraph by de Quincy: "Not one thing, but everything tradition attributes to Judas Iscariot is false" (1857). De Quincy thought that Judas had tried to force Jesus to reveal his divinity and thereby kindle a great uprising against the Roman occupation (which is quite consistent with the Hugh Schonfield interpretation). But Nils Runeberg interpreted differently. With his exacting religious mind, he could not tolerate the apparent superfluousness in the scriptures. To identify a preacher who appeared daily in the temple, there seems no need for a betrayal by a disciple. This nevertheless occurred. To assume a mistake in the scriptures would be intolerable, as it would be to assume arbitrariness in the most important event in history. Thus, the betrayal by Judas could not be arbitrary, but had its mysterious place in "the economy of redemption." When the Word became flesh, it made a sacrifice—which demanded a corresponding human sacrifice. Judas was, in effect, representing all men in making a sacrifice of himself, lowering himself to the despicable role of a traitor. This parallels the sacrifice that Jesus made, and Judas thus reflects Jesus. (And this about parallels how the Gospel of Judas places Judas, except that this Gnostic Gospel placed him above the other disciples.)

At this point in the story, theologians refuted Runeberg's theory for various reasons, and he came up with another, moral, theory. Recognizing in Judas one of the apostles whom Jesus had selected, he rejected the attribution of a base motive to him. Runeberg proposed an opposite motive: the extravagant asceticism of renouncing everything, mortifying his spirit, rather than just his flesh, for the glory of God. Judas sought hell because the felicity of the Lord sufficed for him.

Runeberg then wrote his second book and revised it (this being actually the third version), named it *The Hidden Redeemer,* and then hesitated for two years before taking it to print. "The general argument is not complex, even if the conclusion is monstrous," wrote Borges. If God lowered himself to become human in order to redeem humankind, his sacrifice would have been perfect. Runeberg reasoned that it would not have been possible for God to become a human without being able to sin—"the attributes of *impeccabilitas* and of *humanitas* are not compatible." Thus, the final conclusion that Runeberg reached was that God did not become Jesus—God became Judas.

That second book was received with total rejection. Runeberg intuited from this universal indifference an almost miraculous confirmation—that God did not wish this terrible secret propagated in the world, that the hour had not yet come. Runeberg then realized that he should not have divulged the divine secret, and, having done it, he became a traitor to God. He went mad, running the streets of Malmö, praying aloud that he be given the grace to share Hell with the Redeemer. He himself thus became a Judas.

In "Three Versions of Judas," Borges seems to logically prove Judas to be the Son of God as a hyperbolic way to debunk dogmatic adherence to accepted interpretations of the Gospel story. Note, however, what Borges wrote in the introduction to the story: If these arguments had been pondered elsewhere, by a secular intellectual (like Borges himself), they would not have been as fatal as they were for that stern Swedish theologian. For me, a Jew, born in Palestine that would soon become Israel, the role of Judas did not seem to be totally unredeemable. For me, it seemed that still another version of Judas might be gleaned, and I carried out the task in my *Gospel of Judith Iscariot*.

The Three and the Four–Borges's "Death and the Compass"

Noting the ambiguity in the story about the three or four versions, and in anticipation of our subsequent discussion on the theme of the Three and the Four, it may be useful to recall Borges' masterful treatment of this theme. In one of his earliest and most famous stories, a detective comes to investigate the murder of a Kabbalist rabbi, which took place in a hotel room on the north side of Buenos Aires on the third night of the month. Then on the third of the next month, an apparently similar murder is reported, though in another part of the sprawling city, and then on the night of the third of the third month—a third murder in yet another side of the city. The locations of the three crimes are found to mark on the map of the city a perfect triangle. The police conclude that the gruesome ritual has consumed itself, but the detective—who studied the books of the murdered learned Jew—realizes that by Jewish account (where the day begins in the evening, based on Gen. 1:5), the murders occurred on the fourth of the month and that the pattern is not Trinitarian but Quaternary. On the third night of the fourth month (which is the Jewish fourth day) he takes his gun and rides to a deserted villa on the far south side (in fact, the very same labyrinthine villa of the story "The Shape of the Sword"!), where he confronts the murderer, and it turns out that he himself is the victim.

PART V

THE PROPHECY OF
THE JUDAS GOSPEL:
OUR TIME AS A
MESSIANIC TIME
OF FULFILLMENT

CHAPTER 12

The Gospel of Judas
May Have Been Intended
for Our Time

T HERE IS SOMETHING HAUNTING about the announcement of the Gospel of Judas waiting hidden for some sixteen hundred years and coming out in our generation. Many people view major current events as the fulfillment of some Bible narrative or deriving meaning from it. Thus, the New Testament ends with the Apocalypse—the "uncovering" (dis-covering) of the "Last Things"—and these are interpreted for the most part as dire events (except for the final vision of the New Jerusalem). The Gospel of Judas also purports to disclose how the End will come to pass. Does the Gospel of Judas signal another type of Apocalypse? Could it indicate a new format for "the Second Coming"? Or, in view of the power of "self-fulfilling prophecies," could a new biblical interpretation, supported by the old-new Gospel of Judas, be able even to alter the outcome of the present dire world events?

The scholars who have worked on piecing together and translating the Gospel of Judas have approached it from an academic

historical perspective. As Marvin Meyer sums it up in his introduction to the English version of The Gospel of Judas: "After being
lost for sixteen hundred years or longer, the Gospel of Judas has at
last been found. The authors of this volume hope that the Gospel
of Judas may contribute to our knowledge and appreciation of the
history, development, and diversity of the early Church and shed
light on the enduring issues faced in that formative period." My
aim here, however, is to go beyond the historical studies, and to
suggest what impact this extraordinary find could have on our
present generation. Could this ancient Gnostic text contain a
message intended for us?

Certainly, the work itself seems to claim as much. The very first
pronouncement of the Gospel is that Jesus chose his twelve disciples and that he "began to speak with them about the mysteries
beyond the world and *what would take place at the End.*" Since
that End did not arrive in the second or fourth century—and the
Gospel of Judas reemerged now—it could be that we are now approaching it, in whatever guise it may appear.

Possibly, the central theme of the Judas Gospel is the theme of
Time—the End, eras, ages, aeons, and generations—as they relate
to different types of understanding.

When Jesus walked in the Land of Israel, he acted in the context of the Jewish Messianic expectations of that time. For Jesus'
audience, the "End Days" (**Aharit ha'Yamim**) of which the
prophets of Israel prophesied (for example, Isa. 2:2–4) and the
"Kingdom of Heaven" that Jesus announced were the same thing.
Many people were engaged at those times in various calculations,
both among the Jews and among all the other subjects of the Roman Empire.

For the pagan civilization, time accorded with the astrological
worldview, with its eras of 2,160 years each within a recurring cy-

cle of the "Great (or Platonic) Year," amounting to nearly 26,000 years. This is based on the physical cycle of "the precession of the Equinox." Each 2,160 years, one "month" of that "Great Year" elapses by the movement of the sun's position at the spring equinox through one of the twelve signs of the sidereal zodiac. Each such era—or "Age"—was seen to be connected to one of the signs of the zodiac (which represent 12 constellations of stars) and was expected to derive its character from the abiding nature of that constellation. This was the widely accepted science and cosmology of that period.

The Jews, however, assumed that the history of the world was contained and foretold in the sacred books of the Torah and the Prophets. There can be no doubt that Jesus himself was steeped in the biblical prophecies. There are many prophecies in the Hebrew Bible, and there is also a basic cosmology implied in the Torah, with its own time dimensions.

As I mentioned in the account of Schonfield, among Jews of that period, the dominant way of calculating the "End Days" was to count the "70 weeks" of the book of Daniel (9:24), interpreted as 490 years after the decree of Cyrus to restore Jerusalem (2 Chron. 36:23), which meant at around 46 BCE. But this date came and went, and Jesus' times (0–33 CE) were actually times of subjugation to Rome and mounting threats for Jewish survival. This tended to color the interpretations of the biblical prophecies.

Some of the biblical prophecies for that End of Days are optimistic and "full of light" (for instance, Isa. 2:2–4, 60:1–22), yet this last prophecy ends with ambiguous timing: "I the Lord will hasten it in its time" (Isa. 60:22). Other biblical prophecies, on the other hand, are full of war and destruction (for example, Isa. 59: 17–21), notably Ezekiel 38–39 about the apocalyptic wars of "Gog," which immediately precede the vision of the future temple. The Dead

Sea Sect, about contemporary with Jesus, was expecting a global "War of the Children of Light and the Children of Darkness." The Jewish zealots who rebelled against Rome in 66–73 CE counted on receiving divine help, and the Bar Kokhvah rebellion of 132–135 CE also raised Messianic expectations.

For the Gentiles who adopted Christianity, there was an astrological meaning to Christ's advent. His advent was seen to coincide with the passage of the ages—from the old "Age of Aries" to the new "Age of Piscis" (the Fish). Thus, the early Christians, who were persecuted by the Roman authorities, used the sign of the Fish as their secret identifier, and Jesus himself was esoterically known as "the Fish." The fish symbol was associated with the geometric pattern of the Vesica Piscis, the conjunction of two circles (as parents) that produces a fishlike intersection that symbolizes (in alchemy) the miraculous child. These early Christians saw themselves as the harbingers of that New Age. Jesus himself must have known otherwise. As a Jew himself, he could not have been an astrologer (or certainly not primarily so). The "Kingdom of Heaven" was for him not that of mechanical or animistic stars, but of the stern yet loving "Father in Heaven" who holds a special affinity to Israel and who can overstep the stars. Jesus gave his disciples signs of the End of the Age (Matt. 24:1–31; Luke 21:3–33), yet he said about the time of the coming of the Kingdom of Heaven, "No one knows about the day or hour, not even the angels in heaven, nor the Son, but only the Father. . . . The Son of Man will come at an hour when you do not expect him" (Matt 24:36–44).

This parallels the Jewish teaching of Isaiah 60:22 in the Jerusalem Talmud (tract. Ta'anite 3a), that if Israel repents and merits, then "I the Lord will hasten it," but otherwise the End will come "in its time."

Shortly after Jesus' time (and following the demise of the Great Revolt of 66–73 CE and of the Bar Kokhva revolt [132–135 CE] that spelled the end for their contemporaneous Messianic expectations), the Jewish sages taught publicly and wrote the biblical cosmology: "We have learnt from Elijah: the world exists for six thousand years—two thousand chaos, two thousand Torah, two thousand the Days of the Messiah" (Talmud, tract. Avodah Zara 9a). This division into three ages of some 2,000 years may roughly parallel the astrological scheme—yet it has a definite beginning that is not linked to the immense cycles of astrology, but is related to the chronology of the book of Genesis. In fact, calculations of the generations, from Genesis 4 onward, support the Hebrew calendar, officially used in Israel on all government documents and most private correspondence. In it, for example, the year 2007 CE corresponds to the year 5767, and the "Days of the Messiah" started some 1767 years ago, at about 240 CE. This is about the time that both Judaism and Christianity achieved their definitive formulation. For Judaism, the formulation of the "Oral Torah" into definitive written texts of the Mishna (and then Talmud), which effectively superseded the "Old Testament"; for Christianity, that is also the time it became based on the canonical texts. So even in Jewish terms, Jesus' advent is connected in a certain sense with the onset of the Messianic times.

Promising redemption 2,000 years into the future is hardly a solace for present hard times. When the Gnostics experienced their hard times, they had to assume that their predictions would be vindicated only after the present age/aeon had passed. Thus, they could not hope for world redemption in their own times but only for individual escape from this "vale of tears." So they had to hide their writings for some much later time. The great Argentinean writer Jorge Luis Borges (whose work on Judas we have surveyed) wrote his fantastic tale "Tlön, Uqbar, Orbis Tertius," which tells of a make-believe planet whose synthetic culture is gradually taking over the earth, and in the end the writer has to turn to "urn burial," presumably to preserve his world for coming generations many centuries hence. This seems to be what those Gnostics were doing, hiding the Nag Hammadi Library and, in another place, the Gospel of Judas. But now the situation is changing. Our present is largely different and discontinuous with the past, and we can see the end of the passing age and/or start of another.

The Jesus of the Gospel of Judas shuttles between two ages, or two distinct "generations," and reveals to Judas the secret of the aeons, namely, of the ages.

> They said to him, "Master, where did you go and what did you do when you left us?" Jesus said to them, "I went to another great and holy generation."
>
> Truly [I] say to you, no one born [of] this aeon will see that [generation], and no host of angels of the stars will rule over that generation.

The other generation that Jesus frequented is one that is not ruled by the stars. But of the defective historic generation of Jesus' time, only Judas (the one most connected with Judaism) belongs to the superior generation: "Jesus answered and said, 'You will become the thirteenth, and you will be cursed by the other generations—and you will come to rule over them. In the last days they will curse your ascent to the holy [generation].'"

Now may be those "last days," not in the sense of the destruction of the world but, instead, in the sense that the dire prophecies may not come to fulfillment.

CHAPTER 13

Now May Be the Era
That Can Truly Understand
the Gospel of Judas

MOVING BEYOND THE "cult of Information" to a medium
for acquisition of Wisdom, we may now be approaching that other "great and holy generation," which is ca-
pable of understanding what the generation of those who
founded the Church and the Christian religion could not understand. The Judas Gospel states that only the urbanite Judas Iscariot, the Man of the Cities, could have some inkling of the true
purpose of Jesus' ministry.

So the pertinent question is whether we are now finally
equipped to understand the true nature of the ministry of Jesus,
the thrust of which has been thwarted for a very long time (some
1,600 years or more) by the heirs of the other eleven disciples,
namely, by Christianity! Indeed, the Gospel of Judas implies that
it is by understanding the figure of Judas that we may come to
better understand the true intention of Christ.

The Gospel of Judas gives us a handle for managing the "End
Times" events, even the preparation of a future manner of "the

Second Coming." In the past, Judas was an unhappy accomplice to the decisive public display of Jesus. Now the time has come for him to lead us into a time of happiness and fulfillment.

World Problems Come to a Head in Jerusalem

In order to dramatize the issues, let us assume that the world war has indeed started in the twenty-first century and is already under way to reach a global scale, under the guise of the "Clash of Civilizations." Or perhaps, using biblical terms, the "Wars of Gog" (Ezek. 38) have already started.

Is this World War III? Perhaps it is actually the First—and Last—World War. World War I and World War II were largely European wars, which also involved non-European allies of the warring sides, but the focus stayed on European territory. On the other hand, today, with mass communications and the issue of oil, the scene is global. The "Clash of Civilizations" that drives it is increasingly acquiring a conceptual focus in Jerusalem.

In his seminal book *The Clash of Civilizations,* Michael Huntington counts seven civilizations: (1) Europe and the United States (Christian); (2) Latin America (Catholic); (3) Russia (Orthodox Christian); (4) Islam; (5) Africa; (6) China/Southeast Asia; and (7) Japan. Presumably, only civilizations (1) and (4) and some members of (2), (3), and (5), plus of course the Jews as a special part of (1), have a real interest in Jerusalem.

However, global oil production may have already peaked and may now decline, whereas demand (through the industrialization of the other civilizations, mainly China) is growing. This geopolitical "Malthusian" situation might also draw the other civilizations to the Middle East problems and its contending parties that see the locus of the End of Days scenes is in Jerusalem.

The underpinning of the "Clash of Civilizations" is religious-scriptural as well as ethnic. Both of these factors are present, and focused, in the Israeli-Palestinian conflict, which many fear to be the main precipitator of a world war.

In the midst of this confrontation is Israel and "Zionism." But "Zion" really means Jerusalem, with all its many geopolitical and religious-prophetic associations. It seems that many of the major world problems come to a head in Jerusalem. Thus, the possible world war is likely to be something like the Jerusalem-focused apocalyptic wars detailed in the book of Revelation, and the biblical prophecies of Armageddon (Rev. 16:16) and "the Wars of Gog and Magog" (Ezek. 38–39)—prophesies that also assume a revelation of the Messianic redeemer of Israel and of the whole world.

The Gospel of Judas Offering a Better End to the World than the Book of Revelation

Does our Gospel of Judas—an ancient codex of a long-lost small religious sect, found in an African desert—have anything to do with the present dire world situation? Does it suggest a better, more coherent solution than the book of Revelation? Surprisingly perhaps, the answer is yes! I shall present below several reasons for this affirmation.

The twenty-first century started with a growing feeling of peril facing humankind. There is global warming with its many attendant catastrophes, and there is the ongoing ecological holocaust and environmental degradation. But most menacing, ostensibly, is the mounting "Clash of Civilizations" projected by Huntington and global ultimate war with its threat of nuclear terrorism, global war, and worldwide destruction.

Jesus and his followers in the earliest days of Christianity felt that "the end of the world is at hand." As this did not come about, the Church had to address life in the continued world. The Church spelled out the orthodox doctrines and suppressed the divergent Gnostic texts. However, the canonical inclusion of the book of Revelation repeatedly prompts an "end-time" orientation to Christianity at some unclear future date. The recent finding of an alternative genuine text from the early days of Christianity with views of the distant future is likely to be relevant to the present state of Christianity and to the development of its world-service orientation.

The recent finding of the Gospel of Judas could affect the Christian perception of, and preparation for, the future. This old/new Gospel points to an alternative biblical perspective, which might offer an alternative scenario for world events. To the dire question "Are we going soon to burn inside the mushroom clouds?" it raises an alternative: "Could we take Judas' lead and step into the Luminous Cloud?"

Many, perhaps most, American evangelists are sure about the Second Coming and "the Rapture," when and whereby most of the world will be destroyed (as in C. S. Lewis's *Mere Christianity* and its pedagogic dramatization for children in *The Last Battle* of the Narnia Chronicles). Much of the world's population believes in Armageddon (book of Revelation 16:16). A 2002 CNN/*Time* poll asked the question, "Will the events in the book of Revelation occur sometime in the future or not?" Among U.S. Christians as a whole, 59 percent said yes, and 33 percent thought it would not happen. When presented to born-again, fundamentalist, and evangelical persons, 77 percent believed it would happen, and only 15 percent did not. To the question, "Will the world end in an Armageddon battle between Jesus Christ and the Antichrist?" 45 percent of a population identified as Christian answered yes and 39 percent no. Among evangelical Protestants, 71 percent anticipated the Armageddon end of the world, and only 18 percent did not, whereas among Catholics only 18 percent believe the Armageddon war will take place. A 2002 Gallup survey of religion in the United States found that 40 percent of all Americans believe that Satan exists and more than half believe that people can be possessed by spirits or demons. I have found no surveys of Muslim attitudes yet, but it seems that just as many Muslims believe in some parallel End Time.

Both Christian and Muslim theorists adhere to a theory of time that theologians call "Theodicy"—Divine Justice through tribulations and retribution. I aim, however, at the healing of this theory. Increasing the mental health of the world might be achieved by offering some happy endings to biblical readings that now have catastrophic endings. This is akin to drama—the playing out of a dire situation within a healing framework. In Aristotle's *Poetics*, the function of tragedy is catharsis—purging through pity and terror.

In Jewish tradition, the biblical concept of Tribulation has developed to become *Ḥevlei Mashiaḥ* (חבלי משיח), namely, "The Birth-Pangs of the Messiah." All these troubles can be seen as the needed adjustments that accompany the birth of the Messiah and/or of a new, evolved humankind.

Islam Has a Strong Sense of "End Days"

Islam too has a rich eschatology (belief concerning the end of the world, the Last Judgment, and life after death). Eschatology is called in Arabic **Qiyāma**. The word Qiyāma means the action of rising and of resurrection. The expression *"yawm al-Qiyāma"*—Day of Resurrection—appears in the Qur'an seventy times.

The basic Muslim eschatological scenario includes the annihilation of all creatures, and then the resurrection of bodies, which precedes the Judgment (**Din**). "Day of Judgment"—*Yawm ad-Din*—appears twelve times in the Qur'an. The belief in the end of the world, the resurrection of bodies, and the Last Judgment constitutes one of the five central tenets of Islam and is compulsory—at least in theory—for being a Muslim.

The full scenario is:

1. signs for the End of the World, including earthquakes
2. the first blast of the angel *Isra'fil*, which will bring the annihilation, when "every soul shall taste death" and God alone will remain
3. the second blast, in which all humans who have ever lived would resurrect instantaneously
4. the Gathering for Judgment
5. the Last Judgment itself, for all people, to go to Paradise or hell

Islamic scholars discussed **Qiyāma** in terms of *al-Ma'ād*—"the Return," namely, "the place to which one returns" (a word that appears only once in the Qur'an, Sura 28:85). There is likely a larger proportion of Muslims who believe this literally than of

Christians who believe in the Rapture or even in the Second Coming.

Shi'ite Islam also expects a preliminary "return" that would precede the universal resurrection and gathering; only the virtuous will take part in it, under the guidance of the *mahdi* of the Last Times. One of the differences between Sunni and Shi'ite Muslims is that the latter, which dominate Iran and form the majority in Iraq, believe that there were twelve imams and that the twelfth one, Muhammad al-Mahdi, who disappeared more than a thousand years ago, was shielded or hid by Allah until the end of time. Sunni Muslims also expect a Messianic figure, the Mahdi, to appear at the End Times, but they do not consider Muhammad al-Mahdi to be the Mahdi; many scholars even doubt that he existed at all. They hold that the eleventh imam died at the age of twenty-eight without leaving any offspring. Eighty percent of Shi'ites are called "Twelvers," and they are the largest Shi'a school of thought, predominant in Azerbaijan, Iran, Iraq, Lebanon, and Bahrain. These Shi'ites expect the twelfth imam to return to save the world when it has descended into chaos. Shi'ite orthodoxy has it that humans are powerless to encourage the twelfth imam to return. However, in Iran a group called the Hojjatieh believes that humans can stir up chaos to encourage him to return, and they hold much political power in the present Iranian regime.

The "Second Coming" in Islam

Surprisingly, the Qur'an also asserts Jesus' Second Coming! "And he [Jesus, son of Mary] shall be a known sign for [the coming of] the hour [Day of Resurrection]. Therefore, have no doubt concerning it [that is, the Day of Resurrection], and follow Me [Allah]. This is the straight Path" (Sura 43:61).

Although there are Muslims who explain that Jesus is no Christian and that he would return as a strict Muslim to turn all Christians into Muslims, some Islamic interpreters are not so exclusive. The popular Turkish Islamic teacher Harun Yahya, for example, is ready to concede that the returning Jesus would be of the House of David and identified by "the Star of David."

But where will this Islamic Last Judgment take place? This is clear for Christians and Jews, but the Qur'an itself does not specify a place. Yet there are some traditions (**Ḥadith**) and especially Islamic literature of Praises of Jerusalem—**Fad'ail Beit al-Maqdas**—mainly from the eleventh century (when the Muslims lost Jerusalem to the Crusaders), that maintain that Jerusalem will be the stage for the eschatological events.

Here is a list from the earliest Praises of Jerusalem by Mukatal Ibn-Suleiman of the eighth century, noted in Yitzhaq Ḥasson's *Jerusalem in the Moslem Perspective: The Qur'an and Tradition Literature*, concerning the eschatological Jerusalem:

- The resurrection of the Dead and their gathering will be in the Land of the Temple [**Ard Beit al-Maqdas**, meaning the holy land of Israel];
- Allah, may He be exalted, will come with the angels under a tabernacle of clouds to the Land of the Temple [!];
- On the Day of Resurrection, paradise will be led like a bride to the Temple—**Beit al-Maqdas;**
- The narrow bridge over hell will be placed in the Land of the Temple;
- The Scales of Judgment [**al-mizan**] will be placed at **Beit al-Maqdas;**

- On the Day of Resurrection, the angels will stand in rows at *Beit al-Maqdas;*
- Upon the second blast, all creatures will turn to dust, apart from humans and Jinns;
- The reckoning and judgment [*Din*] will take place at *Beit al-Maqdas;*
- The Holy Sanctuary [the Ka'ba of Mecca] and its Black Stone will be led as brides to *Beit al-Maqdas;*
- Those who were saints will rise from their graves and turn towards Jerusalem while saying the *Talbiyah* [the call of the pilgrims of the *Hajj*];
- The Angel *Israfil* will blow the horn over the Rock of *Beit al-Maqdas*, proclaiming: "You dry bones, torn pieces of flesh, fallen hairs, dispersed skins and torn ligaments! Go to stand for judgment in front of thy Master, who will breathe a spirit of life into you and will reward you for your deeds";
- The people will separate at *Beit al-Maqdas:* some to paradise and some to hell, according to the sayings of Allah [in the Qur'an]: "On that day they will separate" [Sura el-Rum 30:14] and "on that day they will be separate" [Sura el-Rum 30:43].

It was said by the son of the wife of Qab al-Akhbar: "In the Book of Allah that was brought down from heaven by revelation it is told that the exalted Allah says: In you [Jerusalem] there are six virtues—in you is my place of habitation, and the place of my Judgment, and my place of the Gathering, and my Hell and my Paradise and my Scales [of Judgment]." Qab himself is quoted as saying: "In the Day of Resurrection, the *Sakhra* [the Rock under the Dome of the Rock] will be the place for the foot of the Clement One."

The following description is attributed to the prophet Mohammad (PBUH): "[On the Day of Judgment] people will gather in
groups. The believers will not mix with the unbelievers and the
unbelievers will not mix with the believers. The 'Angel of the Horn'
will descend and stand upon the Rock of Jerusalem, and the people will gather barefoot, naked and uncircumcised, and the sun
will near their heads, at a distance of [the walk of] sixty years."

Tsafiya, the wife of the prophet Muhammad, is said to have ascended the Mount of Olives and "stood at the summit of the
mountain and said: From here will the people divide on the Day
of Resurrection, to paradise and to hell."

CHAPTER 14

Anti-Semitism and the Healing Effect of the Judas Gospel

T HE FIRST QUESTION POSED by the discovery of this new ancient text, already posed before, is: Does this newly found "Gospel" really constitute "Good News"? (This is what the word *Gospel* means.) There is little question that it is good news for the Jews.

The bitterest issue related to Judas as presented in the canonical Gospels is anti-Semitism and its consequences for the whole world. Since Jews are by now one of the world's smaller national-ethnic groups, the issue of anti-Semitism may seem to most non-Jews as parochial and of exaggerated significance. But it was much different in Jesus' time—and it would surely have been most important to Jesus himself.

In the time of Jesus, Jews and ex-Israelites were among the largest nations on earth. Research reported in a book by Tsvi Misinai published in Israel in 2006, *The Roadmap to the Third Intifada—The Roots and Solution to the Problem in the Holy Land*, claims that Jews were then the third-largest ethnic group in the

Western world, third only to the Greeks and the Romans. (What is remarkable in Misinai's data is its great detail, giving a view of population dynamics in the Land of Israel/Palestine.) Moreover, if the Jews and long-exiled Israelites had been reunited, they would have been one of the largest nations on earth. But even if we cut those estimates by half or more (about the ratio between Misinai's data and the more conservative accepted estimates), we can still see one reason that Jesus, even though a purported redeemer for the whole world, has appeared not, say, in Rome but in Judea. After Jesus was dead, the Jewish revolt against the Roman Empire took other guises, and within a century more than half of the Jews in the Roman Empire perished in wars and persecution, and Judea ceased to exist. Judea was renamed "Palestine," and the survivors in Judea became "Palestinians." Today, Jewish-Israelite share of the world population is only about 1 percent of what it was in Jesus' time. The chief cause of this was anti-Semitism and the persecution of the Jews, much of it done in the names of Jesus and Judas.

What is the chief cause of anti-Semitism? Is it because Jews are really as vile as some portray them? There are many theories and psychological explanations. But surely it must be connected with the belief (or myth, if you like) that the Jews are "the Chosen People" or that they believe themselves to be. This is not so outrageous by itself. There are scores of peoples in the world convinced they are "the Chosen People"—from small sects such as the Allawis and Druze to large nations such as the Japanese and, in a sense, the Chinese. The problem, however, is not so much that some Jews think they are, or were, "Chosen." It is that many who are not Jews have a creepy feeling that perhaps there is something in it—and they don't like it. As the saying goes,

How odd of God,
to choose the Jews.

Take the case of the worst enemy of the Jews, Adolf Hitler. His insane drive cannot be explained just by his having been an unappreciated artist. When he was still a teenager, he had studied in the same class with a Jewish boy named Ludwig Wittgenstein. I'm sure that, had I been a student there, I might also have contracted an inferiority complex. Not that every Jew is a Wittgenstein, but still, the relative probability for a Jew to win, say, the Nobel Prize is higher than for a non-Jew. Unlike what Hitler believed, this has little to do with "race" or genetics (Jews and "Palestinians" share exactly the same unique "Jewish genes," according to sources M. F. Hammer and Almut Nebel).

But the most pervasive and enduring form of anti-Semitism is likely related to the issue of Jews, Jesus, and Christianity. For a Christian who chose to base his personal salvation and belief on Jesus Christ, there is something uncomfortable in the knowledge that Jesus' own people did not follow him, and, if you believe the canonical Gospels, ended up opposing him. (Something similar happened in India with Buddha, but there it seems not to have generated such feelings among Buddhists.) It just does not make sense—unless there is something inferior or odious about the Jews. But then, was not the historic Jesus himself a Jew? There is a saying that there are people who deny the very existence of the historical Jesus—but they are still convinced that the Jews killed him!

From a Jewish perspective that seeks to respect Jesus, his grand mission (as we have discussed earlier) might well have been to reunite the Jews and the exiled Israelites, "the Lost Ten

Tribes." But it was his very followers, the Gentile church fathers, who thwarted Jesus' dream with their anti-Semitism, using Judas as their tool.

Originally anti-Semitism was a Greek invention, reflecting the major "Clash of Civilizations" at the time of Jesus—between Greek and Jewish cultures, as G. Gager argues in his 1985 work *The Origins of Anti-Semitism: Attitudes towards Judaism in Pagan and Christian Antiquity.* In fact, the whole European civilization, according to Louis Ruprecht in his 1994 book *On Being Jewish or Greek in the Modern Moment,* is a synthesis of these two cultures—the Jewish and the Greek. The Greeks, already conquered by the Romans, were fighting to maintain cultural supremacy in their world. "The Jewish God" that Jesus served had superseded the pagan Greek gods, so the Greek-speaking editors of the New Testament were getting even with the Jews. Despite the fact that Jesus, his family, and all the apostles were Jews, for the readers of the canonical Gospels, the only one branded as a Jew was Judas Iscariot—the traitor to God. (The Gospel of Luke [6:16] mentions another one of the twelve called Judas, but this is not in the other three gospels, which perhaps indicates shoddy editing.) According to *Encyclopaedia Judaica,*

> For Christians, the word "Judaeus" was early on conflated with the name of the villain of the gospel story, Judas Iscariot, who was considered the typical Jew. Judas was linked with the devil (Luke 22:3), and the result was an evil triangle of devil-Jew-Judas. This relationship helped to establish the pejorative meaning of the word "Jew" in popular usage. The noun could mean "extortionate usurer, driver of hard bargains," while the verb was defined as "to cheat by sharp business practices, to overreach."

By a small literary device, a mere wordplay, the whole world history changed. But for this to succeed, the "Gospel of Judas Thomas" had to be suppressed, let alone the Gospel of Judas.

Interestingly, one of the last appearances of anti-Semitism in its old religious garb took place in modern Greece, shortly after its independence. Greeks used to celebrate Easter (and actually are still celebrating it, especially in Crete) with large bonfires in which they would burn the effigy of Judas Iscariot. In Greece, Easter serves more than the memory of the death and resurrection of Jesus; it also serves as a memorial to the part of Judas, the traitor and the representative of all Jews, from his time and to the present.

When founded in the nineteenth century, independent Greece was a poor country, loaded with debts, and its weak regime could not collect taxes properly. Greece had to apply to the Jewish Baron Rothschild to borrow the money needed to start a government. In March 1847, near Easter, the British baron arrived at Athens, which was already famous for its crime and anarchy, to try to collect the debt for the loan he had made to the Greek government ten years earlier. The Greek government could not repay the debt but sought to at least prevent the Burning of Judas Festival, which had always been connected with anti-Semitic manifestations.

Frustrated by the lack of the customary party, hundreds of Athenians broke into the house of the secular head of the local Jewish community, a Jew born in Gibraltar—and hence a British subject—who used to be the general consul of Portugal in Greece until a short time before that incident. For many hours the Athenians looted the house of this man, named Don Pacifico, beat his wife and daughters, destroyed the furniture, and finally set the whole house on fire. It was not just a mob involved but people of the highest strata of society, including the son of the war minister, who eventually became the Greek prime minister. The police who had been called just stood there and did nothing. In this way Don Pacifico, the modern Jew, became a substitute for Judas, the old-time Jew.

This story would have no doubt sunk into oblivion, like thousands of other stories of persecution of Jews, had Don Pacifico not been a British citizen, and had he not sent complaints to the British Foreign Office, and, after he could not get a fair trial in Greece, had Britain not threatened the small and weak Greece with war and sent the British Navy before Greece retreated and agreed to compensate Pacifico the Jew.

Ursula Duba has compiled a list of some two hundred cases of anti-Semitic persecutions in Europe from the first to the nineteenth centuries. These persecutions started with sermons and writings of the church fathers who attacked Jewish practices, such as circumcision, and continued with laws for inferior status (legislated by the Byzantine emperor Theodosius the II in AD 438), which then led to forced conversions (since the seventh century), ending with enslavement of the Jews (in Spain at the end of the seventh and beginning of the eighth centuries) and their expulsion. There was no country in Europe that did not expel its Jews at one time or another, the most dramatic being the expulsion from Spain in 1492, due to the size and status of the Jewish population there.

In the eleventh century the situation was worsening. Jews were accused of witchcraft and causing storms and earthquakes. Pope Benedict VIII found them guilty, and the Inquisition found ways to make the Jews confess those alleged sins and then burned them at the stake. The eleventh century was also the beginning of the Crusades, which were accompanied by massacres of the Jews in Germany and France. The twelfth century added blood libel to the repertoire. These persecutions accompanied the Jews into the twentieth century.

To that list we can add the events in the Land of Israel, such as the burning alive of all the Jews of Jerusalem when the Crusaders conquered it in 1099. After the entry of the Crusaders, Jews were banned from Jerusalem, a ban that persisted until the victory of Saladin.

In the nineteenth century the nature of anti-Semitism seems to have undergone a change. Whereas the old religious anti-Semitism still left the Jews an exit by conversion, modern anti-Semitism bases the blame of the Jews on their racial descent, something they could not change.

Yet in his 2001 book *Unholy War: The Vatican's Role in the Rise of Modern Anti-Semitism,* D. I. Kertzer presents strong evidence that the Nazi persecution of the Jews was merely a continuation of Catholic persecution that had persisted for centuries. He reviews the major tenets of the modem anti-Semitic movement: There is a secret Jewish conspiracy to conquer the world; the Jews have already seized control of the financial centers of Austria, Germany, France, and Italy; Jews are by nature immoral; Jews care only for money; Jews control the press; Jews control the banks and are responsible for the economic ruin of Christians; Jews are responsible for communism (as well as being responsible for capitalism); Jews murder Christian children and drink their blood; Jews seek to destroy the Christian religion; Jews are unpatriotic; Jews must be segregated; Jewish rights must be limited. Kertzer writes:

The Church played an important role in promulgating every one of these ideas that are central to modem anti-Semitism. Every one of them had the support of the highest Church authorities, including the Popes. If the Church bore major responsibility for the inculcation of a dozen of the major ideological pillars of the modem anti-Semitic political movement and a thirteenth came from other sources, are we to conclude that the Church bears little or no responsibility for the flowering of modern anti-Semitism in those areas where the Church had great influence?

Who knows how Jewish history might have fared had Judas Iscariot, the most famous Jew, not been branded as the Traitor.

The Eucharist

One item that enacts subliminally the Christian-Jewish confrontation is the Eucharist ceremony in which eating the Host is seen as eating Jesus' body and participating in a mystical communion with Christ. The Host is a token for the Passover bread (or rather *Matsah*—unleavened bread) that was used at the Last Supper. The original Eucharist must have taken place right after the prediction that one who has been eating with Jesus would betray him (Mark 14:18). "It is one of the twelve . . . one who dips bread into the bowl with me. . . . But woe to that man who betrays the Son of Man. It would be better for him if he had not been born" (14:20–21). That must have been "while they were eating, Jesus took bread, gave thanks and broke it, and gave it to his disciples, saying 'take it: this is my body.'" In the Gospel of John (the most anti-Jewish of the Gospels), the Last Supper is not presented as a Passover ceremony, but a parallel scene is given in which Jesus secretly identifies the traitor as the one to whom he will give a piece of bread when he has dipped it in the dish, "then, dipping the piece of bread, he gave it to Judas Iscariot, son of Simon. As soon as Judas took the bread, Satan entered into him" (John 14:26–27). So here the Eucharistic ceremony becomes tantamount to a Satanic rite, in which the victim is Judas.

During the Middle Ages, there were many pogroms (mob rampages for killing of Jews) right after Jews had been blamed for desecrating the Host. There is a connection between this libel and the blood libel, that the Jews kill Christian boys in order to use their blood for baking their Passover Host-like matzo.

On the other hand, from a Jewish point of view, the eating of the Host was the clearest sign that Christianity is a pagan religion. In his comprehensive 1987 work *Christianity in Perspective*, Robert Wolfe defines the core of Christianity as "the Eating of Jesus," in conformity with cannibalistic traits of the mystery religions of that era, especially in the seedbed of Christianity, Asia Minor (where Paul came from), and claims that the unconscious point of "eating a dead Jew" is anti-Semitism.

The sad fact is that until Hitler in the twentieth century, Jesus was the person responsible for the largest number of Jews who were killed and tortured.

The Jews, for their part, have reciprocated the hatred of Christians with their hatred of Jesus Christ. In fact, the common appellation for Jesus in Hebrew is "*Yeshu,*" which seems an innocent rendering of the Greek name "Yesus," until we are informed that it is also an acronym for *Yimakh Shmo Vezikhro*, meaning "may his name and memory be eradicated."

For Jews, Jesus must appear either as a Jew himself or as an apostate who nevertheless remained a Jew (since Jesus certainly did not consider himself a Christian). For the Christians who deified Jesus, his rejection by the Jews was a constant cause of hatred, as it has always potentially undermined their own belief. But for a Christian who loves Jesus yet realizes that he was a Jew, the hatred of Jesus by his own people (however understandable) is surely a source of grief.

Satan's Invasion and Demonization

The Gospel of John tells how "Satan entered into Judas" to betray Jesus (13:26–29). Now let's ask, where did Satan come from? How did he become a major player in the biblical worldview? Perhaps the rise of Christianity, and then of Islam, required the dramatic threat of the devil and of hell to sell their promise of divine deliverance.

Surprisingly perhaps, Satan (the name means "adversary") or the devil had hardly any place or role in the Old Testament. It is not found in the Hebrew Bible until the late book of Job—and then not as a doctrine but merely as a literary device. The prophets of Israel had no use for the figure of Satan; in the Prophets it is mentioned only once—in the book of the minor prophet Zachariah, who lived at the time of the Persian (today Iranian) rule. Satan never got an official place in the Jewish religion, and entered only with the return to Judea from the Babylonian captivity under Persian-Iranian rule. The dualistic belief in two rival authorities, the Good God and the wicked Satan, was a Persian-Iranian invention and export.

By Jesus' time, some 550 years after Persian rule, Satan had already been established in the popular Jewish imagination.

As Elaine Pagels shows clearly in her 1995 work *The Origins of Satan*, it was the Christian Gospels that employed Satan extensively to demonize "the Jews," namely, the Jewish majority who would not follow Jesus—and with this Satan was lodged deeply into half of the world's inhabitants.

In her book, Pagels adds a chapter about "the social history of Satan," showing how the events told in the Gospels about Jesus, his advocates, and his enemies correlate with the supernatural drama the writers use to interpret that story—the struggle between God's spirit and Satan. And because Christians as they read the Gospels have characteristically identified themselves with the disciples, for some two thousand years they have also identified their opponents, whether Jews, pagans, or heretics, with the forces of evil, and so with Satan. She writes:

> Mark deviates from the mainstream Jewish tradition by introducing "the devil" into the crucial opening scene of the gospel, and goes on to characterize Jesus' ministry as involving continual struggle between God's spirit and the demons, who belong, apparently, to Satan's "kingdom" (see Mark 3:23–27). Such visions have been incorporated into Christian tradition and have served, among other things, to confirm for Christians their own identification with God and to demonize their opponents—first other Jews, then pagans, and later dissident Christians called heretics. . . .
>
> I invite you to consider Satan as a reflection of how we perceive ourselves and those we call "other." Satan has, after all, made a kind of profession out of being "the other"; and so Satan defines negatively what we think of as human.
>
> Conflict between groups is, of course, nothing new. What may be new in Western Christian tradition, is how the use of Satan to represent one's enemies lends to the conflict a specific kind of moral and religious interpretation, in which "we" are God's people and "they" are God's enemies, and ours as well. . . . [R]ereading the gospels, I was

struck by how their vision of supernatural struggle both expresses conflict and raises it to cosmic dimensions.

For nearly two thousand years, many Christians have taken for granted that Jews killed Jesus and the Romans were merely their reluctant agents, and that this implicates not only the perpetrators but (as Matthew insists) all their progeny in evil. Throughout the centuries, countless Christians listening to the gospels absorbed, along with the quite contrary sayings of Jesus, the association between the forces of evil and Jesus' Jewish enemies.

The medieval Christian equation of Judas = Jews = Satan has now become the Islamic equation of Zion = Jews = Satan, and Iran's rulers talk of "the big Satan" (the United States) and "the small Satan" (Israel) and vow to destroy at least the "small Satan," Israel.

What really fuels and sustains this madness is the demonization entertained by both sides, which are locked in a vicious circle. After two thousand years of persecutions, culminating with the Holocaust, the Jews no doubt have paranoid traits. But "even paranoids may have real enemies" who are crazed by their own fanatic belief systems and inferiority complexes. Could Christianity help ameliorate rather than exacerbate these conflicts? It is here, I submit, that the Christian Gnostic traits, especially those of the Gospel of Judas Iscariot, could have a healing effect.

Gnosis gives a different answer to the question of the cause of evil in the world, and it advocates psychological-spiritual development that calls for more personal introspection rather than negative projection on the Other. In the Gospel of Judas, Judas' act, as we have seen, is instigated not by Satan but by Christ himself and is done not as devilish betrayal but for a higher reason. On the other hand, it warns that even Jesus' pious disciples and the Church they founded are liable to cause human sacrifices out of ignorance.

The time of the discovery of the Judas Gospel is the best time for an end to the anti-Semitism inspired by the Christian Church and its misinterpretation of the events at the time of Christ's Crucifixion. Christ's own teachings of love and forgiveness can become reality. And one of the sources of wisdom in Judaism, Qabbalah, can join forces with Christian teachings to bring in a new era on earth.

CHAPTER 15

According to Qabbalah,
Now Is the Time of Redemption

T HE JEWISH CALENDAR of six thousand years (in which 2007
CE is the year 5767) has its own distinct cosmology. When
the sixth millennium of this calendar started (in 1240 CE,
which is the year that the *Mequbal* Abraham Abulafia was born)
there was the great flowering of Jewish mysticism and apocalyptic
teachings of the Qabbalah, which was connected with, and led to,
the publication of the third Jewish canon, the book of the *Zohar*.
In the Qabbalah, the six days of Genesis are considered as six
thousand years, based on Psalms 90:4: "For a thousand years in
thy sight are but like yesterday when it is past." This attribution is
also well known for Christians, for when the early Christians
asked Peter specifically about the End Times and Jesus' return, he
said: "But do not forget this one thing dear friends: With the Lord
a day is like a thousand years, and a thousand years are like a day"
(2 Pet. 3:8). The Qabbalah regards these six thousand years as an
ongoing redemptive process, of which we are very near the end,
and the events of the "Sixth Day of Genesis," including the formation of Adam and the story of the Tree of Knowledge, are still near-
future events! The greatest Jewish scholar, the Gaon of Vilna,

wrote about the Days of Creation: "You should know that all those days are hints to six thousand years, which are six days, as it is written that six thousand years are tied to the primal six, and all the details of those six days are enacted in the six thousand years, each one in its day and hour. From this you can know the final redemption when it is 'in its time' God forbids, which is when they will not merit. And I demand the reader in the [name of the] Lord the God of Israel not to divulge this." This seemingly far-fetched claim that these events are still future events is well supported by the original Hebrew text of the Pentateuch, which is written not in past tense but in "inverted" future tense. This point and the whole logic of this cosmological framework of six thousand years are detailed in the introduction of my Genesis exegesis, see http://www.thehope.org/toreng0.htm.

Does this (un)conventional Jewish calendar with its span of six thousand years make any sense? We are dealing here with "Judas Iscariot," which may literally mean "Judas (or Judaic) of the Cities," and this calendar is the calendar of the urbanization of humankind, in other words, making all the earth one city, "Ecumenopolis," and all humankind one interconnected being— Adam. The decisive incident of "the Tree of Knowledge" is still ahead of us—through the impact of modern science and technology.

According to the Qabbalah, we are in the present age in the time of the Redemption. However, there have already been several false starts whose proponents used the Qabbalah (among them the year 1334 given in the *Zohar;* 1666, which saw the apostasy of the false Messiah Shabbetai Tzevi; and 1840 as noted by the greatest Jewish scholar, the Gaon of Vilna, which brought the formation of a Jewish community in Jerusalem but witnessed a severe earthquake). In the twentieth century, there was a kind of

Marxist **Mequbal**, Rabbi Yehudah Leib Ashlag, who based his prognostications of the nearing redemption on material data.

According to Rabbi Ashlag, we are approaching "the Last Generation"—a term reminiscent of Jesus' promise in the Gospel of Judas. Some validation of Rabbi Ashlag's prognostication is supplied by the current phenomenal success of two competing organizations disseminating his teachings. There is the Kabbalah Center, led by the Berg family, who have purloined and commercialized Ashlag's books by a liberal addition of astrology, reincarnation, and so on, and progressively distancing their Qabbalah from Judaism. The other is the Benei Baruch and Ashlag Research Institute led by Dr. Michael Laitman, who seems a more legitimate successor to Rabbi Ashlag.

My own understanding, however, is that the true origin of the Qabbalah—the book of Genesis—is more a prophecy than a history book, that the formation of Adam (the entire humankind as one conscious creature) is happening right now, and that the crisis of the "Tree of Knowledge of Good and Evil" is already facing us in the form of multiple perils. Now is the time to cleave to the "Tree of Life" in its multiple meanings (such as the Torah, the major Qabbalah text, and the ecological imperative). I believe that the Qabbalah can contribute much to the critical development of modern science in several ways.

Whatever else, the Qabbalah is a "systems science" par excellence. A classic fifteenth-century Qabbalah book is called **Ma'arekhet haElohut** (The System of Divinity), and most Qabbalah concepts and practices involve working with systems in general ways (see Part VI on Qabbalah as Systems Theology).

This writer's hope is to contribute to the development of a "human interaction science" that applies the "Tree of Life" scheme of the Qabbalah, interpreted along the dialogical "conversation theory" formulated by the great cybernetician Gordon Pask. In my 1981 doctoral dissertation I sought to show the correspondence between the Tree of the *Sephirot* of the Qabbalah and Pask's general model of human interaction. It later became apparent that this system is particularly applicable to the all-important areas of self-acceptance and mutual acceptance—and, as mentioned before, Qabbalah literally means "Acceptance." The acceptance of self and other is important in any human realm, and especially in matters of interfaith encounter. All religions, and certainly Judaism and Christianity, advocate the "Golden Rule" of "Love your neighbor as yourself" or "Do not inflict upon another what you hate for yourself." Trouble is, many people do not love themselves enough to offer love. So an art of self-acceptance is part and parcel of a practice of mutual understanding and love.

CHAPTER 16

The Dome of the Rock:
A Gnostic Symbol of World Unity

T THE HEART OF THE PASSION OF CHRIST is Jerusalem, and at
the heart of Old Jerusalem stands one of the world's finest
treasures, one of the world's greatest mysteries—the
Dome of the Rock. The mystery of the Dome of the Rock com-
bines both sacred geometry and the Messianic future we are projecting as well. It also connects past and future for Muslims,
Christian Gnostics, and Jews alike.

The Dome of the Rock has been standing for more than thirteen hundred years and is today known throughout the world as
Jerusalem's most distinct landmark. There is hardly another world
monument that is so prominent—and so utterly misunderstood.

Outwardly and by universal common perception, the Dome of
the Rock is an exclusively Islamic shrine and monument, which
most Muslims believe (erroneously) is the sacred al-Aqsa Mosque
and most Christian and Jews believe usurps the place of the Holy
Temple and thus obstructs the Redemption. In fact, it is not a
mosque and serves no special Muslim religious purpose. It is
commonly thought to commemorate the prophet Muhammad's
ascent, but as research such as that of Amikam Elad shows, this

explanation arose only several centuries after it was built. When we look closer, as if through Gnostic vision, these common views can change.

As for its geomantic position, apart from its north-south axis with the al-Aqsa Mosque and east-west axis with the Church of the Ascension, it is oriented with two symbolic objects on the Temple Mount: the Golden Gate of Mercy (through which the future Messiah is expected to come) and the small Dome of the Spirits (which some claim as the place of the Holy of Holies of the second temple)—two markings that are on the axes that expand the "Abraham Triangle" to the "Jerusalem Cross" discussed in connection with Jesus' claimed travels. With these orientations, it stands at the center of a rudimentary "New Jerusalem Diagram" (somewhat akin to what John Michell observes for Stonehenge and argues for the New Jerusalem of Revelation). Observed closely, this edifice reveals a huge contrast between outer facade and inner contents. Both exterior and interior are magnificent, but they are completely dissimilar and carry different messages. Also, the messages in the interior are graded: some are in clear, though highly ornamental, writings, whereas others are encoded in the "Gnostic" language of sacred geometry, seen only by "those who have eyes to see."

Therefore, I suggest, the Dome of the Rock is one of the deepest secrets of Gnosticism and might well be related to the dreams of our hero, Judas, and to his followers. I shall not interpret here the sacred geometry, those "Gnostic" messages of the Dome of the Rock, but simply state that they designate the place as a temple for the "Holy Wisdom" in the esoteric terms of Judaism, Christianity, and Islam. The Jewish connection can be established by the Sefer Yetsirah, as its chief decoration depicts "the thirty-two wondrous paths of Wisdom" with which it begins, and this corresponds with the thirty-two-fold symmetry of the pattern on the ceiling of the Dome that resolves to thirty-two figures and thirty-two paths between them. The Christian one is quite apparent, as this type of structure was used in Byzantium for shrines of Hagia Sophia (Holy Wisdom, feminine), and there is a record that the site was formerly used for a Hagia Sophia chapel. Accepting the arguments of Israeli architect Tuvia Sagiv, the location of the Dome of the Rock is not that of the second temple but of the Roman Antonia castle. If so, then the apparent "footprints" on the rock, attributed by Muslims to Muhammad's ascent, were earlier attributed by Christians to Jesus. But let us have a first look inside; let us examine the written evidence.

The written messages are placed in graded locations: (1) over the four entrances; (2) in the outer (octagonal) arcades for reading while walking around; (3) in the inner arcade for turning in the opposite direction; and (4) in the inner sanctum, written on the ceiling of the dome in two rings, a lower one and (5) a higher inner one.

The writings in the arcades inside the edifice seem to be polemics addressing the Christians, calling them to acknowledge Muhammad's prophesy. But if so, then that is proof that the edifice was built so that Christians (and Jews) should come there.

Here are the pertinent quotes concerning Christian doctrine and Jesus found inside the Dome of the Rock:

In the name of God, the Beneficent, the Merciful . . . No God exists but God alone, indivisible without peer. Say, God is One, God is central—birthing no child, nor birthed in turn . . .

In the name of God, the Beneficent, the Merciful . . . No God exists but God alone, indivisible. Praise be to God who never fathered a child. No peer exists in all creation, nor has God need of counsel.

> Oh People of the Book! Don't be excessive in the name of your faith! Do not say things about God but the truth! The Messiah Jesus [Issa], son of Mary, is indeed a messenger of God: The Almighty extended a word to Mary, and a spirit too.
>
> So believe in God and all his messengers, and stop talking about a Trinity. Cease in your own best interests! Verily God is the God of unity. Lord Almighty! That God would beget a child? Either in the Heavens or on Earth? Neither Christ nor the angels in heaven scorn servitude and worship of God . . .
>
> The religion before God is Surrender [Islam]: the people who were given the Books [Jews and Christians] did not argue about this until after receiving knowledge and they became envious of one another.

(Just as the Qur'an does not differentiate between Jesus and Esau [Jacob's twin], it also does not differentiate between Mary, Jesus' mother, and Moses' sister.)

So here, right on the hot spot, we find an authoritative Muslim belief in Jesus, not as God, though, but as a prophet, and a Messiah, of both Muslims and of the "People of the Book"—Christians and Jews. This even allows for a belief in the "Second Coming" of Jesus and even of a building to accommodate it.

For an architect, this makes sense. Having a chance of once in a millennium to build on the Temple Mount, in a time that the fortunes of the caliphate were by no means secure, the artisans wanted to make an edifice that would last until the Day of Resurrection, and not suffer the fate of the former temples there (pagan, Israelite-Solomonic, Jewish, and Hadrianic). Oleg Grabar, the recognized expert on Islamic architecture, shrewdly remarks in the 1996 work he coauthored with Said Nuseibeh, *The Dome of the Rock*, that the clear geometrical scheme of this shrine is not identified with one creed and lends itself to accommodate various narratives. This, he notes, happened in the past, and may still happen in the future. So the task of the architects was to build an edifice so beautiful that whichever future ruler of whatever religion prevails, he would want to preserve and renew it. Indeed, the structure is fairly delicate and has collapsed in several earthquakes, but it was always rebuilt to the original pattern, and today, largely due to the Jewish-Muslim competition, it is in its greatest glory ever.

What was the Dome of the Rock built for? Obviously and outwardly, it was built for the glorification of the Islamic caliphate and for validating its legitimacy to rule over Jerusalem. It was built to be more grandiose than the chief Christian holy place in Jerusalem, the Church of the Holy Sepulcher, and indeed this was achieved by exploiting the already existing superb Temple Mount platform (and possibly the foundations of Hadrian's temples there) and making the Dome itself one foot larger and higher than the Dome of the Church of the Holy Sepulchre.

But as noted above, it was also built to attract Christian visitors. How could they be induced? By making it the right and ready stage for the Resurrection and the Second Coming of Jesus as the Messiah! This may explain why the Knights Templar, who occupied the Temple Mount during the Crusaders' reign, did not destroy the Dome of the Rock, but on the contrary renamed it "Templo Domini" and held their secret rituals there. This is reinforced by the argument of Hugh Schonfield that the Templars' *Baphomet* was a code word for *Sophia,* the paragon of the Gnostics and Christian mystics (and *Sophia* is even reminiscent of the Muslim Sufi mystics). In the future the Dome of the Rock might even be the site for the resurrection of a Jesus as Messiah in some way or another.

So let us keep in mind that on the Temple Mount, which is sacred to all the children of Abraham, stands a magnificent building that Christian and Jewish artisans built for the Muslim caliph, to attract the Christian, a building not yet fulfilling its potential, which may be a cause for world destruction—or for its healing. The Gospel of Judas, with its Gnostic message of inner awakening, points to that universal basis of all the religions that can be the fulfillment of the dream of those religions—a time of peace, fulfillment, and harmony on earth.

Epilogue

In the future you will see the Son of Man

Sitting at the right hand of the Mighty One

and coming on the clouds of heaven.

MATT. 26:64; MARK 15:62

THE GOSPEL (GOOD NEWS) that the Gospel of Judas brings us is a whole new look at the Jewish-Christian relationship: a replacement for the Trinity by the *beARBA ELU*, the Quaternary, and the fleeing of Judas into a temple with greenery as a roof and the Luminous Cloud that he enters are for me all indications of a better future for Jerusalem, as well as for the whole world. Instead of total destruction—as the Day of Judgment is perceived by millions of believers—it indicates salvation through the acceptance and acknowledgment of the Dome of the Rock and its rededication (*Ḥanukah*) as a holy temple for all the Abraham faith's believers, and the rest of the world.

It may seem fantastic, but the Gospel of Judas could be the aide and council to neutralize the mounting threat of a world conflagration rising through the desire to realize the biblical prophecies and admonitions concerning the Temple of Jerusalem. The Gospel of Judas indicates the possible addition that would indeed make the whole place into the Universal Temple—the Luminous Cloud as a constructed yet heavenly structure.

When Abraham found Mount Moriah on his way to the binding of Isaac, he recognized it, explains Rashi (Rabbi Shlomoh Yitzhaqi, the almost canonical Bible commentator), by perceiving "a cloud tied upon the mountain" (which his companions apparently could not see). This must have been not just a spiritual but also a prophetic vision. The visions of Ezekiel of the fourfold **Merkavah**, or divine "Chariot," emerged out of a luminous cloud. According to Rashi, the future temple will be a complete "Temple of Fire from the skies." Now in the Gospel of Judas, we see that Jesus summons a luminous cloud from whence emerge the figures of the aeons and angels.

My own design that is prompted by the Gospel of Judas is for the peaceful realization of the Jerusalem Universal Temple of Peace. Recognizing that the current situation dictates that the restoration of the Temple of Solomon cannot and should not proceed by the removal of the Dome of the Rock or the al-Aqsa Mosque, the design I advocate calls for a virtual realization of the Temple that also reassures all Muslims that the actualization of this temple would not disturb a single stone of their extant shrines. This design would use the model of the entire existing Jerusalem Old City, for the welfare of Muslims, Christians, and Jews alike.

The plan is thus to tie a cloud to the Temple Mount, in the form of a transparent giant cube (**Qa'aba**) that would hover over the Old City or would be suspended by the great pylons of a "Tabernacle of Peace over Jerusalem." A cloud would be produced (like the smoke of the sacrifices and the incense burning in the old Temple) from which will emerge light patterns projected by laser beams. This would be a realization of the heavenly temple referred to by Rashi, as presented by Joshua Davis in *Wired* magazine in April 2004.

There would be a worldwide spiritual or "virtual" pilgrimage to this temple via a massive multiplayer network game of intercultural interaction conducted within the scenery of the Jerusalem Old City and Temple Mount. Redemptive, that is, spiritually significant interactions of the actors, such as the production of understandings, would produce signs of "Letters of Light" to be projected inside that tied cloud. These light letters would combine (like Lego bricks) to complete significant figures. The cloud would then serve as a matrix from which there would emerge the redeemer figure. According to the Qabbalah, redemptive interactions are combinations of ***Ben*** (Son) and ***Adam*** (Man). So the emerging figure would be that of the "Son of Man Coming in the Cloud of Heaven" for which so many are yearning—yet without the dire tribulations. Rather, this Temple would offer an ecstatic Rapture instead of the Rupture.

PART VI

EXTRA SECTION ON QABBALAH AS A SYSTEMS THEOLOGY

W<small>E HAVE ALREADY TOUCHED LIGHTLY</small> on the Qabbalah in Chapter 4, "The Role of the Judaic Qabbalah in Gnosis," and a few other places. There I discussed the Qabbalah in a largely anecdotal manner and only as much as was neccessary for the basic account of the Gospel of Judas. This extra section is for people who have a penchant for esotericism and would like to get a more systematic view of the Qabbalah. With this enhanced view, I shall also be able to further amplify the Gnostic message of the Gospel of Judas and its possible relevance for the future as suggested in the Epilogue. For those who may then want a still better acquaintance with the Qabbalah, I also include a special list of books and Web sites, both introductory and more specialized.

I shall present here the more canonical books of the Qabbalah; survey how the elements of these systems operate, providing examples that relate to our discussion of the Gospel of Judas; and then relate the significance of the Qabbalah for our times.

I. The Primary Texts of the Qabbalah

The Sepher Yetsirah—*and the*
Underlying Structure of the Divine Speech

The enigmatic **Sepher Yetsirah** (The Book of Formation/Creation), a rather short text, is a real marvel whose reading (and possibly misreading) is the basis of what came to be known as the Qabbalah and its basic terms. The language of the **Sepher Yetsirah** is beautiful, poetical, and enigmatic Hebrew, and its style is grand and oratory.

There is no agreement on the origin and time of this book. Traditionalists attribute it to the biblical Abraham, some two thousand years before the Common Era. Academic researchers such as Yehuda Liebes in *Ars Poetica in Sepher Yetsira* have placed its authorship from the second-temple times, whereas others assign it to Islamic times and attribute it to various people. So it is a likely contemporary to the Gnostic Gospels. My own assumption it that it is made up of two layers: the earlier one issuing from the secret lore of the Temple attendants (as defended by Liebes) and its later part a sixth-century work of an astrological healer (as proposed by Meir Bar Ilan in *Astrology and Other Sciences among the Jews of the Land of Israel in the Byzantine Period*).

The opening words of the **Sepher Yetsirah** are arrayed in the order of the opening verse of Genesis: "In Thirty-two Wonderful

Paths of Wisdom the Divinity [a set of Ten Holy Names] engraved and created His World [*Olamo*] in three Accounts/Books/ Ciphers." These opening words, and especially the opening letter B'e (In), in which the *Sepher Yetsirah* resembles Genesis ("In the Beginning . . ."), are also our key for understanding the meaning of *Barbelo* in the Gospel of Judas. They all relate to what means it takes to create the world. The *Sepher Yetsirah* presents these basic elements as the letters of the Hebrew language. The Gospel of Judas, through the indication of the names Barbelo and Judas, must refer to four special letters of these twenty-two that have special relevance to forming the redeemed world and to the true mission of Jesus.

These thirty-two archetypal "Wonder Paths" are presented as ten so-called *Sephirot* and twenty-two "Foundation Signs" (*Otiyot Yesod*), represented by the ten ciphers and the twenty-two letters of the Hebrew Alphabet.

The term *Sephirot* came eventually to mean many concepts, including "Ciphers," "Spheres," "Sapphire-like," and "Accounts" or even "Narratives." The point of the *Sepher Yetsirah*, however, is that the *Sephirot* are arranged in a definite way as the ten perpendicular coordinates of a five-dimensional space, giving account and control (*Blimah* [harnessing]) of the possibly infinite runways in those ten directions.

The basic space that serves modern science was determined by the philosopher Descartes as the three-dimensional cubical space of corporeal-material extension, completely distinct from the possible measures or accounts of the soul world. In the early twentieth century Einstein used notions of four-dimensional geometry to show that the physical universe is a four-dimensional "space-time continuum." The Qabbalah offers an expansion of the current scientific paradigm to include also the

dimension of the soul, or of a "soul-time continuum" that ani-
mates the 3D physical space.

Take, for instance, a time axis of "Beginning to Completion" as
running from Above to Below, and form a cross with a transcendental Soul axis running Right to Left as if between "Right and
Wrong," thus marking a plane hyperspace of Soul-Time, or Moral-
Time. This hyperspace plane is beyond, or "perpendicular" to, the
six-sided three-dimensional space our bodies inhabit, formed by
six **Sephirot**—the measures of East and West, North and South,
Height and Depth.

The **Sepher Yetsirah** describes the process of the formation of
our world, conceived as a five-dimensional created universe of
Space-Time-Soul, which is essentially (hyper)cubical space. Noting that the four-dimensional hypercube ("Tessaract") has thirty-
two edges and the five-dimensional hyper-hypercube has
thirty-two vertices, we can now understand why "In Thirty-two"
are the first words about the Creation of the World.

The book is traditionally attributed to Abraham because its
conclusion deals with Abraham, who had mastered all the arcane
arts treated in the book: "And as Abraham, Peace Be On him,
looked and saw and investigated and understood and engraved
and hewed and combined and formed and thought and accomplished, was revealed to him the Master of All may His Name be
Blessed and He set him in His lap and kissed him on the head and
called him 'Abraham my lover' and made a covenant for him and
his seed for ever."

The **Sepher Yetsirah** has set the stage for all subsequent Jewish
mysticism, whose basic elements are the ten **Sephirot** and the
twenty-two Hebrew letters. Genesis says that all creation was
made through ten utterances of divine speech, and the **Sepher
Yetsirah** offers to explain the underlying structure of the divine

speech and of the whole Torah. In creating the world (and quite likely in generating all human thought and speech) the elementary letters are "carved, hewed, weighed and permutated" (and also joined and counted), recalling the scheme of joining atoms to form molecules in the current worldview.

In its second part, the original poetical text becomes a manual or textbook of quasi-astrological anatomy, where the twenty-two letters (in their three sets of three, seven, and twelve) are identified with the elements in the realms of "World" (Space), "Year" (Time), and "Soul." In Hebrew, these dimensions are *Aolam-Shanah-Nefesh*, their acronym is עשן—*AShaN*—which means "Smoke" (close to our concern here with the Cloud). For example, the Seven in the domain of World are the planets, in the domain of Time they are the days of the week, and in the domain of "Soul" are the eyes, ears, nostrils, and mouth; the Twelve in the domain of the World are the zodiac constellations, and in the human domain they correspond to Conversation, Thought, Walking, Sight, Hearing, Action, Coitus, Smell, Sleep, Anger, Eating, and Laughter—as well as twelve bodily organs. Most Jewish mystical attempts to form a *Golem* (Homunculus in alchemical parlance, artificial android in current sci-fi and cyberpunk) involved such letter operations as suggested in the *Sepher Yetsirah*.

The Zohar and the Tree of the Holy ARI

Among the thousands of Qabbalah books and manuscripts, there are two compendiums: the *Zohar* ("Brilliance"), which has become quasi canonical for Judaism, and the *Etz Hayim* ("The Tree of Life"), which gives the main teachings of the Holy ARI.

The book of the *Zohar* is attributed to the disciples of second-century Rabbi Shim'on Bar Yoḥay, but actually appeared (and likely was written) in thirteenth-century Castilia, Spain. The name **Zohar** is based on Daniel's vision of the End Times (12:3): "Those who are wise (or who impart wisdom) will shine like the brightness [**Zohar**] of the heavens." It has the form of an exegesis of the Pentateuch and the Song of Songs by Rabbi Shim'on and his disciples. Its style is sort of a wedding between the Gospel stories and the Talmudic discourses of the sages.

Here is a description of the **Zohar** from an experiential study by Melila Hellner-Eshed, in *A River Issues forth from Eden: On the Language of Mystical Experience in the Zohar:*

The Book of the Zohar is the jewel in the crown of the esoteric literature of Israel. It has no equal in terms of its acceptance [that is, Qabbalah], sanctity and influence over the conception of generations, and this in spite of its apparently sudden appearance at the end of the 13th century. The mysterious style of the Zohar and the special religious-mystical experience it offered the Jew soon won the hearts of its readers. The imagination and the mythical and erotic creativity that burst out from this book made the Zohar into a world by itself. The surprising explanations that the Zohar offers for the Biblical verses, and its deep insights into the human soul in her joys and pains, have found an echo with many souls. And maybe most of all, its worldview left an indelible impression on its readers—a worldview that sets a system of mutual relationship between the human world and the divine world. This system of relationship exists in infinite movement in which the divine plenitude [**Shefa** or **Ḥayut**] seeks to become revealed and saturate the human world, while the human being from his side seeks to reach, take apart and cleave to the divine world. Still more significant is the fact that the Zoharic world formed a worldview that grants the human being the capacity and responsibility to mend, establish and repeatedly beautify the Image of God, and thereby also the image of himself and his world. The Zohar invites the reader to a journey in various secret worlds through an intricate game of hide-and-seek, which demands of the reader an effort, albeit pleasant, to extricate and reveal its moves. This invitation is a significant factor in the secret of its magic. The protagonist of the Zohar, Rabbi Shim'on bar Yoḥay, became a mythological figure in the conception of the reader and in the popular conception. His figure as the great Teacher, the mysterious Man of God who reveals the secret light in the world, had impressed its mark in the conception of the readers and became a source of inspiration and emulation for creative writers and lovers of the Torah and of God.

The most mysterious and ceremonial sections of the *Zohar* are called the *Idrot* (which have to do with a circular threshing ground, recalling the site of the future Temple [2 Sam. 24; 1 Chron. 21]), where Rabbi Shim'on imparts the greatest divine secrets to the circle of his beloved wise students. For a start, he reveals that the greatest secrets of the Torah are hinted in the obscure listing of "The kings who reigned in the Land of Edom before there was a King for the Children of Israel" (Gen. 36:31; 1 Chron. 1:43). There were seven short-lived kings without progeny, and the eighth—called *Hadar* (Chivalry), the sole one for whom it is mentioned that he had a wife, called *Mehetavel bat Matred bat Mei-Zahav* (roughly, "God's Betterment, Daughter of Annoyance, Daughter of the Golden Waters")—apparently survived. These enigmatic insights were some three centuries later contemplated at length, understood, mastered, and then shortly taught by the Holy ARI, Rabbi Yitzhaq Luria (1514–1552).

It can be said that the life of Holy ARI strangely resembles the life of Jesus. He was born in Jerusalem in the sixteenth century, spent his boyhood and got his education in Egypt, and had two public and fruitful years in Galilee (in the town of Zefat) before he died at the age of thirty-eight, and his teachings are known from his circle of students. His teachings are detailed in the book *Etz Hayim* (Tree of Life) of his foremost disciple, Hayim Vital, which took him decades to write. However, this book is extremely entangled, and very few understand it.

It is quite likely that the **Zoharic** references to the short-lived "Kings of Edom" reflect the Messianic expectation in the wake of the Crusades (historically, there were eight major Crusades and eight Christian kings of Jerusalem, and all were finally defeated), as Edom was associated in Judaism with Christianity, that now should come the time for the new Kingdom of Israel. However, in the interpretation of the ARI, these Kings of Edom refer to a whole cosmology of former ancient ages (or, in Gnostic terms, aeons) that resulted in catastrophes (a bit like the current myths of Mu and Atlantis promulgated by theosophists and many others). All those ancient aeons that are now gone have left their debris, and from this debris we can and ought to build our corrected world, **Olam haTiqun**, in which the divine image is restored and feeds all the world with its enlivening wisdom-energy (**Hayut**).

The ARI gives the history of how the balanced figure of the Tree of Life came about, as the result of complicated, and even traumatic, processes of "Shattering of the Vessels" until the configuration achieved its balance. This may be likened to C. G. Jung's finding that when people are in a shifting and confusing state, they automatically generate in their dreams and artwork the balanced fourfold form of the Mandala. In fact, we shall see that the ARI advanced a fourfold **Merkavah**-like scheme of divine personae—which were somehow already implied in the Gnostic Gospel of Judas.

According to the *Etz Hayim*, initially the Divine Glory filled the entire universe, and nowhere was empty of it. When "it rose in His Will" to create the world, it was as if the creator contracted himself and in the space created by that Contraction created the worlds and all that is in them and the "vessels," or the *Sephirot*. The death of the ancient Kings of Edom is a reference to a primordial "Shattering of the Vessels": The plethora of Light went through all the *Sephirot* to the center. Only the first three *Sephirot* could contain the intense light coming directly from the Infinite. But the lower *Sephirot* could not receive the great flow and broke. Through the Shattering of the Vessels the sparks of holiness became scattered into "shells" and Good and Evil mixed, so that we have since had in our world no good without bad and no bad without some good. The function of humans in their lifetime is to select the sparks of holiness inside the evil in this world and to raise their quality. The rectification of these damages in the *Sephirot* and the raising of the holy sparks from among the shells are achieved through our fulfilling the commandments and living in purity and good manner and remorse over wrongdoings and true Spiritual Return (*Teshuvah*).

This Shattering of the Vessels, therefore, was not done accidentally, but happened for the rectification and completion of the world. If the vessels had remained whole and the divine *Shefa* had arrived regularly, humans would have resembled angels, which cannot evolve, and there would have been no sin and no rules, pay, and retribution, so that humans would not have been able to reach further perfection through overcoming their egoistic passions and passing through the crucible of life to rise morally to the intended ideal.

Elements of Qabbalah

One of many ways to characterize the Qabbalah is that it is largely a creative grammar of the divine and spiritual systems, evidenced by the detailed interactions of their elementary entities—of Letters, Words, *Sephirot*, and *Partsufim* ("Divine Faces" or Personae).

The Hebrew Letters as "Letters of (Inter)Action"

The ancient Qabbalah of the *Sepher Yetsirah* (from which the concept of the "*Sephirot*" originated) is mostly concerned with the Hebrew letters. These letters are seen as the very "building blocks" out of which the universe was created. So, alongside the Qabbalah of the *Sephirot*, there also developed systems of Qabbalah based on work with the letters, their combinations, permutations, and pronouncement. The two Qabbalah systems of the *Sephirot* and of the letters were sometimes rival systems and sometimes complementary, and the great Qabbalah synthesizers (notably Moses Cordovero in the fifteenth century and the author of the Tanya in the eighteenth) integrated the two currents as they developed, and Qabbalistic explorations of the letters are still going on. The most basic integration, hinted at already in the *Sepher Yetsirah*, is when the twenty-two letters of the Hebrew alphabet denote the connections between the ten *Sephirot*, and hence the letters stand for the relations between the *Sephirot* and for the specific processes that transfer their states and unite them.

The basic premise of the Qabbalah of letters is that since the Hebrew scriptures teach that God created the universe by speech, the letters of which those (ten) divine utterances are made are those elementary units out of which the manifest elements of this world came into being, or even was called into being. It is related to the notion mentioned earlier that the whole Torah is the Great Name of God, and hence by studying and reading from the Torah, one is actually calling God by his proper name (the same Hebrew word, *qri'ah*, means both reading and calling). Therefore, most of the meditation methods of the Qabbalah and especially those of Abraham Abulafia employ work with letters and names, such as visualization, chanting, contemplation, or letter permutations, in order to re-create or simulate in the psyche of the mediator some of these divine processes.

Words, Letter Permutations, Gematria, and Holy Names

In the Gospel of Judas, the names of the various angels are of great importance. In the beginning of Jewish mysticism, in the **Heikhalot** texts, we find those mysterious names of angels, which are largely lost to us today, and even no academic researcher understands them.

One of the chief methods of working with the letters, common to Christian Gnosis and to Jewish as well as Muslim mysticism, is the use of gematria—the assigning of numerical values to the letters, adding up the values of the letters of a word or an expression, and associating this word or expression with another one that has the same numerical value.

The following is a table for the gematria of the letters of the Hebrew alphabet, in which the original Hebrew Bible is written. The Hebrew alphabet has twenty-two letters plus five "final letters," used where these letters occur at the end of a word (the sign "]" here signifies final letters). The "Full Gematria" (which is more frequently used) counts the letters in units, tens, and hundreds, and final letters can be counted alternatively as common letters. The "Small Gematria" is the sequential order of the Hebrew letters. See below.

Gematria of the Letters of the Hebrew Alphabet

Letter	ט	ח	ז	ו	ה	ד	ג	ב	א
Translit.	T	Ḥ	Z	V/U/W	H	D	G	B/Bh/V	A/E
Pron.	Tet	Khet	Zayin	Waw	He'	Dalet	Gimmel	Bet	Alef
Full G.	9	8	7	6	5	4	3	2	1
Small G.	9	8	7	6	5	4	3	2	1

Letter	צ	פ	ע	ס	נ	מ	ל	כ	י
Translit.	Ṣ/Ts	P/Ph	A/E	S	N	M	L	K/Kh	I/Y
Pron.	Tsadiq	Peh	Ayin	Samekh	Nun	Mem	Lamed	Kaf	Yud
Full G.	90	80	70	60	50	40	30	20	10
Small G.	18	17	16	15	14	13	12	11	10

Letter	ץ	ף	ן	ם	ך	ת	ש	ר	ק
Translit.	Ṣ/Ts	P/Ph	N	M	K/Kh	T	Sh/S	R	Q
Pron.	Tsadiq]	Peh]	Nun]	Mem]	Kaf]	Tav	Shin	Resh	Qof
Full G.	900	800	700	600	500	400	300	200	100
Small G.	–	–	–	–	–	22	21	20	19
Alt.	90	80	50	40	20				

NOTE: Translit. = Transliteration; Pron. = Pronunciation; Full G. = Full Gematria; Small G. = Small Gematria; Alt. = Alternatively

(In the following examples, as mentioned in the text, I use the ⇔ sign to signify correspondence by gematria.)

Thus, the numerical value of the Hebrew letters of **BeARBA ELU—בארבע אלו** ⇔ 312, and 312 = 13 × 24 and 12 × 26. The first three are all significant numbers in the Gospel of Judas. As men-

tioned, Jesus promises Judas in the Judas Gospel, "You will become the thirteenth." The fourth number here, 26, is the gematria
value of the unutterable Name of **YHWH**. Also 312 = 4 × 78; 4 (in
Hebrew **ARBA̱**) is what **BeARBA̱ ELU** means, and 78 = 26 × 3.
Thus, 78 ⇔ בן הויה—"Son of Being" (or, if you like, "Son of God").

Let us look now at a novel example of gematria constructs. In
the wake of Dan Brown's *Da Vinci Code* there is much interest and
debate about Mary Magdalene—her role and her relationship to
Jesus. Some even speculate that the two have engaged in ceremonial lovemaking in the style of some pagan rites. But there is really
no need to send them to paganism in order to associate them
with the expression of love. Let's consider what her name may
represent, in the manner it would perhaps have been treated in
the book of the *Zohar*.

Mary is surely the Hebrew **Miryam** (מרים), name of the sister of
Moses. The name "Magdalene" (**Migdalit**—מגדלית), namely, a
place called **Migdal**, which means "Tower," suggests she was attractive. In the Canticles, the beloved quotes: "I was a wall, and
my breasts were like towers (**Migdalot**), then was I in his eyes as
one who finds content" (Cant. 8:10).

By counting and "Weighing" the letters of the name of the
Tower—מגדל (**MiGDaL**; the Hebrew consonant letters are rendered in capitals)—we get its gematria value as 77 (which is 7 ×
11, both meaningful numbers in esoteric systems, 7 for Judaism
and 11 for Islam—where the name **Allah** comes to 66). But the
beauty is that the gematria of מרים מגדלית (**MiRYaM MiGDaLIT**)
⇔ 777. This puts Mary Magdalene in a very interesting company
of characters of the New Testament: on her Left is the (in)famous
666 and on her Right 888, which is the Christian-Gnostic gematria
number of the Greek name of Jesus—'Ιησους. These three significant numbers are multiples of 111—the gematria of **Aleph**, the

first letter of the Hebrew alphabet and a word meaning "teaching" or "training."

The trinity thus formed, of the bearer of the 666, of Mary Magdalene, and of Jesus, somewhat resemble the trinity of the Genesis story of the Tree of Knowledge—of the serpent, Eve, and Adam. Note also that the Hebrew text also explains the nature of these three as the methods for gaining knowledge, namely, Gnosis: (1) the Serpent is **Naḥash** (נחש), related to **Niḥush** (נחוש), that is, Guessing, which is often erroneous; (2) Eve is **Ḥavah** (חוה), related to **Ḥavayah** (חויה), that is, Experience, which is open to temptation; and (3) **Adam** (אדם), with gematria value of 45 (to which we shall return), related to **Dimyon** (דמיון) or Analogy, and especially similitude to God, as it is written (Isa. 14:14) **E'ele al Bamotey Av, Adame le'Eliyon:** "I will ascend over the stages of the Cloud: I will resemble [God] the most High." The word **Av** here is the very same (Luminous) Cloud that we have been discussing all along.

The Letters of the Tetragrammaton

The creed of Israel is the **Shema** testimony: **Shema Yisra'el YHWH Elohenu YHWH Eḥad!**—"Hear O Israel: the Lord our God, the Lord is One" (Deut. 6:4). This is the assertion and the conviction that behind all the multiplicity in the world and in life there is underlying Unity. The prophetic expectation is for the revelation of this unity: "And **YHWH** shall be king over all the earth; on that day shall be **YHWH** (הויה) **One** (אחד) and His Name One" (Zech. 14:9).

The Tetragrammaton—the four-letter-name of הויה is made of three letters—a demonstration of the principle of the three-that-are-four. אחד is a three-letter word. Since הויה (or, as often rendered, ידוד) is a four-letter word that is made of three different

letters, therefore there are just 12 permutations of these four letters (which in the Qabbalah of the ARI correspond to the Twelve
Tribes of Israel as twelve channels for the Divine).

Let us examine these concepts by gematria:

- אחד ⇔ **13**
- הויה ⇔ **26** = 2 × אחד
- ב"ן (**Son**) ⇔ **52** = 2 × הויה

We shall meet this name of 52 soon.

We can now add to the gematria also a geometrical examination: What is the special inherent significance to the number 26?
It is the number of directions in three-dimensional cubical space.
Imagine space as made of tightly packed cubes. Each one is en-
closed inside a cube of 3 × 3 × 3 (= 27 cubes). So to move out or
communicate from a cube there are 26 directions to turn, making
26 the sum of possible movements.

These three-as-four letters of this Holy Name have special geometrical forms: They mark the elements that build all spatial (and
hyperspace) constructs: י corresponds to a point; ו to a line; and ה
to a surface. A second ה can be seen as if its short vertical line is
perpendicular to the surface, thus corresponding to a volume. So
the different sequences of these letters can be seen as trajectories
of relations in space, and especially in the 5D hyperspace of
Space-Time-Soul.

The Tenfold Pattern of the Sephirot

The **Mequbalim** follow the biblical saying: "From my flesh . . . I
would see God" (Job 19:26) and employ an anthropomorphic

model to describe divine and spiritual phenomena. The generic human form is seen as a tenfold structure of nodes with 22 specific connections between them, which is often called the "Tree of the **Sephirot**" or the "Tree of Life." This is actually the five-dimensional scheme of the **Sepher Yetsirah**, but it is generally depicted as a two-dimensional chart, forming three vertical lines—right, left, and center. There are three nodes on the right, three corresponding nodes on the left, and four nodes on the center. These nodes on the center line are always above or below the level of the peripheral nodes (*see opposite, at right*), and their 12 connections are thus diagonal. The seven lower nodes are regarded as the more visible and manifest, or pertaining to "This World" (**Olam haZeh**), and can be shown as corresponding to the two arms, trunk (the solar plexus), the two thighs, the genitals, and the ground. (*See opposite, at left.*) The three upper ones are regarded as more hidden, or "inside one's head," and can be regarded as corresponding to the two sides of the brain and the crown of the head. In the Qabbalah, they pertain to the yet unseen "World to Come" (**Olam haBa**).

The anthropomorphic correspondence of the Qabbalah can be compared with the Indian model of the chakras. Regard each vertical pair of nodes on the right and left as having their weighted balance on the center, and we have the system of the seven chakras. This is true enough, but then we can also start to appreciate what is gained by the specific reference to the right and left sides of man, and even to "the right and left side of God."

Continuing the comparison with the classic Oriental models, we can see that the Qabbalah scheme of the two sides encompasses the Taoist notions of yin and yang. The right side is seen as male (the expansive and giving side), whereas the left side is seen as female (the contracting, constricting, and receiving side).

Crucifix Lying on the Tree of Life   **The Tree of the *Sephirot***

Thus, the Qabbalah anthropomorphic ***Sephirot*** model integrates elements from the chakras and the Taoist models. This view of the sides may help us to appreciate the significant, sometimes paradoxical, nature of the center.

We may also add the most famous human figure drawing, that of the man on the cross (*see above, at left*). Again we find that the "Tree of Life" diagram can accommodate this figure as a particular instance. This does stretch the Tree of Life figure to the sides, which were not stressed in the Oriental models.

Coming back to the left, right, and central lines, we should better consider what these sides mean. Take the notion of the right side as Love or Grace (**Ḥesed**), giving because it is its nature to give, even without regard to the recipient's needs. The left side is the side of Judgment (**Din**) and Rigor (**Gevurah**), which weighs and restricts. Their proper balance is the quality of Compassion (**Raḥamim**), of giving judiciously to the extent of need.

Also note that the correspondence of the Tree of the **Sephirot** with the human body is only one application of the general structural fractal model that repeats at each level. Each node contains all the ten-node structure, which is, using the current language of fractal mathematics, a self-similar structure. It is like the famous Mandelbrot set with its Buddha-like figure repeated endlessly—only that here it is an erect figure, geared for action. Thus, the tenfold structure can be found again just in the head, and even in each of the limbs and so on to the smallest details, and the principles gained from the general structure provide insights as to the workings and the balance, or lack thereof, of the parts. It is a nested holistic structure of wholes within wholes.

If the right-hand path entails moving from the top down and the left-hand path entails going from the bottom up, then the middle path entails moving both ways at once, and the ascent along this middle path means transcending. The middle line of the Tree of Life is the path of comprehension and transcendence, going up from conflict to agreement to understanding and finally to realization of the divine, of a true Self that is not limited to the subjective self. As Martin Buber has shown, the divine is the realm of the You (or Thou) in the I-Thou relationship. God is thus the "Eternal Thou," and a genuine turning to the other is to the divine in him/her.

Partsufim: *The Faces of the Godhead*

The most wildly mythical and anthropomorphic elements of Qabbalah are the *Partsufim*, the Faces or Figurations of the Godhead. Although the earliest mystical Jewish texts were anthropomorphic in giving the enormous dimensions of the divine anthropos, the mysticism of the *Partsufim* is mostly concerned with the Godhead(s), even though a body stature (*Qomah*) and even genitals are implied. The discussion of the *Partsufim* issues from the book of the *Zohar*, though the name and the detailed theosophy belong to the ARI.

In the *Zohar*, these divine faces are presented in the *Idrot*, in which Rabbi Shim'on reveals the secrets hidden even from the angels, and have to do with an assortment of Divine Faces and Skulls (*Gulgolet*, the Aramaic Golgotha); there are revelations about the supernal Trinitarian Godhead, and the Faces that issue from it, with their brow, eyes, and nose. The detailed didactic discussion, however, is about the hairs of the beards of two Faces, the white-bearded Long Face (*Arikh Anpin*) and the black-bearded Small Face (*Ze'er Anpin*) of God. These accounts culminate with the face-to-face Union of the *Ze'er Anpin* with his feminine counterpart and the ecstatic departure of Rabbi Shim'on from this world.

In the mystical cosmology of the ARI referred to above, in order to enable the Broken Vessels to renew their Function, the Holy One changed the position and composition of those vessels and made *Partsufim* ("Faces" or Configurations). The first *Sephirah*, *Keter* (crown), became *Arikh Anpin* (the Long Face). The second *Sepfirah*, *Ḥokhmah* (Wisdom), became *Partsuf Abba* (Father). The *Sephirah Binah* (Understanding) became *Partsuf Imma* (Mother). The next lower six *Sephirot*, which were shuttered, became the *Partsuf Ze'er Anpin* (the Small Face), and the *Sephirah* of *Malkhut* (Kingdom), identified with the *Shekhinah* and *Knesset Yisrael* (the feminine side of the creator), became the *Partsuf Nuqba* (Female) or the *Bat* (Daughter). In addition, connecting the supernal three *Sephirot* and the seven lower ones there is also a virtual *Sephirah* of *Da'at* (Knowledge), and, likewise, in the Qabbalah of the *Partsufim* there are also *Partsufim* that intermediate between the *Partsufim* of *Abba* and *Imma* and their Child, the *Ze'er Anpin*. These are the *Partsufim* of *Yisra'el Saba* (Grandfather Israel) and of *Tevunah* (Intelligence) that supply spiritual food.

Connection between the Partsufim *and the Human Soul*

This vast mystical vista of divine faces issuing one from each other is reminiscent of the cosmological teachings of Jesus in the Gospel of Judas, demonstrated by figures emerging from the Luminous Cloud. But the picture presented in the Qabbalah is not only more positive; it is also more developed and leads to much spiritual insight.

Building on the preceding schemes of the Qabbalah, the ARI regarded the human soul as a series of control levels on an axis or ladder with five levels, which are called (Genesis Raba, portion 14) *Nefesh, Ru'ah, Neshamah, Hayah,* and *Yehidah.* These five animate the five "Worlds" of the Qabbalah as expanded by the ARI: *Assiyah* (Action), *Yetsirah* (Formation), *Bri'ah* (Creation), *Atzilut* (Divine Emanation), and *Adam Qadmon* (Primordial Human). These five types of souls are nourished by the strict interactions of the corresponding *Partsufim.*

There may seem a similarity between the mythical-mystical visions of the Gnostics, with all their confusing array of lesser gods, and the array of divine *Partsufim* in the Tree of Life Book. Both activate the mythical imagination. But there are significant differences: The plurality of Godheads of the Qabbalah not only does not imply two authorities—for Good and for Evil—but also shows that this plurality has meaningful yet only apparently different faces of the One, and, more precisely (as shown below), different combinations and assemblies of the letters of the same Divine Name.

The corollary is that processes of spiritual-psychological developments are related not to mythical entities (like in paganism and the archetypes of the Jungian psychology) but to strict and precise operations that could be enacted ritually.

The Partsufim *as the Different Combinations of the Divine Name*

The expansion of the *Sephirot* to *Partsufim*, each containing the array of ten *Sephirot* (a self-similar or "Fractal" form) is a "Second Order" operation. The ARI was also fond of doing such second-order operations of gematria with the letters of the Holy Names. This is done through the practice of *Miluy* ("Filling")—rendering these Hebrew letters by the words of their names, where each such word is made up of two to four letters. For example, the name of the first letter *Aleph* א is made of three letters (אלף), and so is the second letter, *Bet* ב (בית).

Another remarkable thing about the letters of the Name of the Lord is that they are not just consonants but actually also vowels (in other words, made up of the softest and most subtle letters that create the voice that precede speech). Note that Hebrew words are normally written only in their consonants, and the vowels are assumed from prior knowledge. So in fact a word can be pronounced in a variety of ways, using different vowels between the consonants.

There are four such Hebrew letters that are not really consonants but vowels: Alef (א), He (ה), Waw (ו), and Yud (י), and these are the letters that make up the holiest names in the Bible. For the ARI, these letters also "fill in" the Tetragrammaton so that the degrees of manifestation of the Divine Name in the Four Worlds are expressed, and might even be explained, by the fulfilling of these letters of the Tetragrammaton.

Degrees of Manifestation of the Divine Name in the Four Worlds

World	Name/ Partzuf	Value	Hebrew Rendering	English Rendering
Atzilut	*AaB* ע"ב	72	יוד הי ויו הי	*Yud Hy Wyw Hy*
Bri'ah	*SaG* ס"ג	63	יוד הי ואו הי	*Yud Hy Waw Hy*
Yetsirah	*MaH* מ"ה	45	יוד הא ואו הא	*Yud He Waw He*
Assiyah	*BeN* ב"ן	52	יוד הה וו הה	*Yud Hh Ww Hh*

This reveals four additional divine Names based on the Tetragrammaton, which are really alternative depictions of what is meant by the ***Partsufim***. Therefore, those apparently distinct "faces of God" are actually different arrangements of the same One entity denoted by the Tetragrammaton. So the Qabbalah of the ARI makes much use of the terms "Name of 72," "Name of 63," and so on. But this is by no means the end of the story. Through gematria, these numbers themselves become names or are related to significant names—and with these, suddenly the key names and concepts of the Gospel of Judah and of the Christian eschatology can emerge in a new light.

Displaying the "Son of Man in the Cloud of Heaven"

The actual mystical perception of these ***Partsufim*** follows their emanation—the Divine first appears in the Name of 72, in the *Av*—which we have been associating with the Cloud of Glory. From this emerges "the Name of 63," where 63 ⇔ סבא, that is, ***SaBA*** (literally, "Grandfather"). This can correspond to the ***Partsuf*** of "Grandfather Israel" (***Yisra'el Saba***) whose wisdom and understanding offer guidance to the new generation. Then may appear the two ***Partsufim***, one corresponding to "the Name of 52," or **BeN** (ב"ן), meaning "Son" (and also the same gematria of ***Behemah***, namely, "Beast"). The other one is the "Name of Rectification" (***Shem haTiqun***) as "the Name of 45" (***Shem MaH***), which has the gematria of **Adam** (אדם), namely, "Man."

So finally, this system of faces-names of the Qabbalah allows the mystical perception of the eschatological revelation of the "Son of Man in the Clouds of Heaven"—especially when we consider the quality of "Heaven" with ***Havannah***, Hebrew for "Understanding."

The Once and Future Qabbalah:
Global Mutual Acceptance

Remarkably, the Qabbalah has retained its name for a thousand years (and maybe two), though its meaning has changed considerably. The same word suggested different meanings and perspectives for different generations, each of which could innovate while trusting they were keeping the true inner meaning.

Qabbalah originally meant "trusted transmission," from a true sage verbally to the few deserving disciples, of the secrets of *Ma'ase Bereshit* and *Ma'ase Merkavah*, namely, the Workings of Creation and the Workings of Assembly.

Written texts of what was called "Qabbalah" appeared only from the eleventh century CE—after the appearance of what eventually became the third canon of Judaism, the *Mishne Torah* of Maimonides and its auxiliary religious philosophy book the *Moreh Nevukhim* ("Guide for the Perplexed"). In his guide, Maimonides referred to *Ma'ase Bereshit* as Aristotelian natural science and to *Ma'ase Merkavah* as Aristotelian metaphysics. So the keepers of the secret verbal transmissions about the meaning of *Ma'ase Bereshit* and *Ma'ase Merkavah* likely felt they must publish and explain their traditional true meanings. Within a century, more than a thousand Qabbalah texts appeared, and since then the Qabbalah has no longer been an oral tradition but just as likely learned from books.

Currently, there are at least three novel understandings of what the Qabbalah means. First, related to its meaning of "Receiving," the Qabbalah is advocated as the "Art of Receiving"—a moral education system for turning egoism (receiving for self) into altruism, or "Receiving in Order to Give," generally characterized by four aspects (as defined by Rabbi Yehuda Ashlag and currently promoted by Michael Laitman).

Second, **haQabbalah** is understood as **Haqballah**, namely, "Paralleling," or the act of building metaphors (promoted by Yitzhaq Ginsburgh, in a redemptive Jewish context). Yet in this sense, the Qabbalah is much the same as general systems theory or cybernetics (defined by the master cybernetician Gordon Pask as "the art or science of building defensible metaphors"). The significance of the Qabbalah for our times may be in being a kind of "general systems science" and a systems theology. This implies the knowledge of patterns and development of "a Methodology of Pattern in Consciousness" (for example, by Julius Stulman's four stages of singular perspective, systems, systems of systems, and metamorphosis and by Christopher Alexander's "Pattern Language of Design").

Then there is also the third meaning, the one that I would like to advocate. Understood by its literal meaning of "Acceptance," I construe the Qabbalah to indicate a science and art of "Mutual Acceptance" (**Qabbalah hadadit**) or "Self and Other Acceptance," a systemic, sociopsychological spiritual discipline for nurturing the fruitful interaction of diverse actors—both individuals and collective entities. In particular, as I have tried to indicate in this book, the Qabbalah may well become a tool for effecting Jewish-Christian reconciliation. This approach will accept the constructs of "Conversation Theory," as put forth by Pask in *Conversation, Cognition, and Learning,* for facilitating multilevel communications and of the Lurianic Qabbalah of four relations: going from "back to back" to "face to face" interactions and giving birth to an enlightened new face (**Partsuf**).

Conclusion

We can take the Luminous Cloud of the Gospel of Judas as *Partsuf Av*—a primordial face from which emanate the other faces. From it, we may then see *Partsuf SaG*—the sagacity of "Grandfather Israel" as (in)forming luminous "Clouds of Heaven" from aggregations of instances of Understandings (*Havanot*). In this medium there may shine the *Partsufim* of *BeN* and of *MaH-ADaM*, so "with these Four"—or *BeARBA ELU*—we would even be able to see the coming of the "Son of Man in the Clouds of Heaven." Whatever the form this apparition takes, it will constitute a collective face of redeemed humanity—allowing humankind to observe its own ideal reflection, feeding back a new vision for humankind and the Living Earth—*Adam* and *Adamah*. The artificial luminous cloud over the Temple Mount proposed in the Epilogue could then accommodate the Revelation of the collective Face of redeemed universal New Israel.

READINGS

Readings Mentioned in the Book

Bar Ilan, Meir. *Astrology and Other Sciences among the Jews of the Land of Israel in the Byzantine Period* (in Hebrew). Bialik Institute, in press.

Biasiotto, P. R. *History of the Development of Devotion to the Holy Name.* New York: St. Bonaventure College and Seminary, 1943.

Borges, Jorge Luis. *Collected Fictions: A New Translation by Andrew Hurley.* New York: Allen Lane, Penguin Press, 1998; or *Labyrinths,* Penguin Books, Modern Classics. (Original in Spanish: *Artificios,* included in the book *Ficciones.* Buenos Aires: Sur, 1944.)

Coudert, Allison. *The Impact of the Kabbalah in the 17th Century: The Life and Thought of Francis Mercury Van Helmot, 1614–1698.* Leiden: Brill Academic Publishers, 1999.

———. "Leibniz, Locke, Newton, and the Kabbalah." Paper presented at the conference "Christian Kabbalah and Jewish Thought." University of Arizona, Tucson, April 1996.

———. *Leibniz and the Kabbalah.* New York: Springer, 1995.

Cousins, Ewert. *Christ of the Twenty-first Century.* Rockport, Mass.: Element Books, 1992.

Davis, Joshua. "Apocalypse Now—How a Hologram, a Blimp, and a Massively Multiplayer Game Could Bring Peace to the Holy Land." *Wired,* April 2004, 144–49, 179–81. Available online at http://www.wired.com/wired/archive/12.04/holyland.html.

Duba, Ursula. "Persecution of Jews over 1900 Years." Article 61 of search for "Duba" at http://www.h-net.org.

Elad, Amikam. "Why Did Abd al-Maliq Build the Dome of the Rock?" In "al-Haram ash-Sharif—Abd al-Malik's Jerusalem." *Oxford Studies in Islamic Arts* 9 (1992): 33–53. (Expanded and improved version will appear in *Jerusalem Studies in Arabic and Islam* by 2008.)

Farmer, Philip José. *The Night of Light.* New York: Berkley Paperbacks, 1966.

Fine, Lawrence. *Physician of the Soul, Healer of the Cosmos: Isaac Luria and His Kabbalistic Fellowship.* Stanford: Stanford University Press, 2003.

Freke, Timothy, and Peter Gandy. *The Laughing Jesus.* Oakland, Calif.: O Books, 2006.

Gager, G. *The Origins of Anti-Semitism: Attitudes towards Judaism in Pagan and Christian Antiquity.* Oxford: Oxford University Press, 1983.

Gallup, G., Jr. *Religion in America, 1996.* Princeton: Princeton Religion Research Center, 1996.

Gardner, Martin. "666 and All That." In *The New Age: Notes of a Fringe-Watcher.* Amherst, N.Y.: Prometheus Books, 1991.

Gershom, Rabbi Yonassan. "Antisemitic Stereotypes in Alice Bailey's [*sic*] Writings" (2005). http://www.pinenet.com/rooster/bailey.html.

Godwin, Joscelyn, Chanel Christian, and John Patrick Deveney. *The Hermetic Brotherhood of Luxor: Initiatic and Historical Documents of an Order of Practical Occultism.* York Beach, Maine: Weiser Books, 1995.

Grabar, Oleg, and Said Nuseibeh. *The Dome of the Rock.* London: Thames and Hudson, 1996.

Gurdjieff, G. I. *Meetings with Remarkable Men.* 1963. Reprint, New York: Penguin, 1991.

Hammer, M. F., A. J. Redd, E. T. Wood, M. R. Bonner, H. Jarjanazi, T. Karafet, S. Santachiara-Benerecetti, et al. "Jewish and Middle Eastern Non-Jewish Populations Share a Common Pool of Y-Chromosome Biallelic Haplotypes." *PNAS* (Proceedings of the National Academy of Sciences, USA) 67, no. 12 (June 6, 2000): 6769–74.

Hasson, Yitzhaq. "Jerusalem in the Moslem Perspective: The Qur'an and Tradition Literature" (in Hebrew). In *The History of Jerusalem: The Early Islamic Period,* edited by J. Prawer. Jerusalem: Yad Izhak Ben-Zvi Publications, 1987.

Hayut-Man, Yitzhaq. "From Tel Aviv to the Temple: The Restoration of Israel according to the Book of Ezekiel" (in Hebrew). In *Am Levadad: Moledet uPzurah,* edited by Lau Benyamin. Tel Aviv: Yedi'ot Aharonot Books, 2006. Available online at http://www.thehope.org/Ezekiel1.htm.

———. "Genesis Exegesis" (2005). http://www.thehope.org/toreng0.htm.

———. *The Gospel of Judith Iscariot: An Ecofeminist Passion Play* (1994). http://www.thehope.org/jud1–1.htm.

Hellner-Eshed, Melila. *A River Issues forth from Eden: On the Language of Mystical Experience in the Zohar* (in Hebrew). Tel Aviv: Am Oved, 2005. (English version expected in early 2008.)

Al-Hilali, Dr. Muhammad Taqi-ud-Din, and Dr. Muhammad Muhsin Khan, trans. *The Noble Qur'an*. Riyadh: Maktaba Dar-us-Salam, 1994.

Hoeller, Stephan. *The Gnostic Jung and the Seven Sermons to the Dead*. Wheaton, Ill.: Quest Books, 1982.

Huntington, Samuel. *The Clash of Civilizations and the Remaking of World Order*. 1996. Reprint, New York: Free Press, 2002.

Hurtak, J. J., and D. Hurtak. *"Pistis Sophia": A Post Gospel Dialogue on Consciousness, Light, and the Spirit of Wisdom*. Los Gatos, Calif.: Academy of Future Science, 1999. Available online at http://www.pistissophia.org.

Idel, Moshe. *Studies in Ecstatic Kabbalah* (in Hebrew). Jerusalem: ACADE-MON Publishers, 1990.

———. *Messianism and Mysticism* (in Hebrew). Tel Aviv: Broadcast University, 1992.

———. "Ramon Lull and Ecstatic Kabbalah: A Preliminary Observation." *Journal of the Warburg and Courtould Institutes* 51 (1988): 170–74.

———. "Abraham Abulafia and the Pope." Chap. 3 in *Studies in Ecstatic Kabbalah*. Albany: SUNY Press, 1988.

Irenaeus, Saint. *Irenaeus against Heresies*. Whitefish, Mont.: Kessinger Publishing, 2004.

Jensen, Robin Margaret. *Understanding Early Christian Art*. London and New York: Routledge, 2000.

Jung, C. G. "Gnostic Symbols of the Self." In *Aion: Researches into the Phenomenology of the Self*. Vol. 9, pt. 2 of *The Collected Works of C. G. Jung*. Translated by R. F. C. Hull. London: Routledge and Kegan Paul, 1959.

———. *Memories, Dreams, and Reflection*. New York: Vintage, 1989.

———. "A Psychological Approach to the Trinity." In *Psychology and Religion East and West*. Vol. 11 of *The Collected Works of C. G. Jung*. Translated by R. F. C. Hull. Princeton: Princeton University Press, 1969.

———. *Psychology and Religion*. Terry Lecture Series. New Haven: Yale University Press, 1960.

Kaplan, Arieh. *Meditation and the Bible*. York Beach, Maine: Samuel Weiser, 1978.

Kasser, Rudolphe, Meyer Marvin, and Wurst Gregor. *The Gospel of Judas*. Washington, D.C.: National Geographic, 2006.

Kersten, Holger. *Jesus Lived in India*. Shaftsbury, Dorset, UK: Element Books, 1986.

Kertzer, D. I. *Unholy War: The Vatican's Role in the Rise of Modern Anti-Semitism*. London: Pan Books, 2001.

Khayutman [Hayut-Man], Yitzhak. "The Cybernetic Basis for Human Recon-
    struction: An Application for the Middle-East." Ph.D. diss., Brunel Univer-
    sity, 1981.

Khunrath, Heinrich. *The Amphitheatre Engravings of Heinrich Khunrath.*
    Translated by Patricia Tahil. Edited byAdam McLean. Edinburgh: Magnum
    Opus Hermetic Sourceworks, 1981.

Klossowski de Rola, Stanislas. *The Golden Game: Alchemical Engravings of the
    Seventeenth Century.* London: Thames and Hudson, 1997.

Krosney, Herbert, and Bart D. Ehrman. *The Lost Gospel: The Quest for the
    Gospel of Judas Iscariot.* Washington, D.C.: National Geographic, 2006.

Lewis, C. S. *Mere Christianity.* San Francisco: Harper, 2001.

Maccoby, Hyam. *Judas Iscariot and the Myth of Jewish Evil.* New York: Free
    Press, 1992.

Maymon, Y. L. *The GRA Book* (in Hebrew). Jerusalem: Rav Kook Institute,
    1954.

Michell, John. *The Dimensions of Paradise.* London: Thames and Hudson,
    1988.

Michell, John, and Christine Rhone. *Twelve-Tribe Nations and the Science of
    Enchanting the Landscape.* London: Thames and Hudson, 1991.

Misinai, Tsvi. *The Roadmap to the Third Intifada: The Roots and Solution to
    the Problem in the Holy Land* (in Hebrew). Rehovot, Israel: Li'ad Publish-
    ers, 2006.

Nebel, Almut, Dvora Filon, Bernd Brinkmann, Partha P. Majumder, Marina
    Faerman, and Ariella Oppenheim. "The Y Chromosome Pool of Jews as
    Part of the Genetic Landscape of the Middle East." *American Journal of
    Human Genetics* 69 (2001): 1095–112.

Nebel, Almut, Dvora Filon, Deborah A. Weiss, Michael Weale, Marina Faer-
    man, Ariella Oppenheim, and Mark G. Thomas. "High-Resolution Y Chro-
    mosome Haplotypes of Israeli and Palestinian Arabs Reveal Geographic
    Substructure and Substantial Overlap with Haplotypes of Jews." *Human
    Genetics* 107 (2000): 630–41.

Pagels, Elaine. *The Gnostic Gospels.* New York: Random House, 1979.
————. *The Origins of Satan.* New York: Random House, 1995.

Pask, Gordon. *Conversation, Cognition, and Learning.* Amsterdam: Elsevier,
    1975.

Patey, Richard. "Jesus and the Theatre." *New Testament Studies* 30 (1984).

Phillips, Kevin. *American Theocracy: The Peril and Politics of Radical Religion,
    Oil, and Borrowed Money in the 21st Century.* New York: Viking, 2006.

Pico de la Mirandola, Giovanni. *Oration on the Dignity of Man: Heptaplus.*

Translated by Paul J. W. Miller, Charles Glenn Wallis, and Douglas Carmichael. Indianapolis: Hackett, 1998.

Prophet, Elizabeth-Claire. *The Lost Years of Jesus.* Gardiner, Mont.: Summit University Press, 1984.

Reuchlin, Johannes. *De Arte Cabalistica* [On the Art of Kabbalah]. Translated by Martin Goodman and Sarah Goodman with an introduction by Moshe Idel. 1517. Reprint, New York: Abaris Books, 1983.

Richer, Jean. *Sacred Geography of the Ancient Greeks: Astrological Symbolism in Art, Architecture, and Landscape.* Translated by Christine Rhone. SUNY Series in Western Esoteric Traditions. Albany: SUNY Press, 1994.

Robinson, James M. *The Nag Hammadi Library in English.* Rev. ed. San Francisco: Harper, 1990.

———. *The Secrets of Judas: The Story of the Misunderstood Disciple and His Lost Gospel.* San Francisco: Harper, 2006.

Roerich, Nikolas. *Shambhala: In Search of the New Era.* Rev. ed. Rochester Vt.: Inner Traditions, 1990.

Rudolph, Kurt. *Gnosis: The Nature and History of Gnosticism.* New York: Harper and Row, 1987.

Ruprecht, Louis. "On Being Jewish or Greek in the Modern Moment." *Diaspora* 3, no. 2 (1994).

Sagiv, Tuviah. Several articles available online at http://www.templemount.org.

Scholem, Gershom. *Jewish Gnosticism, Merkabah Mysticism, and Talmudic Tradition.* New York: Jewish Theological Seminary, 1965.

———. *On the Kabbalah and Its Symbolism.* Rev. ed. New York: Schocken Books, 1969.

———. *On the Mystical Shape of the Godhead.* New York: Schocken Books, 1991.

Schonfield, Hugh. *The Essene Odyssey: The Mystery of the True Teacher and the Essene Impact on the Shaping of Human Destiny.* Shaftsbury, Dorset, UK: Element Books, 1984.

———. *The Passover Plot: New Light on the History of Jesus.* London: Hutchinson, 1965.

———. *The Politics of God.* 2d ed. Santa Cruz, Calif.: University of the Trees Press, 1978.

———. *Those Incredible Christians.* New York: Bernard Geis Associates/Grove Press, 1968.

Smith, Morton. "Clement of Alexandria and the Secret Mark: The Score at the End of the First Decade." *Harvard Theological Review* 75 (1982): 449–61.

———. *The Secret Gospel.* London: Gollanz, 1974.

Trompf, Garry. "Isaac Newton and the Kabbalistic Noah: Natural Law between *Mediaevalia* and the Enlightenment." *Aries* 5, no. 1 (2005): 91–118.

Trungpa, Chogyam. *Shambhala: Sacred Path of the Warrior.* Rev. ed. Boston: Shambhala Books, 1995.

Wechsler, Tuvia. *Tsfunot beMasoret Yisra'el* [Hidden Codes in the Tradition of Israel: On the Secrets and Hints of Our Ancients]. Jerusalem: Rubin Mass, 1968.

Winnicott, Donald. *Playing and Reality.* London: Routledge, 1982.

Wirszubski, Chaim. *Pico della Mirandola's Encounter with Jewish Mysticism.* Cambridge: Harvard University Press, 1989.

Wolfe, Robert. *Christianity in Perspective.* New York: Memory Books, 1987.

Yahya, Harun. "The Second Coming of Jesus (PBUH) the Messiah." Chap. 7 of *A Call for Unity.* Istanbul: Global Publishing, 2004.

———. *An Index to the Qur'an.* Istanbul: Global Publishing, 2003.

———. *The Signs of Jesus' Second Coming.* Istanbul: Global Publishing, 2004.

Yates, Frances. *The Occult Philosophy in the Elizabethan Age.* London: Routledge and Kegan Paul, 1979.

Zeleny, Milan. "What Is Autopoiesis?" In *Autopoiesis: A Theory of Living Organization,* edited by Milan Zeleny. New York: North Holland, 1981.

Additional Readings

Almond, G., S. Appleby, and E. Sivan. *Strong Religion: The Rise of Fundamentalism around the World.* Chicago: University of Chicago Press, 2003.

Aloni, Nehemiah. "The Time of the Writing of *Sefer Yetsirah*" (in Hebrew). *Temirin* 2 (1982): 41–50.

Aptowitzer, Avigdor. *Bet haMiqdash shel Ma'alah lefi ha'Aaddah* [The Heavenly Temple according to the Agaddah] (in Hebrew). *Tarbits* 2 (1931).

Ashe, Geoffrey. *Dawn behind the Dawn: A Search for the Earthly Paradise.* New York: Henry Holt, 1992.

Baigent, Michael. *The Jesus Papers: Exposing the Greatest Cover-up in History.* San Francisco: Harper, 2006.

Barnstone, Willis. *The Other Bible: Jewish Pseudepigraphia, Christian Apocrypha, Gnostic Scriptures, Kabbalah, Dead Sea Scrolls.* San Francisco: Harper, 1984.

Bloom, Harold. *Jesus and Yahweh: The Names Divine.* New York: Riverhead Books, 2007.

Brandon, S. G. F. *Jesus and the Zealots.* Manchester: Manchester University Press, 1967.

Charles, Robert H. *Eschatology: The Doctrine of a Future Life in Israel, Judaism, and Christianity: A Critical History.* New York: Schocken Books, 1963.

Davis, Alan, ed. *Anti-Semitism and the Foundation of Christianity.* New York: Paulist Press, 1979.

Deardorff, James. "Survival of the Crucifixion: Traditions of Jesus within Islam, Buddhism, Hinduism, and Paganism" (1998). http://www.tjresearch.info/legends.htm.

Deutsch, Daniel. *The Gnostic Imagination: Gnosticism, Mandaeism, and Merkabah Mysticism.* Leiden and New York: E. J. Brill, 1995.

Duncan, Ronald. *Judas: A Poem in 13 Chapters.* Illustrated by John Piper. London: Anthony Blond, 1960.

Eisenmann, Robert. *James, the Brother of Jesus: The Key to Unlocking the Secrets of Early Christianity and the Dead Sea Scrolls.* London: Faber and Faber, 1997.

Fitzmyer, S. J. *Essays on the Semitic Background of the New Testament.* London: Geoffrey Chapman, 1971.

Flusser, David. *Jewish Sources in Early Christianity.* Translated by John Glucker. Tel Aviv: MOD Books, 1989.

Fox, Mathew. *The Coming of the Cosmic Christ.* New York: Harper and Row, 1988.

Freeman, Charles. *The Closing of the Western Mind.* New York: Vintage Books, 2005.

Friedman, Thomas. *The World Is Flat: A Brief History of the Twenty-first Century.* New York: Farrar, Straus, and Giroux, 2006.

Geyser, A. S. "Jesus, the Twelve, and the Twelve Tribes in Matthew." *Essays on Jewish and Christian Apocalyptic* 12 (1981).

———. "The Twelve Tribes in Revelation." *International Journal of Studiorum Novi Testamenti Societas* 28, no. 3 (1982).

Gorenberg, G. *The End of Days: Fundamentalism and the Struggle for the Temple Mount.* Oxford: Oxford University Press, 2000.

Graves, Kersey. *The World's Sixteen Crucified Saviors: Christianity before Christ.* 1875. Reprint, Kempton, Ill.: Adventures Unlimited Press, 2001.

Guénon, René. *The Lord of the World.* 1972. Reprint, Ripon, North Yorkshire: Coombe Springs Press, 1983.

Guillaumont, A. Puech, H. Quispel, G. Till, W. Till, and Yassah 'abd al-Masiḥ. *The Gospel according to Thomas.* Leiden: Brill; London: Collins, 1959.

Harris, Sam. *The End of Faith: Religion, Terror, and the Future of Reason.* New York: W. W. Norton, 2004.

Hopkins, Keith. *A World Full of Gods: Pagans, Jews, and Christians in the Roman Empire.* Phoenix: Weidenfeld and Nicolson, 2000.

Johnson, R. Paul. *The Masters Revealed: Madame Blavatsky and the Myth of the Great White Lodge.* Albany: SUNY Press, 1994.

Jonas, Hans. *The Gnostic Religion.* 2d ed. Boston: Beacon Press, 1990.

Kessler, Edward, and Melanie Wright, eds. *Themes in Jewish-Christian Relations.* Cambridge: Orchard Academic, 2005.

Khalidi, Tarif. *The Muslim Jesus.* Cambridge: Harvard University Press, 2003.

Kim, Seyoon. *"The Son of Man" as the Son of God.* WUNT, no. 30. Tübingen, Germany: Mohr/Siebeck, 1983.

Kirby, Peter. "Gospel of Judas" (2006). http://www.earlychristianwritings.com/gospeljudas.html.

Klassen, William. "The Contribution of Jewish Scholarship to the Quest for the Historical Jesus." In *Themes in Jewish-Christian Relations,* edited by Edward Kessler and Melanie Wright. Cambridge: Orchard Academic, 2005.

———. *Judas: Betrayer or Friend of Jesus?* Minneapolis: Fortress Press, 1996.

LePage, Victoria. *Shambhala: The Fascinating Truth behind the Myth of Shangri-la.* Wheaton, Ill.: Theosophical Publishing House, Quest Books, 1996.

Levine, Baruch. "Mythic and Ritual Projection of Sacred Space in Biblical Literature." *Journal of Jewish Thought and Philosophy* 6 (1996).

Makiya, Kanan. *The Rock: A Tale of Seventh-Century Jerusalem.* New York: Vintage Books, 2002.

Malachi, Tau. *Gnosis of the Cosmic Christ.* St. Paul, Minn.: Llewellyn Publications, 2005.

———. *Living Gnosis.* St. Paul, Minn.: Llewellyn Publications, 2005.

Nicholls, William. *Christian Antisemitism: A History of Hate.* Lanham, Md.: Jason Aronson, 1993.

Osman, Ahmed. *Jesus in the House of the Pharaohs: The Essene Revelations of the Historical Jesus.* Rochester, Vt.: Inner Traditions, 2004.

Pagels, Elaine. *Adam, Eve, and the Serpent.* New York: Vintage Books, 1989.

Palazzi, Shaykh Abdul Hadi. "Anti-Zionism and Anti-Semitism in the Contemporary Islamic Milieu" (2005). http://www.amislam.com/racism.htm.

Panas, Henryk. *The Gospel according to Judas.* Translated by Marc Heine. London: Hutchinson, 1977.

Parkes, James. *Voyage of Discoveries.* London: Gollanz, 1969.

Price, Randall. *The Coming Last Days Temple.* Eugene, Ore.: Harvest House, 1999.

Ridge, Ian. *Jesus: The Unauthorised Version.* London: Profile Books, 2006.

Sanders, E. P. *The Historical Figure of Jesus.* Harmondworth: Penguin, 1993.

Sandmel, Samuel. *Anti-Semitism in the New Testament.* Philadelphia: Fortress Press, 1978.

Saperstein, Marc. "Religious Intolerance and Toleration in the Middle Ages." In *Themes in Jewish-Christian Relations,* edited by Edward Kessler and Melanie Wright. Cambridge: Orchard Academic, 2005.

Schneider, Michael. *A Beginner's Guide to Constructing the Universe: The Mathematical Archetypes of Nature, Art, and Science.* New York: Harper Collins, 1994.

Shahan, Avigdor. *Towards the Sambatyon River: A Journey in the Footsteps of the Ten Tribes* (in Hebrew). Tel Aviv: Hakibbutz Hame'uchad Publishing House, 2003.

Sim, David. "Christian Judaism: A Reconstruction and Evaluation of the Original Christian Tradition." In *Themes in Jewish-Christian Relations,* edited by Edward Kessler and Melanie Wright. Cambridge: Orchard Academic, 2005.

Strachan, Gordon. *Jesus: The Master Builder.* Edinburgh: Floris Books, 1998.

Suares, Carlos. *The Passion of Judas: A Mystery Play.* Boulder: Shambala, 1973.

Urbach, Ephraim. *The Sages: Their Concepts and Beliefs.* Jerusalem: Magnes Press, 1975.

Vermes, Geza. *The Changing Faces of Jesus.* New York: Viking, 2001.

Walsh, James, ed. *The Cloud of Unknowing.* Classics of Western Spirituality Series. New York: Paulist Press, 1981.

Wehr, Demaris S. *Jung and Feminism.* Boston: Beacon Press, 1987.

Werblowsky, R. J. Zwi. "Milton and the *Conjectura Cabbalistica.*" *Journal of the Warburg and Courtould Institutes* 18, no. 1/2 (1955): 90–113.

Wistrich, R. S. *Anti-Semitism: The Longest Hatred.* New York: Schocken Books, 1991.

RESOURCES FOR FURTHER STUDY OF QABBALAH

Books of Introduction to the Qabbalah or to the Zohar

Aaron, David. *Endless Light: The Ancient Path of the Kabbalah.* New York: Berkley Books, 1997.

———. *Seeing God: Ten Life-Changing Lessons of Kabbalah.* New York: Berkley Books, 2001.

Jacobs, Louise. *Jewish Mystical Testimonies.* New York: Schocken Books, 1976.

Liebes, Yehuda. *Ars Poetica in Sefer Yetsira* (in Hebrew). Tel Aviv: Schocken Books, 2000.

Matt, Daniel. *The Essential Kabbalah: Heart of Jewish Mysticism.* San Francisco: Harper, 1996.

———. *Zohar: The Book of Enlightenment.* Classics of Western Spirituality Series. New York: Paulist Press, 1983.

Scholem, Gershom. *Kabbalah.* Jerusalem: Keter Publishing House, 1974.

———. *Major Trends in Jewish Mysticism.* Rev. ed. 1954. Reprint, New York: Schocken Books, 1961.

———. *Zohar: The Book of Splendour.* 1945. Reprint, New York: Schocken Books, 1995.

Steinsaltz, Adin. *The Thirteen Petaled Rose.* 1980. Reprint, New York: Basic Books, 1991.

Tishby, Isaiah, and F. Lachower. *The Wisdom of the Zohar.* Translated by D. Goldstein. Oxford: Oxford University Press for the Littman Library, 1989.

Books That Augment Discussion of the Qabbalah

Bar Lev, Rabbi Yechiel. *Song of the Soul: Introduction to the Kaballah, Based on Rabbi Chaim Moshe Luzatto's "Kalach Pitchei Choschma."* Brooklyn: Moznaim Press, 1994.

Fossum, Jarl. *The Image of the Invisible God: Essays on the Influence of Jewish Mysticism on Early Christology.* Freiburg, Switzerland: Universitätsverlag; Göttingen, Germany: Vandenhoek and Ruprecht, 1995.

———. *The Name of God and the Angel of the Lord: Samaritan and Jewish Mediation Concepts and the Origin of Gnosticism.* WUNT, no. 36. Tübingen, Germany: Mohr/Siebeck, 1985.

Gikatilla, Rabbi Joseph. *Sha'are Orah* [The Gates of Light]. Translated by Avi Weinstein. New York: Harper Collins, 1994.

Ginsburg, Y. *The Hebrew Letters: Channels of Creative Consciousness.* Jerusalem: Gal Einai, 1990.

Goldish, Matt. "Newton on Kabbalah." In *The Books of Nature and Scripture,* edited by James E. Force and Richard H. Popkin, 89–104. Dordrecht: Kluwer, 1994.

Green, Arthur. "Bride, Spouse, Daughter: Images of the Feminine in Classical Jewish Sources." In *On Being a Jewish Feminist,* edited by S. Heschel. New York: Schocken Books, 1983.

Hames, Harvey. *The Art of Conversion: Christianity and Kabbalah in the Thir-teenth Century (Medieval Mediterranean)*. Leiden: Brill Academic Publishers, 2000.

Idel, Moshe. *Kabbalah: New Perspectives*. New Haven: Yale University Press, 1988.

———. *Messianic Mystics*. New Haven: Yale University Press, 1998.

———. *The Mystical Experience in Abraham Abulafia*. Albany: SUNY Press, 1987.

———. *"Pardes*: The Quest for Spiritual Paradise in Judaism" (1991). http://www.kheper.net/topics/Kabbalah/Idel/Pardes.htm.

Karr, Don. "The Study of Christian Cabala in English" (2006). http://www.digital-brilliance.com/kab/karr/ccinea.pdf.

Schaefer, P., and Joseph Dan, eds. *Gershom Scholem's Major Trends in Jewish Mysticism, 50 Years After*. Tübingen, Germany: Mohr/Siebeck, 1993.

Scholem, Gershom. *The Messianic Idea in Judaism, and Other Essays of Jewish Spirituality*. New York: Schocken Books, 1971.

———. *Origins of the Kabbalah*. 1987. Reprint, Princeton: Princeton University Press, 1991.

Steinsalz, Adin. *In the Beginning: Discourses on Chasidic Thought*. York Beach, Maine: Jason Aronson, 1992.

———. *The Long Shorter Way: Discourses on Chasidic Thought*. York Beach, Maine: Jason Aronson, 1988.

———. *The Sustaining Utterance: Discourses on Chasidic Thought*. York Beach, Maine: Jason Aronson, 1989.

Wirszubski, Chaim. *Between the Lines: Kabbalah, Christian Kabbalah, and Sabbatianism* (in Hebrew). Edited by Moshe Idel. Jerusalem: Magnes Press, 1990.

Qabbalah Web Sites

http://www.kabbalah.info (the Bnei Baruch Web site)
http://www.kheper.net/topics/Kabbalah/
http://www.marquette.edu/maqom/

INDEX